THE CANONICAL INSTALLATION OF PASTORS

THE CATHOLIC UNIVERSITY OF AMERICA
CANON LAW STUDIES
No. 273

THE CANONICAL INSTALLATION OF PASTORS

A Historical Synopsis and a Commentary

BY
REVEREND FREDERICK W. FREKING, A.B., S.T.B., J.C.L.
PRIEST OF THE DIOCESE OF WINONA

A DISSERTATION

SUBMITTED TO THE FACULTY OF THE SCHOOL OF CANON LAW OF THE CATHOLIC UNIVERSITY OF AMERICA IN PARTIAL FULFILLMENT OF THE REQUIREMENTS FOR THE DEGREE OF DOCTOR OF CANON LAW

THE CATHOLIC UNIVERSITY OF AMERICA PRESS
WASHINGTON, D. C.
1948

Nihil Obstat:
CLEMENS V. BASTNAGEL, S.T.L., J.U.D.
Censor Deputatus
Washingtonii, D. C., die 2 martii, 1949.

Imprimatur:
✠ LEO BINZ
Episcopus Pinarensis
Administrator Apostolicus Ecclesiae Winonensis
Winonae, die 4 martii, 1949.

THE COLWELL PRESS, INC.
MINNEAPOLIS 15, MINN.

To

MY MOTHER AND FATHER

TABLE OF CONTENTS

PAGE

FOREWORD xi

PART ONE—HISTORICAL SYNOPSIS

CHAPTER I

PRELIMINARY CONSIDERATIONS 3

Article 1. The Meaning of *Parochus* 3

Article 2. The Notion of Installation 5

CHAPTER II

INSTALLATION TO THE TIME OF GRATIAN 8

Article 1. Early Legislation Regarding Institution 8

Article 2. The Proprietary Church and Investiture 12

Article 3. The Gregorian Reform and the Investiture Struggle 17

CHAPTER III

INSTALLATION FROM THE TIME OF GRATIAN TO THE COUNCIL OF TRENT 25

Article 1. The Decretals of Gregory IX 26

Article 2. The *Liber Sextus* of Boniface VIII 31

Article 3. The *Clementinae* 35

CHAPTER IV

LEGISLATION ON INSTALLATION FROM THE COUNCIL OF TRENT TO THE CODE OF CANON LAW 39

Article 1. Decrees of the Council of Trent Indirectly Affecting Installation 39

Article 2. The Profession of Faith 41

Article 3. Responses of the Sacred Roman Congregations 42

Article 4. Legislation of Provincial Councils after the Council of Trent 47

Article 5. The Oath against Modernism 50

CHAPTER V
DOCTRINE OF THE COMMENTATORS 53
Article 1. The Necessity of Corporal Institution 54
Article 2. *Ius in Re* and *Ius ad Rem* 56
Article 3. Verbal and Actual Installation 57
Article 4. Validity or Lawfulness 59

PART TWO—CANONICAL COMMENTARY

CHAPTER VI
THE DEFINITION OF TERMS 67
Article 1. An Explanation of Canonical Installation 67
Article 2. The Pastoral Office and Installation 71
A. Pastors (*Parochi*) 72
B. Quasi-pastors (*Quasi-parochi*) 75
C. Acting Vicars (*Vicarii Actuales*) 77
D. Administrators (*Vicarii Oeconomi*) 81
E. Substitute Vicars (*Vicarii Substituti*) 82
F. Adjutant Vicars (*Vicarii Adiutores*) 82
G. Assistant Pastors (*Vicarii Cooperatores*) 84

CHAPTER VII
THE NECESSITY OF INSTALLATION 85
Article 1. Necessity for Validity or for Lawfulness 89
Article 2. Dispensation from the Law of Installation 104
Article 3. Customs Contrary to the Law of Installation 107
Article 4. Penalties for Unlawful Occupation of the Pastoral Office 110

CHAPTER VIII
THE MANNER OF CANONICAL INSTALLATION 119
Article 1. The Rite of Installation 120
Article 2. The Installing Officer 126
Article 3. The Time of Installation 128
Article 4. The Profession of Faith 131
Article 5. The Oath against Modernism 134
Article 6. Installation by Proxy 135

CHAPTER IX

THE JURIDICAL CONSEQUENCES OF INSTALLATION 138

Article 1. The Rights and Obligations of the *Cura Animarium* 139

Article 2. The Right to the Income of the Benefice 154

Article 3. The Obligation of the Administration of the Temporal Goods of the Parish 159

Article 4. The Tacit Renunciation of an Incompatible Benefice 162

Article 5. The Presumption of Actual Possession and Restrictions Concerning Petitory Actions 164

Article 6. The Right to Possession through Prescription after Three Years of Peaceful Possession 166

CONCLUSIONS 175

APPENDIX I

A TYPICAL RITE OF THE FORMAL INSTALLATION OF PASTORS 177

APPENDIX II

AN INFORMAL MANNER FOR THE INSTALLATION OF PASTORS 181

APPENDIX III

SUGGESTED FORMS FOR THE DOCUMENTS USED IN INSTALLATION 182

BIBLIOGRAPHY 184

ABBREVIATIONS 193

ALPHABETICAL INDEX 194

BIOGRAPHICAL NOTE 197

CANON LAW STUDIES 198

FOREWORD

SINCE the Church established by Christ is a visible, living, teaching organization whose purpose is to carry the work of salvation to "all nations," it is a natural development of history that the more intimate care of souls should gradually be assigned as a specific office, so that each might have his proper pastor to guide him in the paths of the Good Shepherd.

Because of its importance, therefore, the pastoral office has been shaped, guided and protected by various types of legislation against the pitfalls of human ambition as well as for the good guidance and government of the souls committed to the pastor's care. To impress upon him and upon the faithful alike the importance and the dignity of the obligations of his office, as also to establish without doubt his rights and duties in it, the institution of the installation of pastors in office has had its gradual development.

To trace the history of this legislation it is necessary to study the pages of many turbulent and trying years in the Church's history. As in many other types of laws, the abuse of power by both civil and eccleciastical authorities has had much influence on the present form of that legislation. The so-called Investiture Struggle of the early Middle Ages, while it touched upon far more fundamental issues, nevertheless was responsible for much of the importance attached to installation.

As the Church in the United States advanced from the various stages of missionary endeavor to its present firmly established and flourishing position, there was a hesitancy to put into effect in this country the canonical legislation requiring the installation of pastors in office. This reluctance no doubt arose from the fact that it was generally felt that the conditions of the Church in Europe which had made this legislation advisable did not in reality exist in this country. Indeed, it was not until the advent of the Code of Canon Law in 1918 and the subsequent interpretations of the Pontifical Commission for the Authentic Interpretation of the Code that the pastoral office in this country was given the stable character intended for it in ecclesiastical law. Before that time parishes in this country were not generally considered as benefices in the strict canonical sense.

In more recent years diocesan synods and extra-synodal legislation in an increasing number of dioceses have required a definite manner for the induction of pastors in office. As yet, however, the canonical installation of pastors is not observed in many sections of the country.

Discussions on this subject range from the viewpoint that this legislation does not apply in this country to the extreme view that a large number of the pastors are in reality only putative pastors, whose strictly parochial ministrations are in many cases valid only by virtue of the factor of common error. It is hoped that the present study may contribute in some measure to a clarification of ideas concerning this subject, and to a better understanding of the nature of this canonical institute.

In the preparation of this treatise the writer has had the opportunity to study the various methods employed in the induction of pastors into office in most of the dioceses in this country. For this opportunity he wishes to express his deep gratitude to the chancery officials of the various dioceses, who so kindly provided this information. A special expression of gratitude is due and sincerely accorded to the Very Rev. Howard V. Smith, Vicar General of the Diocese of Fargo, for the permission to reprint in Appendix I the formal Rite of Installation which is contained in the *Liber Synodalis* of the Diocese of Fargo.

The writer also wishes to take this occasion to manifest his sincere gratitude to His Excellency, the Most Rev. Leo Binz, D.D., Coadjutor Bishop and Apostolic Administrator of the Diocese of Winona, for making available to him the opportunity to pursue an advanced course in Canon Law; to the Faculty of the School of Canon Law at the Catholic University of America for their profitable instruction, patient direction and kind assistance; and finally, to all those who in any way have helped in the preparation of this dissertation.

PART ONE
HISTORICAL SYNOPSIS

CHAPTER I

PRELIMINARY CONSIDERATIONS

Article 1. The Meaning of *Parochus*

To understand and properly circumscribe the history of the canonical installation of pastors it is necessary to have a clear concept of the ecclesiastical office of pastor, which likewise has had its own historical development. A full treatment of this history can be found in many contemporary writings as well as in the commentaries.[1] It will suffice here to give a brief historical outline of the office of the one who is now called pastor.

In the early ages of the Church the bishop took personal charge of the faithful committed to his care, and the sacred functions were carried on by him personally.[2] This was easily possible when the Christians were only a comparatively small group in the larger cities, but as the numbers of the faithful increased and the Church began to spread into the outlying and rural areas, it became necessary for the bishop to share his duties with others whom he had associated with him. Thus, early in the second century some of the parochial functions were given to the priests who made up the so-called College of Presbyters, to members of the College of Deacons and to the *chorepiscopi.*[3]

---

[1] Augustine, *A Commentary on the New Code of Canon Law* (8 vols., St. Louis: Herder & Co., 1919-1931), II, 505-508; Bastnagel, *The Appointment of Parochial Adjutants and Assistants,* The Catholic University of America Canon Law Studies, n. 58 (Washington, D. C.: The Catholic University of America, 1930), pp. 3-22; Barbosa, *De Officio et Potestate Parochi, Animadversiones et Addimenta Ubaldi Giraldi* (Romae, 1831), pp. 3-6; Bouix, *Tractatus de Parocho* (3. ed., Parisiis, 1880), pp. 16-21; Galvin, *The Administrative Transfer of Pastors,* The Catholic University of America Canon Law Studies, n. 232 (Washington, D. C.: The Catholic University of America Press, 1946), pp. 6-32; Hinschius, *System des katholischen Kirchenrechts,* (6 vols., Berlin, 1869-1897), II, 261-269.

[2] Bouix, *Tractatus de Parocho,* pp. 16-21.

[3] Hinschius, *System des katholischen Kirchenrechts,* II, 162, 183, 261; Coronata, *Institutiones Iuris Canonici* (5 vols., Taurini: Marietti, 1939-1947), I (2. ed., 1939), 365.

These associates, however, whether they were simple clerics or priests, acted only in the name of the bishop and under his immediate authority. This is evident from the fact that in the earlier periods they lived with the bishop, and also because the faithful were required to come to the principal church for the more important functions.[4] It is generally agreed among authors that the first resident priests outside the bishop's city with designated powers as pastors did not come until the latter part of the fifth century in the rural areas,[5] and at a much later date in the urban centers.[6]

The historical development of the status of the churches other than the church of the bishop coincided in large measure with the development of the pastoral office. Early in the second century it was customary to erect oratories in places at a distance from the bishop's church for the convenience of the faithful. Some religious functions were permitted in them, but the fulfillment of religious obligations and the administration of the sacraments were reserved to the bishop's church. During the third century in the East and the fourth century in the West the oratories and churches which had been erected in the rural areas began to enjoy a certain independence.[7]

When the Church became free of the dangers of persecution and Christianity began to spread, larger numbers of these churches were built, especially by the monks and nobles. To accommodate the increasing numbers of Christians, more functions were allowed in some of the larger of these churches. They became known as *"ecclesiae maiores vel baptismales"* from the fact that it was permitted to administer solemn baptism there. Conciliar legislation from the fourth century onward speaks of the functions which were permitted to be held there as well as of those whose exercise was denied.[8]

The titles given to those who first acted in the name of their bishop and later in their own name are found in the various types of early ecclesiastical legislation. Among them are the following:

---

[4] Hinschius, *op. cit.,* II, 262.

[5] Coronata, *op. cit.,* I, 365, 562.

[6] Coronata, *loc. cit.*; Hinschius, *op. cit.,* II, 277.

[7] Galvin, *The Administrative Transfer of Pastors,* pp. 12-14.

[8] Galvin, *loc. cit.*

curatus (one intrusted with the care of souls), *ecclesiasticus* (sacristan), *rector ecclesiae, pastor, plebanus* (folk-priest), *presbyter parochialis* and simply *sacerdos.*[9]

It was not until the Council of Trent (1545-1563) that the division of the diocese into distinct parishes with proper and perpetual pastors was made universal.[10] It is from this time that the word *parochus* has the precise meaning which it has today in the Code of Canon Law, namely, the priest or moral person to whom a parish has been given in title with the care of souls to be exercised under the authority of the local ordinary.[11]

From this brief outline it is obvious, then, that a historical treatise on the subject of the Canonical Installation of Pastors must deal with legislation governing other offices as well, particularly in its earliest stages. Since the office of pastor also partakes of the nature of an ecclesiastical benefice,[12] there will be frequent uses of that terminology.

Article 2. The Notion of Installation

The English word "installation" is used to designate the formal granting of possession of an office or position. Hence it adequately describes the canonical institute described in the Code of Canon Law as *"missio in possessionem seu institutio corporalis."*[13] The Latin word *"installatio"* seems not to have been used very frequently in this connection in the early sources, although the words *"installeretur"* and *"installentes"* are used in a letter of Pope Innocent III to the Archdeacon of Richmond.[14] DuCange (1610-1688)

---

[9] Galvin, *op. cit.*, p. 6; Hinschius, *op. cit.*, II, 291; Sägmüller, *Lehrbuch des katholischen Kirchenrechts* (4. ed., Freiburg im Breisgau: Herdersche Verlagshandlung, 1925-1934), p. 378.

[10] Conc. Trident., sess. XXIV, *de ref.*, cc. 1, 2, 7; Hinschius, *System des katholischen Kirchenrechts,* II, 295; Cappello, *Summa Iuris Canonici* (3 vols., Vols. I-II, 2. ed., Romae: Apud Aedes Universitatis Gregorianae, 1932-1936), II (1934), 10, 11; Wernz, *Ius Decretalium* (3. ed., 6 vols., Prati, 1913-1915), Tom. II, pars II, 685, footnote 3.

[11] *Codex Iuris Canonici,* lib. II, tit. VIII, cap. IX, can. 451, § 1 (hereafter cited by the number of the canon only); Hinschius, *loc. cit.*

[12] A juridical entity, permanently constituted or erected by the competent ecclesiastical authority, and consisting of a sacred office and the right to receive the revenue accruing from the endowment of such office—Can. 1409.

[13] Can. 1443, § 2.

[14] C. 7, X, *de concessione praebendae et ecclesiae non vacantis,* III, 8.

cited examples from the thirteenth century in which the word was used to designate the assigning of a place or stall in choir.[15] The more frequent expressions are *investitura, institutio, institutio corporalis* or *missio in possessionem.*[16]

These terms are sometimes misleading in the sources, inasmuch as the first two especially are often used to indicate the conferring of an office in its much wider phases. This difficulty was already apparent to the glossators in their study of the earlier legislation. The *Glossa Ordinaria* to *Regula Juris* 1, contained in the *Liber Sextus,* discusses in detail the various meanings of *Institutio.*[17]

The glossator there indicated a triple signification of the word, namely, *institutio tituli collativa, institutio auctorizabilis,* and *institutio realis et actualis.* He explained the first as the assignment of an office holder by the bishop to a benefice which was not vested with the right of patronage; the second as that by which the commission of the care of souls is given to one presented for the office; and the last as the induction into the real and corporal possession of the office, which, he said, was also called investiture.[18] This triple distinction seems to be generally followed by the later writers.[19]

The word investiture, as indicated in the preceding paragraph, also has a variety of meanings. Sometimes it was used in indication of the actual canonical institution. At other times it was used for the technical term *collatio,* or the complete conferring of an office. Abbas Panormitanus (1386-1453) adverted to this variable attachment of meaning to the term, and then explained by means of an example how the confusion often arose inasmuch as the three acts integral to the conferral of office could at times occur simultaneously.[20]

---

[15] DuCange, *Glossarium Mediae et Infimae Latinitatis* (9. ed., 10 vols., Paris: Librairie des Sciences et des Arts, 1938), V, 382, s. v., *installare*; cf. also VII, 577, s. v., *stallum,* 2.

[16] Wernz, *Ius Decretalium,* Tom. II, pars II, p. 195; Hinschius, *System des katholichen Kirchenrechts,* II, 654.

[17] Reg. 1, R. J., in VI°, s. v., *Beneficium.*

[18] *Loc. cit.*

[19] Reiffenstuel, *Ius Canonicum Universum* (5 vols. in 7, Parisiis, 1864-1870), lib. III, tit. 7, n. 5; Wernz, *Ius Decretalium,* Tom. II, pars II, p. 195.

[20] Nicholaus de Tudeschis (Abbas Panormitanus), *Commentaria in*

The simultaneous occurrence of the three elements was verified if the bishop chose to grant an office by giving to the person some symbol of that office, such as a ring or a biretta. If he did this without any previous appointment of the person, the action could also be called a *collatio*. If the previous conferring of the office in some other way preceded the act of presenting the symbol of the office, the latter implied simply a confirmation of appointment to the office. Finally, if the presenting of the symbol of the office occurred at the seat of the benefice, it pointed to the fact that an actual corporal possession was executed.[21]

From these illustrations it becomes evident that many references to institution or investiture do not necessarily refer to what is understood by installation, namely, the actual taking of the possession of a benefice, or the physical induction into office.[22]

Quinque Libros Decretalium (5 vols. in 8, Venetiis, 1581-1588), lib. III, tit. 7, c. 4, n. 9 (hereafter cited as Panormitanus).

21 Panormitanus, *loc. cit.*

22 Wernz, *Ius Decretalium,* Tom. II, pars II, p. 195.

CHAPTER II

INSTALLATION TO THE TIME OF GRATIAN

Article 1. Early Legislation Regarding Institution

Since the development of corporal institution must logically come after the establishment of true parochial offices, it is to be expected that there will be found little early legislation which has a direct bearing on corporal institution. It is generally agreed among authors that the introduction of benefices in the Church did not come until the sixth or seventh century, though there is some disagreement regarding the system from which they took their origin.

Some have maintained that the origin of benefices is rooted in the sixth century, when priests were allowed a certain portion from the common fund of the diocese for their support. Sometimes this took the form of the income from a piece of land or property, which was called the *precaria.*[1] Others have held that the origin of benefices stems from the system of proprietary churches, which originated in the Frankish Kingdom in the seventh century.[2]

Likewise it was only gradually that corporal institution emerged as a distinct step in the act of the conferring of an office, and it was frequently referred to in the same terms as the conferral of office.[3] Consequently there are some early regulations which may be considered as indicating the course of legislation in this direction. An early example of this is the reference in Gratian's *Decretum* to the thirty-first canon of the *Canones Apostolorum.*[4] This canon states that bishops who obtained a church through the

---

[1] Wernz, *Ius Decretalium,* Tom. II, pars II, pp. 12-14; Claeys-Bouuaert, *De Canonica Cleri Saecularis Obedientia* (Lovanii, 1904), p. 286.

[2] Stutz, "The Proprietary Church as an Element of Medieval Germanic Ecclesiastical Law," *Studies in Medieval History, Medieval Germany (911-1250),* translated by Geoffrey Barraclough (2 vols., Oxford: Blackwell, 1938), II, 55 (hereafter referred to as "The Proprietary Church").

[3] Cf. *supra,* p. 6.

[4] C. 14, C. XVI, q. 7; Bruns, *Canones Apostolorum et Conciliorum Saeculorum IV-VII* (2 vols., Berolini, 1839), I, 5 (hereafter cited Bruns).

secular powers were to be deposed and segregated, and also those who communicated with them.

It is more than likely that this canon referred to a bishop who wrongfully received his appointment from secular authority, rather than to the corporal institution itself, but the manner in which it was reproduced many times in later collections indicates that it was given a wide interpretation. Friedberg (1837-1910) in the footnotes of his edition of the *Decretum*[5] indicated that the canon was incorporated in the *Decretum* of Burchard of Worms (c. a. 1012), in the Collection of Cardinal Deusdedit (a. 1083-1087) and in the *Decretum* of Ivo of Chartres (a. 1094-1096). It was used also at the time of the Gregorian Reform, for it is found incorporated in the General Council of Rome over which Pope Gregory VII presided in the year 1080.[6]

Such was the case with much of the early legislation and with some of the conciliar decrees regarding corporal institution. It will be helpful, therefore, to study some of these decrees to gain an understanding of the historical background of this topic without attempting to present all of the legislation which helped to shape the pastoral office and the incumbent's canonical institution in it.

As was indicated in the previous chapter, the bishop in the early centuries was the only pastor of the diocese. He alone exercised the full authority in the functions of the ministry. Other clerics who assisted him, whether priests, deacons or simple clerics, did so only by his specific authorization. This can be gathered from canon 39 of the *Canones Apostolorum,* which commanded deacons and priests to do nothing without the direction of the bishop, since he was the one to whom the people had been entrusted by God and who had to account for their souls.[7]

It became necessary for the bishop to share these powers with others when the Church began to spread from the cities into the rural areas. In the fulfillment of this need there were appointed "rural bishops," who enjoyed a certain independence from the urban bishops in the care of souls. Mention of these was made in

---

[5] *Corpus Iuris Canonici* (2 vols., Lipsiae, 1879-1881), I, 804.

[6] C. 2—Mansi, *Sacrorum Conciliorum Nova et Amplissima Collectio* (53 vols. in 60, Parisiis, 1901-1927), XX, 532.

[7] Bruns, I, 6.

the synodal letter of the Bishops of the Council of Antioch in the year 269.[8]

At a later date these "rural bishops" came to be known as "*chorepiscopi.*" They were thus mentioned for the first time in the Council of Ancyra (314),[9] and this canonical institute as then extant seems to have received confirmation from the I Council of Nicaea (325), which provided that the Novatian bishops who had returned to the profession of orthodoxy should be instituted as *chorepiscopi.*[10]

The exact extent of the powers of the *chorepiscopi* is not entirely clear. They evidently enjoyed a certain amount of independence, but were still under the authority of the urban bishops.[11] Whether because of conflicts of authority or because of the spread of Christianity which made it inadvisable to consecrate bishops for each new church, the number of the *chorepiscopi* decreased, and *periodeutae* or visiting priests were appointed in their place.[12]

These so-called *periodeutae* became in the course of time attached to individual churches, as is evident from the legislation of the Council of Chalcedon in the year 451, which forbade the ordination of clerics without a tile of ordination, or, in other words, apart from an implied assignment to a particular church which they were to serve permanently.[13]

As the number of these churches and the clerics attached to them increased, their relationship to the bishop of the diocese was more closely defined by conciliar legislation. Gratian reproduced a number of the early decrees which show this trend, and which also had their application at his time. He quoted canon 17 of the I Council of Orleans (511), which insisted that all basilicas which

---

[8] Eusebius, *Historia Ecclesiastica,* lib. VII, cap. 30—Migne, *Patrologiae Cursus Completus, Series Graeca* (161 vols., Parisiis, 1857-1866), XX, 709-720 (hereafter cited with the letters *MPG*).

[9] C. 13—Hardouin, *Acta Conciliorum et Epistolae Decretales ac Constitutiones Summorum Pontificum* (12 vols., Parisiis, 1714-1715), II, 275 (hereafter cited as Hardouin).

[10] C. 8—Mansi, II, 671-672.

[11] Hinschius, *System des katholischen Kirchenrechts,* II, 162-169.

[12] Council of Sardica (343), c. 6—Mansi, III, 10; Council of Laodicea (343/381), c. 57—Hardouin, I, 792.

[13] C. 6—Hardouin, II, 603.

had been built in various places were to remain under the authority of the bishop in whose territory they were located.[14]

Gratian likewise quoted an early letter of Pope Damasus I (366-384) to Paulinus, Bishop of Antioch, written in the year 378. In this letter the Pontiff took a strong stand against those priests who left their churches and then, while roaming about, associated themselves with some other church. He ordered that they be considered as outside the communion of the Church until they returned. If in the meantime someone else was ordained in their place, the deserters were upon their return to forego the exercise of their priestly ministry throughout the lifetime of those who had supplanted them.[15]

Gratian furthermore reproduced a letter of Pope Gregory the Great (590-604), written in the year 592. This letter strictly forbade any ministers of the Church to usurp the office of another. Anyone who assented to such a usurpation in his own favor incurred deposition from the office he held. Anyone who with further presumption injected himself into another's ministry was barred from all participation in the bond of clerical communion.[16]

Provincial and General Councils enacted many laws governing the residence of clerics at the church for which they were ordained.[17] It seems, however, that these legislative restrictions were enacted not so much with a view to a rightful claim upon a residential ecclesiastical office, but rather in consideration of the obligation incident to ordination itself.[18] Permanence of residence in office and the title of ordination as the seal of a cleric's claim to it were considered as requisite conditions for the very act of receiving ordination, and not simply as elements which entailed obligations

---

[14] C. 10, C. XVI, q. 7; Mansi, VIII, 354.

[15] C. 43, C. VII, q. 1; Mansi, III, 425; Jaffé, *Regesta Pontificum ab condita Ecclesia ad annum post Christum natum MCXCVIII* (2. ed., cura G. Wattenbach, S. Loewenfeld, F. Kaltenbrunner, P. Ewald, 2 vols. in 1, Lipsiae, 1885-1888), n. 235 (hereafter cited Jaffé).

[16] C. 40, C. VII, q. 1; Jaffé, nn. 1173 and 1175.

[17] Council of Elvira (ca. 305), c. 18—Mansi, II, 9; Council of Rome (402), cc. 13-15—Mansi, III, 1138; Council of Chalcedon (451), c. 6—Mansi, VII, 394; Council of Tarragona (516), c. 7—Mansi, VIII, 542; II Council of Seville (619), c. 3—Mansi, X, 557.

[18] Claeys-Bouuaert, *De Canonica Cleri Saecularis Obedientia,* p. 287.

upon the granting of jurisdiction through the act of appointment.

In the absence of any other evidence in this matter it may be concluded that corporal institution as such did not yet exist by the end of the sixth century. Among the signs which did exist as leading to a future development one may, of course, point to the traditionally acknowledged necessity of a title for ordination, to the postulated permanence of residence at the church to which the cleric was assigned, and to the insistence upon the bishop's authority over all the churches in his diocese to the exclusion of interference from the civil authority.

Article 2. The Proprietary Church and Investiture

The decline of the Roman Empire with the advent of the barbarian invasions and the resultant rise of the Frankish and Germanic Kingdoms could not but have some effect upon many ecclesiastical institutions. Though the ecclesiastical legislation of the earlier period was still in effect, the influence of the Teutonic legal concepts was bound to be felt. This was especially true in the matter of ecclesiastical appointment, and it resulted in many difficulties for the maintenance of church discipline.

To understand this development a briefly summarized discussion of some of these concepts will be helpful. Because of its lack of clearness in distinguishing between the basic concepts of public and private law,[19] the Germanic concept of the powers and rights of the kings was based partly on their military leadership and partly on their ownership of the largest portions of the land. The rights of the kings were considered in many respects as a composite of individual rights, and royal prerogatives could, therefore, be alienated or given to others.[20]

According to this concept of land ownership churches were regarded simply as pieces of property, as objects or things which existed minus any juristic personality of their own. Whoever owned the land owned the church as well.[21] There is also evidence

[19] Stutz, "The Proprietary Church," p. 43.

[20] *Loc. cit.*

[21] Capitulary of Lothaire I in the year 823, c. 2—"Si quis homo liber per consensum episcopi sui ecclesiam in sua construxerit proprietate, fontesque in eadem ab episcopo fuerint consecrati, ideo non suam perdat hereditatem

that the churches were often sold and even given away as a dowry by the lords.[22]

The institution which perhaps contributed most in bringing about this deplorable situation has come to be known as the *proprietary church*, the *Eigenkirche*.[23] This new system seems to have had its inception during the later part of the sixth century in the reign of the Merovingian kings. Stutz (1868-1938) held the view that it derived its basic concept from the ancient patriarchial idea, so strong in the Germanic household, which gave the head of the family group a priestly character.[24] But, since the patriarchial concept was prevalent in other regions as well, it is more likely that it was rooted in the Germanic concept of property rights (*Eigentum*).

In order to consolidate their power, the Merovingian kings had to control the power of the dukes and the lords who had been their military leaders. This they accomplished by means of land grants together with the bestowal of property rights which were called *seisin* or *gewere*.[25] These included the *bannus*, or the right to issue an order under threat by legislation, administration or purely judicial acts. Originally the lords were considered as rulers in the name of the king, but later this office became secondary, and the tenure of the land was considered as the most important prerogative of these lords.

The lords in turn granted the *seisin* to the minor lords and those who lived on the land. This gave rise in about the ninth century to the feudal system or the law of fiefs. It was the product of two elements, the personal type of land lease which became known as the *beneficium, feudum, fief* or *Lehn*, and the corresponding per-

. . ."—*Monumenta Germaniae Historica, Leges in 4°*, Sect. II (*Capitularia Regum Francorum*), I (ed. A. Boretius, Hannoverae, 1883), 316 (hereafter cited *MGH*).

[22] Agobard, Bishop of Lyons (d. 840), *Liber de dispensatione ecclesiasticarum rerum* (828): "Nunc non solum possessiones ecclesiae sed etiam ipsae ecclesiae cum possessionibus vendantur."—*Patrologiae Cursus Completus, Series Latina* (221 vols., Parisiis, 1844-1864), CIV, 237 (hereafter cited *MPL*).

[23] Stutz, "The Proprietary Church," p. 44.

[24] *Loc. cit.* Cf. Fuchs, *Der Ordinationstitel von seiner Entstehung bis auf Innozenz III* (Bonn: Kurt Schroeder Verlag, 1930), pp. 152-153.

[25] Stutz, *ibid.*, p. 57.

sonal obligation of fealty and service, sometimes called vassality.[26]

Because of its bearing on this subject, a detailed description of the manner of operation of this system will not be amiss. Sir Paul Vinogradoff (1854-1925) in his article on "Feudalism" described it as follows:[27]

> "The acts constituting the feudal contract were called *homagium* and *investitura*. The tenant had to appear in person before the lord surrounded by his court, to kneel before him and to put his folded hand into the hand of the lord, saying: 'I swear to be faithful and attached to you as a man should be to his lord.' He added sometimes: 'I will do so as long as I am your man and as I hold your land.' To this act of homage corresponded the 'investiture' by the lord, who delivered to his vassal a flag, a staff, a charter or some other symbol of the property conceded. There were many variations according to localities, and, of course, the ceremony differed in the case of a person of base status. Yet even a villein received his yard-land or oxgang from the steward of a lord after swearing an oath of fealty and in the form of an 'admittance' by the staff, of which a record was kept in the rolls of the manorial court . . ."

It was in this system that the "proprietary church" gradually grew and flourished. The church, built on the manorial property by the lord, being considered in this respect as any other piece of property, was treated in the same manner. Usually the *focus* of the church property was the ground on which was built the altar, which contained the relics of the saint to whom it was dedicated. It was under the title of this saint that the lord acted as owner of the church's possessions, including the fixtures, vestments, etc., and also the offerings levied for the services of the priest.[28]

It is easy to understand how in this system the clergy gradually came under the influence and power of the lords. Gradually also the baptismal churches and cathedral holdings of the bishop came into this same category, with the bishop himself sometimes in the position of the lord.[29]

---

[26] Vinogradoff, "Feudalism," *The Cambridge Medieval History,* planned by J. Bury and edited by Gwatkin and Whitney (8 vols., New York: Macmillan & Co., 1911-1936), III, 464.

[27] *Op. cit.,* p. 459.

[28] Stutz, "The Proprietary Church," pp. 41-42.

[29] "Art. cit.," p. 49.

These conditions were bound to effect a radical change in the manner of ecclesiastical appointments. Previously the candidates for ordination were presented to the bishop by the archdeacon, and at the time of ordination they received the title of the church which they were destined to serve. The archdeacon as head of the College of Deacons had the duty of training, educating and examining the candidates for ordination. For the rural parishes this duty was shared by the archpriest, who likewise superintended the education and preparation of candidates.[30]

Now it became the custom, though by no means generally sanctioned, for the lords to appoint priests from other churches and dioceses for the service of their private chapels without first obtaining their own bishop's approval. Sometimes candidates for the priesthood were selected from their own household and presented to a neighboring or a vagrant bishop for ordination, if their own bishop refused to yield to their demands.[31]

These priests were then invested in the churches by the lords themselves in ceremonies similar to that presented above.[32] Usually a ring, a staff, a biretta, the book of Gospels or some other symbol of office was used in this ceremony together with the words: *Accipe ecclesiam,* or some similar expression.[33]

To believe that this system developed without protest on the part of the church authorities would be unthinkable. A vehement denunciation against the usurpation of the lay powers was decreed by the Bishops at the Synod of Chalon-sur-Saône (650).[34] It was specifically decreed that oratories constructed by laymen were still under the bishop as well in regard to the placing of the clergy as in regard to the property and the ordering of the divine services.[35]

---

[30] Bastnagel, *The Appointment of Parochial Adjutants and Assistants,* p. 31.

[31] *Op. cit.,* p. 33.

[32] *Supra,* p. 14. Cf. Mourret-Thompson, *A History of the Catholic Church* (6 vols., St. Louis: Herder Book Co., 1930-1946), IV, 16-18.

[33] Mourret-Thompson, *A History of the Catholic Church,* IV, 16-18.

[34] C. 14—*MGH, Leges in 4°*, Sect. III (*Concilia*), I (*Concilia Aevi Merovingici*) (ed. F. Maassen, Hannoverae, 1893), 211.

[35] Hefele-Clark, *A History of the Councils of the Church* (2. ed., 5 vols., Edinburg, 1883-1896), IV, 464 (hereafter referred to as Hefele).

Gratian listed the decrees of the earlier councils which indicated that from the beginning of these abuses the Church made efforts to control them. At the Council of Lerida (524) it was decreed that laymen who wished basilicas which they had built to be consecrated were not to attempt to have them separated from the diocesan law under the guise of considering them as monasteries.[36] The III Council of Toledo (589) recited the abuses of those who wished to have churches consecrated in order to make possible the derivation of income from them, and demanded that all churches be placed under the authority of the bishop according to the ancient rule.[37] This rule was also repeated in the IV Council of Toledo (633).[38]

The so-called German Council (742), at which St. Boniface presided, ordered that every priest should be subject to the bishop in whose diocese he resided, and also required him to give a report of his ministry to the bishop during the season of Lent. Likewise no unknown priests or bishops were to be admitted to the ecclesiastical ministry without synodal approbation.[39]

Four councils held in the year 813 indicate the spread of these abuses, but reflect also the efforts to restore church discipline during the Carolingian period through what is often called the Carolingian Reform. At the II Council of Chalon-sur-Saône (813) clerics were required to swear obedience to the bishop who ordained them and to the church for which they were ordained.[40] The Council of Mainz (813) ordered not only that laymen should not eject priests, but also that they could not institute them in their churches without the consent of their bishops, and that the bishops should diligently inquire about all clerics in their dioceses and return fugitives to their proper diocese.[41] At Tours (813) the evil practice of priests going from one church to another for a price was recognized as widespread, and both lay persons and

---

[36] C. 3—Mansi, VIII, 612 (under the year 524); c. 1, C. X, q. 1.; Peltier-Migne, *Dictionnaire des Conciles* (2 vols., Paris, 1847), I, 1112.

[37] C. 19—Mansi, IX, 998; c. 2, C. X, q. 1.

[38] C. 26, 32—Mansi, X, 627-628; c. 6, C. X, q. 1.

[39] C. 3, 4—*MGH, Leges in 4°*, Sect. III (*Concilia*), II (*Concilia Aevi Karolini*) (ed. A. Werminghoff, 1904), 3.

[40] C. 13—*MGH, Leges in 4°*, Sect. III (*Concilia*), II, 276.

[41] C. 28, 31—*MGH, Leges in 4°*, Sect. III (*Concilia*), II, 268.

clerics who presumed to grant a church to a priest without the permission and consent of the bishop who interdicted.[42] Similar canons were also decreed at Arles (813).[43]

From the decrees of these councils and of others it is obvious that a bitter struggle was already in progress to maintain church discipline in accord with the older traditions.[44] It was in this period that the Pseudo-Isidorian Collections appeared. These attempted, in part even by means of cleverly disguised forgeries, to aid in the reforms of ecclesiastical discipline.[45] This was also the period during which such men as Hincmar, Archbishop of Rheims (845-882),[46] Abbot Regino of Prüm (d. 915),[47] and Burchard, Bishop of Worms (1000-1025),[48] attempted by various means to bring about the reform of clerical morals and conditions in general. Unfortunately they did not seem to recognize with adequate clarity that the root of these evils was lay investiture.

The subsequent heroic efforts of Pope Gregory VII (1073-1085) were to achieve only a partial success against this evil, and the conflict was destined to endure until the twelfth century before order was completely restored.

Article 3. The Gregorian Reform and the Investiture Struggle

At the outset of this article it must be noted that the Gregorian Reform and the Roman Pontiff's part in the Investiture Struggle

---

[42] C. 15—*MGH, ibid.*, p. 288.

[43] C. 4, 5—*MGH, ibid.*, p. 251.

[44] Council of Rome (826), c. 7—Mansi, XIV, 494, 999; Council of Pavia (850), c. 18—Mansi, XIV, 936; Council of Rome (853), c. 6, 7—Mansi, XIV, 1003; III Council of Valence (855), c. 9—Mansi, XV, 8; Council of Vienne (892), c. 1, 4—Mansi, XVIII, 121-122; Council of Tribur (895), c. 28—Mansi, XVIII, 146; Council of Ingelheim (948), c. 4, 5—Mansi, XVIII, 421; Council of Augsburg (952), c. 9—Mansi, XVIII, 438; Council of Seligenstadt (1022), c. 13—Mansi, XIX, 398; Council of Bourges (1031), c. 21, 22—Mansi, XIX, 505.

[45] Cicognani, *Canon Law* (2. rev. ed., authorized English version by O'Hara and Brennan, Westminster, Maryland: The Newman Bookshop, 1946), pp. 239-248.

[46] *Op. cit.*, p. 245; Mourret-Thompson, *A History of the Catholic Church*, III, 465-467.

[47] Cicognani, *Canon Law*, p. 252.

[48] *Loc cit.*

are by no means to be identified. The latter was in reality only a part of the broad program initiated by Pope Gregory VII, which included a vigorous aggression against the immorality of the clergy, against simoniacal practices in the conferring of offices, against lay domination in all fields of Church discipline, and against the disruption of discipline in general.[49] The deplorable events of history during this period are well known. It is the purpose here to trace in this outline only the legislation and the events which had an important bearing on the subject of canonical installation in ecclesiastical offices.[50]

For almost a quarter of a century before he ascended the papal throne, Gregory had an opportunity to observe the difficulties of the times at close range. Having entered the papal court in the reign of Gregory VI (1045-1046), he frequently, at the behest of the succeeding Popes, functioned as a legate in the various countries to which he had been sent. His influence was undoubtedly felt in the Roman Synod of 1059, held under Nicholas II (1059-1061), which reenacted the ancient Canon of the Apostles which forbade clerics to obtain churches from the laity, and which insisted upon the authority of the bishop over all churches in his territory.[51] The same canons were repeated in the Council of Rome in the year 1063 under Alexander II (1061-1073). It was from this Council as his source that Gratian incorporated the pertinent legislation.[52]

When Gregory ascended the papal throne after the death of Alexander II in 1073, he immediately pursued his reform efforts with determined zeal. In March, 1074, a council was held at Rome. The abuses of simony in the obtaining of ecclesiastical offices were

---

[49] Haydt, *Reserved Benefices,* The Catholic University of America Canon Law Studies, n. 161 (Washington, D. C.: The Catholic University of America Press, 1942), pp. 11-12.

[50] For a concise history of this period cf. Mourret-Thompson, *A History of the Catholic Church,* IV, 186-382; Löffler, "Conflict of Investitures," *The Catholic Encyclopedia* (15 vols. with Index and 2 Supplements, New York, 1907-1922), VIII (1910), 84-89; Scharnagl, *Der Begriff der Investitur in den Quellen und der Literatur des Investiturstreites,* Kerchenrechtliche Abhandlungen, (hrsg. von U. Stutz, Stuttgart: Verlag Enke, 1902-1938), Heft 56 (1908), pp. 1-141 (hereafter cited as *Der Begriff der Investitur*).

[51] Cc. 6, 7—Mansi, XIX, 897.

[52] C. 20, C. XVI, q. 7; c. 6, 7—Mansi, XIX, 1025.

condemned, clerics who had obtained churches in this manner were ordered to forfeit them, and the laity were forbidden to attend the functions of clerics who did not comply.[53]

In the following year (1075) a council held at Rome decreed that bishops or abbots who in the future would receive their bishoprics or abbacies from the hands of a layman were to be considered as under interdict, and emperors, dukes, counts, or any lay powers or persons who dared to grant investiture were to be considered under the same condemnation.[54] These decrees were repeated in the following years in successive councils, and excommunications were pronounced against those who did not comply.

The tragic events which followed the excommunication of Emperor Henry IV (1056-1106) in the Council of 1076 are well known.[55] Henry first attempted to depose the Pope in a National Council at Worms, and again at Mainz. When he discovered that the bishops were not in sympathy with his plans, he feigned repentance at Canossa before he could be judged at the national diet which was to have been held at Augsburg. As soon as the excommunication was lifted, he returned to his previous scheming, and so he was excommunicated a second time in the Roman Council of the year 1080.

In the famous *"Si quis deinceps"* decree of that Council the excommunications previously enacted against the lay investiture of bishops and abbots were repeated, and the decree was declared to apply also with reference to lay investiture granted for the lesser churches and eccleciastical dignities.[56]

Gregory's prudence in attempting to destroy the evil of lay investiture with these bold strokes may be questioned, but there can be no doubt of his sincerity and zeal. Despite the grave dangers to his person and the terrible suffering of the siege of Rome, he remained firm in his stand and reiterated the excommunication. In the end he felt it wiser to leave Rome, but he

---

[53] C. 7—Mansi, XX, 410.

[54] Mansi, XX, 443.

[55] Mansi, XX, 468; Mourret-Thompson, *A History of the Catholic Church,* IV, 215-236.

[56] C. 12, C. XVI, q. 7; c. 12—Mansi, XX, 531.

continued to carry on the struggle until he died at Salerno in 1085.[57]

During the reign of Urban II (1088-1099) councils were held at various places, often in the presence of the Pope, and the condemnations against investiture were repeated.[58] In practice, however, the emphasis in the opposition to existing abuses was related to the investiture of the bishops and abbots of the larger churches and abbeys, and less vigorous aggression was shown in relation to the smaller churches. Urban also took occasion at the Council of Clermont (1095) to make it known to the princes that by forbidding the practice of lay investitures with reference to ecclesiastical benefices as such, the Church did not intend to take away all rights of the princes to participate in the election of bishops as the chiefs of their people.[59]

Likewise in the Council of Nimes (1096) it was the receiving of the *cura animarum* from the bishop, rather than the granting of the church itself, that was vindicated for the spiritual authority of the Church.[60] This change in the approach to the problem was to be the basis for the later compromise. It was largely the result of changing circumstances.

Changing political situations had made the princes rebellious against the lordship exercised by the king, especially in the investitures attending the bestowal of the larger churches which had considerable land holdings. The saturation point of land ownership under ecclesiastical dominion had also made the lords envious of the properties owned by many of the bishops. By appealing to the good will of the princes and the laity, the popes were able to bring many of the bishops into conformity with church

---

[57] The statement of this paragraph seems warranted in view of the fact that succeeding popes adopted less strenuous measures and proceeded less vehemently in coping with the situation.—Haydt, *Reserved Benefices*, p. 12.

[58] Council of Melfi (1089), c. 8—Mansi, XX, 723; Council of Piacenza (1095), c. 15—Mansi, XX, 813; Council of Clermont (1095), cc. 15-18—Mansi, XX, 817; Council of Rouen (1096), c. 6—Mansi, XX, 924; Council of Nimes (1096), c. 8—Mansi, XX, 936.

[59] Mourret-Thompson, *A History of the Catholic Church*, IV, 281; Ivo of Chartres, *Epistola 60,—MPL,* CLXII, 73; Scharnagl, *Der Begriff der Investitur*, p. 31.

[60] C. 9—Mansi, XX, 936.

discipline, and thus at the same time became able to exert pressure on the kings.[61]

In dealing with the question of investiture as related to the lesser churches a different method was used. The basic conception of ownership of the church complex had gradually broken up into many particular rights such as the *ius fundi,* the *ius petitionis,* the *ius praesentationis,* the *ius decimationis,* the *ius regaliae,* the *investitura ecclesiae,* etc.[62] The ownership of the church had become a less profitable venture than the certified income deriving through the holding of these various rights.

The gradual effect was that the lords began to lose interest in the "proprietary church." This situation made possible the rise of new ecclesiastical institutions. As the "proprietary churches" fell into the hands of ecclesiastical owners, e.g., of a diocese or an abbey, the entire church property with all the particular rights incident thereto became incorporated as a juridic or moral person in law. The pastor, thereafter, received the right to the income of his office which was called a benefice, but the ultimate control of the property remained with the bishop.

In other cases the particular rights of the owners were no longer acknowledged, but instead they were given the right of patronage, the *ius patronatus.* This custom had been prevalent in Spain for some time. The patron had the right to derive personal support from the church if he was poor, but conversely he had the obligation to contribute his support to the church if it needed help. In return for this favor he was given the right of precedence, the right of presentation, the right of burial inside the church, etc., but the appointment and investiture remained with the bishop.

Such radical changes were not effected over night or without a struggle. During the reign of Pope Paschal II (1099-1118) the condemnations of the past were repeated in the Council of Troyes (1107).[63] Gratian quoted also a letter of Paschal, in which the Pope insisted that the clerics who received investiture from laymen were barred from exercising the divine offices in the churches,

---

[61] Scharnagl, *op. cit.,* pp. 60-62.

[62] Stutz, "The Proprietary Church," p. 68.

[63] C. 1—Mansi, XX, 1223; c. 13, C. XVI, q. 7.

and the churches themselves were no longer a place for the conduct of the divine offices.[64]

When Henry V (1106-1125) marched on Rome in the year 1111, Paschal tried to establish peace by constraining the bishops to return to the crown many of their estates and privileges, but without success. Consequently he was imprisoned at Sutri, and under threats to his life he was forced to grant the right of investiture to the king.[65] After the immediate dangers had been removed, the Pope in the Council of the Lateran in the year 1112 revoked this privilege for the reason that it had been obtained by force.[66]

Peace was finally restored by the Concordat of Worms (1122) between Henry V and Calixtus II (1119-1124).[67] The basis of the concordat was a clear distinction between the ecclesiastical and secular elements in the appointments of bishops. The Pope permitted the elections to be held in the presence of the king, provided that there was no simony or violence. The king was to use his influence in the election only in the event of a dispute. Within six months after the election the king had the right to invest the bishop with the secular elements of his benefice (*regalia*) through the symbol of the scepter, and could require of the bishop the oath of loyalty in secular matters.

The king in turn renounced all claim relative to the investiture of the bishops with the ring and crosier, and guaranteed free and canonical elections in all the churches of his kingdom. Those properties of the Church which he had confiscated he promised to return, and he also agreed to assist in regaining control of those then held by others. A similar concordat was signed in England between St. Anselm, Archbishop of Canterbury (1093-1109), and King Henry I (1100-1135) in the year 1107,[68] and in France the less centralized authority gradually fell into line.[69]

The General Council of the Lateran convoked by Calixtus in the

---

[64] C. 19, C. XVI, q. 7; Jaffé, n. 6610; Mansi, XX, 1072.

[65] Mansi, XXI, 42-44.

[66] Mansi, XXX, 69.

[67] Mansi, XXI, 273-274; Scharnagl, *Der Begriff der Investitur*, pp. 76-80.

[68] Mourret-Thompson, *A History of the Catholic Church*, IV, 336-339; Scharnagl, *op. cit.*, pp. 125-132.

[69] Mourret-Thompson, *op. cit.*, IV, 335.

year 1123 confirmed the agreement at Worms with the lay authorities, and set about to establish proper order within the ecclesiastical jurisdiction itself. It was decreed anew that priests were to be instituted in the parish churches through the bishops, and they were required to report to the bishop regarding the care of souls and other matters which pertained to him.[70]

Now that lay investiture had been abolished, it seemed that certain ecclesiastics also needed curbing. The archdeacons and archpriests had attained undue power in the period of the investitures and were usurping the powers of the bishops. In canon 7 the Council ordered that no archdeacon or archpriest should bestow on anyone the care of souls or other prebends without the decision and consent of the bishops, since the care of souls and the disposition of ecclesiastical funds remained under the authority and power of the bishop. Those who presumed to vindicate to themselves these or other powers of the bishop were to be refused admittance to the church (*ab ecclesiae liminbus arceatur*).[71]

It is interesting to see the attitude of canonists of the time as recorded by Rufinus (+ ca. 1190) in his *Summa Decretorum,* which he wrote between the years 1160 and 1170.[72] In discussing the right of the Church in the matter of investiture he insisted that it had to be most vehemently defended as an exclusive prerogative of the Church (*usque ad sanguinem defendere debemus*), yet he cited examples from Gratian in which the popes themselves seem to have granted the use of that power to non-ecclesiastics. The act in which Pope Adrian I (772-795) appears to have given to King Charles (Charlemagne, 768-814) the right of investing bishops and archbishops[73] he dismissed by stating that it was an old law which since had become obsolete. Furthermore, he added, if this privilege as granted by Pope Adrian was to be understood in the same sense of granting the right of investiture, it would certainly have been cited oftener in defense of the later practice of lay investiture. The second case, in which certain kings and princes had been

---

[70] C. 18—Mansi, XXI, 285.

[71] C. 11, C. XVI, q. 7; Mansi, XXI, 283.

[72] *Summa Decretorum* (ed. H. Singer, Paderborn, 1902), pp. 368-369.

[73] C. 22, D. LXIII; Jaffé, n. 2406.

given the right to hand over one monastery to another monastery,[74] he explained by saying that it referred to the (*ius patronatus*), and not to the right of investiture as such.

In concluding this chapter the writer deems it necessary to point out that the historical treatment up to this point of time dealt with the complete process of canonical institution, and not only with the element of corporal installation, since the distinction between the various acts integral to the notion of a canonical institution in office was not always clearly defined. The strong emphasis in legislation on the manner in which the physical possession of the office was granted seems to indicate, however, that the person who granted the investiture in office often controlled the appointment to the office as well.

Much of the legislation here recounted was directly concerned with investiture relative to the episcopal office, but its principles were usually applied to the pastoral office as well. It is through the historical developments already considered that the question of installation in office arose. Eventually the act of installation was to become a separate element in a composite act of the conferral of office. Hence it is necessary to have a clear understanding of this period.

---

[74] C. 40, C. XVI, q. 7; Jaffé, n. 903.

CHAPTER III

INSTALLATION FROM THE TIME OF GRATIAN TO THE COUNCIL OF TRENT

With the Concordat of Worms in 1122 a solid basis was recognized for the solution of the lay investiture struggle. By it also an official sanction was given to the practice which had gradually been adopted by ecclesiastical authority from the secular custom, namely, that of conferring a benefice or office through the handing over of the symbols of that benefice or position, that is, by means of an installation in office.

As yet, however, there was no clear delineation between the granting of the jurisdiction of the office (*institutio tituli collativa*) and the installing of the cleric in the possession of the office (*institutio corporalis* or *missio in possessionem*). Evidence of this is furnished in the numerous conflicts between bishops on the one hand and archdeacons and archpriests on the other. The latter maintained that it was their right to induct the prospective beneficiary into office in the manner indicated above, while the bishops held that they alone had the right to confer a benefice or ecclesiastical office.

The twelfth and thirteenth centuries, which saw a great development in the field of canon law, not only in the enactment of new laws but also in the organizing of existing legislation into a complete juridic pattern, also produced a solution of the problem between the bishops and the archdeacons. Protection was accorded to the authority of the bishop to grant jurisdiction in all the churches of his diocese through the recognition that he alone had the right to confer an office in its fullest sense. The position of the archdeacon was upheld through the fact that for him there was recognized the right to induct into office by means of a corporal institution or installation those whom the bishop had appointed.

The history of this development is recorded in the various collections of decretals which contain numerous excerpts of papal letters and decrees formulating this policy. It was during the post-

Gratian period that it became customary to formulate legislation by means of decretal letters.[1]

Before passing on to a consideration of these decretal letters, one must first advert to the legislation of two general councils. In the II General Council of the Lateran (1139), held under Innocent II (1130-1143), clerics were again forbidden to receive prebends or any ecclesiastical benefices from laymen under pain of losing the benefice.[2] This penalty was further increased in the III General Council of the Lateran (1179), held under Alexander III (1159-1181), to include deposition for such clerics who persisted in the practice. Lay patrons who continued to grant these offices were to be excommunicated.[3]

It was also decreed in the III General Council of the Lateran that benefices were not to be promised to anyone before they became vacant, and, when vacant, they were to be conferred within six months, lest the delay should give rise to abuses.[4] These decrees as well as various decretal letters indicate that the old practice of lay investiture was not yet completely eradicated.

Article 1. The Decretals of Gregory IX

An analysis of the legislation regarding installation as found in the Decretals of Gregory IX indicates that the primary objective was to eradicate the practice of the conferring of jurisdiction by anyone other than the bishop himself. Besides the non-ecclesiastics who had arrogated this power to themselves through the practice of lay investiture, the archdeacons also had frequently usurped this power. Their subsequently acknowledged right of conferring corporal institution was in turn protected against the lay patrons who simply were accorded the right of presentation.

The subject of investiture was specifically treated in Book III, Title 7, *de institutionibus*; the office of the archdeacon in Book I, Title 23, *de officio archidiaconi*; and the rights and duties of patrons in Book III, Title 38, *de iure patronatus*. Various letters

[1] Cicognani, *Canon Law*, p. 289.

[2] C. 25—Mansi, XXI, 532.

[3] C. 14—Mansi, XXII, 226; c. 4, X, *de iure patronatus*, III, 38.

[4] C. 8—Mansi, XXII, 222; c. 2, X, *de concessione praebendae et ecclesiae non vacantis*, III, 8.

bearing on these subjects are also to be found in other places. Without attempting a comprehensive enumeration of all these passages, the writer now proposes to present such passages as illustrate the mentioned objectives.

In a letter to the Archbishop of Canterbury and his Suffragans, Alexander III (1159-1181) reproved the *"consuetudinem pravam admodum et enormem"* by which clerics had received churches and ecclesiastical benefices without the consent of the bishop of the diocese or of his officials who *"de iure"* possessed this right. He ordered the Archbishop by force of the apostolic letter to punish with excommunication which barred every appeal those who had knowingly occupied churches in this manner, and not to absolve them unless they had made suitable satisfaction.[5]

In a similar letter to the Archbishops and Bishops of England the same pope decreed that those who had accepted churches or benefices without the consent of the bishop were to be removed if they did not give up these offices after being admonished to do so.[6] The Bishop of Tournai was ordered by Alexander III to punish with canonical penalties those who dared to occupy a benefice or to renounce it without his permission.[7] And in another letter patrons were forbidden to give churches to their sons or to anyone else by their own authority. Likewise clerics could not lay claim to a church by hereditary right.[8] A letter of Pope Honorius III (1216-1227) to the Bishop of Reggio instructed him to remove clerics who had been instituted in churches by inferior prelates without his consent.[9]

It is to be noted, however, that in all these letters the question seems to turn directly on the actual conferral of the title of the benefice, so that the primary consideration was the *institutio tituli collativa* rather than the *corporalis institutio.*

However, the possessed rights of patrons to present candidates were accorded a full protection. A group of religious (*Hospitalarii*) had received possession of a benefice with the consent of only one

---

[5] C. 3, X, *de institutionibus,* III, 7; Jaffé, n. 13,817; Mansi, XXII, 378.

[6] C. 21, X, *de iure patronatus,* III, 38; Jaffé, n. 13,744; Mansi, XXII, 440-441.

[7] C. 4, *de renunciatione,* I, 9; Jaffé, n. 14,117.

[8] C. 15, X, *de iure patronatus,* III, 38; Mansi, XXII, 340.

[9] C. 3, X, *de excessibus praelatorum et subditorum,* V, 31.

of the two brothers who were the patrons of the church. The right of the second brother, who had complained to the Holy See, was upheld by Pope Alexander III, and accordingly the religious group was ordered to relinquish the benefice, the order being imposed under threat of excommunication and interdict.[10]

Similarly the rights of the archdeacon were protected within their due bounds. At this time it had also become customary for the Popes to confer benefices through delegated judges in cases of appeal, etc.[11] In a letter to the Bishop of Le Mans, Pope Alexander III treated the question of a delegated judge's right to induct a cleric in office when upon an unappealable judicial sentence it had been determined which of the contending presentees was to be instituted in office. The precise question was whether in such a case the right of appeal was denied also to the bishop or the archdeacon to whom by law the right of installing the cleric in office belonged. The Pope replied that there still remained the possibility of appeal on the part of the bishop or the archdeacon regarding the presentee's right of receiving installation or corporal institution in the office, since he did not intend that the delegated judge's decision should prejudice their rights in this regard, inasmuch as the right of appealing the decision was denied simply to the litigant parties themselves.[12]

On the other hand, the archdeacon of Ely in England was severely taken to task for having presumed without the mandate of the bishop to grant the care of souls on his own authority, or, in other words, for having arrogated to himself the act of the *institutio auctorizabilis*.[13]

Innocent III (1198-1216) found it advisable to define in detail the duties of the archdeacon.[14] Calling the archdeacon "the eye of the bishop," an old expression frequently used, he stated that in

---

[10] C. 14, X, *de iure patronatus,* III, 38; Mansi, XXII, 340.

[11] Haydt, *Reserved Benefices,* pp. 14-15.

[12] C. 15, X, *de officio et potestate iudicis delegati,* I, 29; Mansi, XXII, 413; Jaffé, n. 13,842.

[13] C. 4, X, *de officio archidiaconi,* I, 23; Mansi, XXII, 364; Jaffé, n. 13, 898.

[14] C. 7, X, *de officio archidiaconi,* I, 23; Potthast, *Regesta Pontificum Romanorum inde ab anno post Christum natum MCXCVIII* ad annum MCCCIV (2 vols., Berolini, 1874-1875), n. 5031 (hereafter cited as Potthast).

general his duties were to correct abuses under the authority of the bishop. In particular he listed among his duties the right of corporal institution in benefices as well as in other offices, and the duty to examine clerics and to present them to the bishop for ordination and appointment.

He similarly, in a letter to the Archbishop of Milan, who evidently had allotted these duties to the chancellor, defended the rights of the archdeacon to examine and to present candidates for ordination. He stated further that it pertained to the office of the archdeacon to install abbots and abbesses in their office.[15]

Several other matters pertaining to institution in office were treated by Pope Innocent. In a letter to the archdeacon of Paris he enunciated the principle that those who have the authority to confer positions cannot institute themselves in that office, since there must be a personal distinction between the giver and receiver.[16] In a vehement letter to the Bishop of Tournai he condemned the election of anyone to an office when he already possessed several others.[17]

Another matter authoritatively determined by the same pope is reflected in his decision that the six months within which the conferring of a benefice was to ensue were not to be regarded as having lapsed when the bishop had been impeded from performing his office.[18] Of considerable importance even to the present legis-

Potthast, n. 678.

lation is a letter of the same pope to the Bishop of Zamora, in which letter it was indicated that a cleric could be invested with a benefice by proxy.[19]

The interpretation of these decretal letters in the schools and universities along with their application to the solution of canonical cases can be found in the writings of the decretalists. Bernard of Pavia (d. 1213), the author of the First Compilation of Decretals, called also the *Breviarium Extravagantium,* defined institution as the induction into the corporal possession of an office or prebend, and he stated that it is often not inaccurately called investiture.

15 C. 7, X, *de officio archidiaconi,* I, 23; Potthast, nn. 377 and 5031.

16 C. 7, X, *de institutionibus,* III, 7; Potthast, n. 3122.

17 C. 18, X, *de praebendis et dignitatibus,* III, 5; Potthast, n. 1186.

18 C. 5, X, *de concessione praebendae et ecclesiae non vacantis,* III, 8;

19 C. 24, X, *de praebendis et dignitatibus,* III, 5; Potthast, n. 1066.

He then delineated a two-fold division of investiture, *"in re praesenti"* and *"in re absenti."* It could be bestowed at the site of the benefice, namely, when a person was inducted into corporal possession of the benefice, and then it was properly called the institution in the benefice. On the other hand, if a bishop conferred a benefice in his palace by the handing over of a book or by means of some other symbol of office, then the act of conferral was less properly called an institution of the cleric in his benefice.[20]

Bernard also stated that the bishop alone had the native power of instituting clerics in office. Those under him could do so only with his delegated authority. Laymen could not invest or institute anyone in office under any circumstances. In all appearance Bernard did not distinguish sharply between the elements of appointment and installation. In his day the archdeacon's right to induct a cleric into the corporal possession of his benefice or office was fully recognized.[21] He also taught that the effect of institution was that, once the cleric was instituted in his benefice or office, he was its incumbent in full right and thereafter could not be dismissed from it without a reasonable cause.[22]

Henricus de Segusio (a noted glossator of this period who died as Cardinal Bishop of Ostia in 1271 and is generally referred to as Hostiensis) described investiture as the cleric's induction into the corporal possession of his benefice or office. In his *Summa Aurea* he distinguished it from institution in the proper and technical sense by comparing it to the enthronization of a bishop or the assigning of a *feudum,* both of which acts required a previously made appointment.[23] In his *Commentaria* he defined institution as the granting of the canonical right to a church or to an ecclesiastical benefice, and investiture as a conferring of the quasi-possession of that right. He added, however, that one term was used indifferently for the other.[24]

---

[20] *Summa Decretalium* (ed. E. Laspeyres, Ratisbonae, 1860), lib. III, tit. 7, n. 1.

[21] *Ibid.,* n. 2.

[22] *Ibid.,* n. 4.

[23] *Summa Aurea* (Venetiis, 1570), p. 231 (recto), q. 2.

[24] *Commentaria in Quinque Libros Decretalium* (5 vols. in 8, Venetiis, 1588), lib. III, tit. 7, *de institutionibus,* c. 4, n. 3 (hereafter cited *Commentaria*).

In the summary at the beginning of the title, *de institutionibus,* he stated that the conferral of a prebend alone was of itself of little import unless it was accompanied with the act of taking corporal possession.[25] He explained that the confusion in the use of the term investiture arose from the fact that sometimes a benefice was granted simply through the bestowal of a ring. He implied that such an act was the equivalent of the act of taking corporal possession, since it was acknowledged that in such circumstances a bodily installation in the benefice was no longer necessary for the appointee in order to gain possession of his benefice.[26]

This author again adverted to the consideration of corporal institution in his treatment of the office of the archdeacon. There he stated that, when there exists no custom to the contrary, then the right of bestowing corporal institution belongs *"de iure communi"* to the archdeacon.[27] However, before he used his right the archdeacon had to have recourse to the authority of the bishop in all dubious cases, and then had to abide by the bishop's directions.[28]

These views of Hostiensis may well be taken as furnishing a true picture of the practice regarding installation during the later part of the twelfth and the earlier part of the thirteenth centuries.

Article 2. The *Liber Sextus* of Boniface VIII

Further evidence of the problems regarding institution is found in the *Liber Sextus,* the official collection of Boniface VIII (1294-1305), which was published with the Bull *Sacrosanctae,* of March 3, 1298, inasmuch as the same trend is apparent in this legislation. The bishop's authority in the conferring of office was firmly upheld.

---

[25] "Parum prodest collatio praebendarum . . . nisi haberetur possessio corporalis. . . . A quocumque fiat beneficii collatio, semper debet fieri episcopo praesentatio, et per episcopum, vel officialem suum debet approbari, antequam administrat."—*Ibid.,* n. 1.

[26] "Hac autem institutione facta per episcopum, quae et quandoque investitura appellatur eo quod in signum approbationis, seu collationis, plerumque anulus traditur. . . . Et quandoque collatio scilicet, quando ad praelatum pertinet conferre beneficium, sicut . . . post electionem . . . Sequi debet alia investitura, seu installatio corporalis, quae de iure communi ad archidiaconum pertinet. . . . Et in hoc multi delinquunt hodie . . ."—*Loc. cit.*

[27] *Commentaria,* lib. I, tit. 23, *de officio archidiaconi,* c. 4, n. 2.

[28] *Ibid.,* c. 6, nn. 6, 18.

Two particular cases were treated. In one case the right of the bishop to grant institution in office was defended; but during the vacancy of the see the cathedral chapter, during the time of its government of the diocese, could grant confirmation to the one presented by a lay patron if the presentee was deemed qualified.[29] The second case dealt with those who by force or other unjust means sought to intrude themselves in a benefice to which was attached the care of souls. In the event of any such effort there followed an *ipso facto* incurred deprival of any right to the benefice, regardless of whether or not the benefice had been unlawfully occupied by them.[30] Contemporary and later authors interpreted this law as referring to the fact of installation as well as to that of actual appointment.[31]

Another passage in the *Liber Sextus* reproduced a decree of the II Council of Lyons (1274), held under Pope Gregory X (1271-1276). It stated that one who was elected to a benefice was not to assume to administer the benefice in any manner whatsoever before he had received confirmation of his right.[32] While it is evident that this decree referred primarily to the election of bishops, yet it undoubtedly applied also in the event of elections to lesser churches.[33]

The gradual decline in the power of the archdeacon is reflected in the chapter *"Licet episcopus."* There it was indicated that, when someone had gained peaceful possession of a second parochial benefice, the bishop was allowed to confer the earlier possessed parochial benefice to another.[34] The archdeacon's diminishing authority seems implied in the last part of the chapter, for the decretal there stated that the bishop should not grant corporal possession of the earlier possessed benefice to the new appointee unless he had previously advised the former beneficiary of it, since the latter might

---

[29] C. 1, *de institutionibus,* III, 6, in VI°.

[30] C. 18, *de praebendis et dignitatibus,* III, 4, in VI°.

[31] Cf. Garcia, *De Beneficiis Ecclesiasticiis* (Venetiis, 1618), pars IV, c. 2, n. 9; Ioannes Andreae, in *Glossa ordinaria,* s. v., *Eum qui*; Hostiensis, *Commentria in Quinque Libros Decretalium,* lib. III, tit. 5, c. 28, n. 11.

[32] C. 4—Mansi, XXIV, 86-87; c. 5, *de electione et electi potestate,* I, 6, in VI°.

[33] Cf. *Glossa ordinaria,* s. v., *Ecclesiarum,* and s. v., *Casus.*

[34] C. 28, *de praebendis et dignitatibus,* III, 4, in VI°.

perhaps have some right to the retaining of possession of the benefice. The context seems to assume that it was the bishop who was to grant the corporal possession rather than the archdeacon. Later authors explained this decretal by pointing out that it contemplated a special case in which there was a possible conflict of rights, and that therefore it belonged to the bishop, rather than to the archdeacon, to institute the new appointee in the relinquished parochial benefice.[35] It was through the special provision that was made for such and similar cases, so it seems, that the earlier recognized power of the archdeacon in this matter gradually disappeared.

Of special importance to the subject of installation are the *Regulae Juris* listed at the end of the *Liber Sextus.* Though some have held that these did not have the force of law, it is generally admitted that they were part of the official collection and therefore constituted true legislation.[36]

Five of these *Regulae* may be listed here as having special bearing on the subject of installation. They are as follows:

> "Regula 1. Beneficium ecclesiasticum non potest licite sine institutione canonica obtineri.
> Regula 2. Possessor malae fidei ullo tempore non praescribit.
> Regula 3. Sine possessione praescriptio non procedit.
> Regula 68. Potest quis per alium, quod potest facere per seipsum.
> Regula 72. Qui facit per alium, est perinde, ac si faciat per seipsum."[37]

The possible use of a proxy or procurator, as indicated in the last two rules just listed, has already been mentioned with reference to installation.[38] Likewise it has been shown that the second and the third of these principles were applicable in the matter of canonical installation.[39]

The *Glossa ordinaria* to *Regula 1* also showed that these rules had reference to installation when it stated that institution proceeded from the acts of others. For its validity certain things were

---

[35] Reiffenstuel, *Ius Canonicum Universum,* lib. III, tit. 7, n. 45.
[36] Cicognani, *Canon Law,* p. 311.
[37] R. J., in VI°.
[38] C. 24, X, *de praebendis et dignitatibus,* III, 5; *supra,* p. 29.
[39] C. 18, *de praebendis et dignitatibus,* III, 4, in VI°; *supra,* p. 32.

required. First, the person needed to have the authority to grant the institution. Secondly, the one to be appointed or installed had to be capable of receiving the benefice in question; neither a layman nor the cleric if he were himself the one who granted the institution (*ipse idem instituens*) could receive it. Thirdly, the authority to grant the institution had to proceed either from a right which derived *ex iure proprio* or from a right which had been acquired through an act of delegation. Fourthly, the proper form had to be observed.[40]

Regula 1 had a special significance, and hence deserved a special consideration. Ioannes Andreae (d. 1348), the author of the *Glossa ordinaria* to the *Liber Sextus,* offered a lengthy discussion on the question of institution in that section wherein he treated the opening *Regula* of the *Regulae Iuris.*[41] Reference has already been made to the threefold distinction which he used in explaining institution, namely, *institutio tituli collativa, institutio auctorizabilis,* and *institutio realis et actualis.*[42] He maintained that the execution of the first two pertained to the bishop. This he explained by indicating that the act of institution in office, when taken strictly, could be twofold in character. One case obtained when someone was presented by a patron, and the bishop then granted the title by confirming the presentation. A second case obtained in the event of an election which likewise required the confirmation of the bishop. Undoubtedly both of these cases referred to the *institutio auctorizabilis.* He then defined *collatio* as the act of the appointment to a benefice which did not have the right of patronage attached to it, and which accordingly was left *pleno iure* within the free disposal of the bishop.

He upheld the right of the archdeacon by insisting that the third type of institution in office, the *institutio realis et actualis,* which he also called investiture, pertained to this diocesan official. He stated specifically that when the bishop had appointed someone to an office or benefice, he was to command the archdeacon to induct him into the corporal possession of this office or benefice. The expression which he used, *"debet mandare,"* could be interpreted,

---

[40] *Glossa ordinaria,* s. v., *Obtineri.*

[41] S. v., *Beneficium.*

[42] *Supra,* p. 6.

however, to mean that the bishop could personally proceed to the corporal institution without the archdeacon, and that accordingly the latter no longer had this right *de iure communi*. This same author expressed similar views when he discussed the office of the archdeacon in his separate commentary.[43]

Article 3. The *Clementinae*

As has been indicated, the legislation concerning installation became crystallized in the twelfth and thirteenth centuries. It remained for these concepts to take root in general practice. Hence it is to be expected that there would be little new legislation in the period to follow. The Constitutions of Clement V (1305-1314), however, are deserving of mention. Though the legislation contained therein was enacted during the reign of Clement, the Constitutions were not promulgated until the year 1317 during the reign of John XXII (1316-1334).

In the matters pertaining to installation the application of legal prescription is indirectly mentioned. In the single chapter on sequestration, a decree of Clement published at the Council of Vienne (1311-1312) receives mention. It implies that the peaceful possession of a benefice for three years begot prescription, inasmuch as sequestration was allowed within that time in case of a conflict. It appears, of course, that the beneficiary had to be in good faith.[44]

Another chapter indicated further that upon the peaceful possession of a second benefice the first became vacant *de iure*.[45] The next following chapter, however, stated that this did not necessarily apply if the second benefice was granted by the pope *motu proprio* and he made no mention of the first benefice.[46]

With these brief references in the Clementine Constitutions the legislation on installation prior to the Council of Trent seems to have been completed, for no further legislative enactments regarding installation are to be found in the *Extravagantes* of John

---

[43] Ioannes Andreae, *In Decretalium Libros Novella Commentaria* (5 vols., Venetiis, 1584), lib. I, *de officio archidiaconi*, c. 4, n. 6, and c. 8, n. 1.

[44] C. un., *de sequestratione possessionis et fructuum*, II, 6, in Clem.

[45] C. 3, *de praebendis et dignitatibus*, III, 2, in Clem.

[46] C. 4, *de praebendis et dignitatibus*, III, 2, in Clem.

XXII or in the *Extravagantes Communes*. A final picture, however, of the interpretation of this legislation in practice is useful for the purpose of this treatise.

Among the best known of the glossators and commentators of this period was the Abbas Panormitanus, the Benedictine canonist Nicholaus de Tudeschis (1386-1453). He discussed the matter of canonical institution in office at considerable length in his commentary.[47] Acknowledging the difficulties because of the confusion of terms, he offered the following explanations:

Electio, properly understood, occurred when the canons of a church chose a prelate. This gave to the person elected only a *"ius in habitu"* and not a *"ius in actu,"* and consequently confirmation of the election by the superior was required.

Praesentatio as a right properly pertained to a patron, but this act did not connote any transfer of spiritual authority to the presentee. If the person presented was duly qualified for the office or the benefice, he was still to be instituted in the office or the benefice by a superior, whose act alone sufficed to endow the presentee with spiritual power and authority.

Confirmatio was properly to be associated with elections. Since the person elected gained radically the possession of authority through the act of confirmation, it was not necessary for him to be instituted by a superior. It sufficed that his election received the superior's confirmation.

Institutio was threefold in character. Properly it implied the necessary transfer of a right made by a superior when one had been presented by a patron. Such a transfer of right was properly called institution, since the mere act of presentation did not connote the transfer of any authority. The transfer of right was necessitated inasmuch as the superior was under legal constraint to confer the right on the one presented if he was duly qualified. Secondly, in the act of free appointment to a benefice the institution of the prospective incumbent in it was designated as a free *collatio* or conferral. In such an event the granting of the office pertained solely to the bishop. Thirdly, institution in an office or a benefice pointed to a cleric's induction in the corporal possession of his office or benefice.

[47] Panormitanus, lib. III, tit. 7, *de institutionibus,* c. 4.

Investitura was sometimes identified in its meaning with the corporal institution, but sometimes also with the act of free conferral. The latter identification was juridically admissible if the bishop granted the institution through the bestowal of a ring or of a biretta, as long as no grant of the right to the office or benefice had previously been made. If there was a previous act of conferral, of institution, or of confirmation, then in the absence of any actual bestowal of right (*in absentia rei*) the investiture was simply an act of quasi-confirmation of the previously bestowed right. Some canonists, he stated, held that, when an act of conferral, of institution, or of confirmation had been executed, then the one designated for the benefice had the right to take possession of it on his own authority. Others, he declared, insisted that the investiture as pointing to an actual bestowal (*in re praesenti*) of the right was still demanded as a means for entering upon the possession of the office or the benefice.[48]

Other points mentioned by Panormitanus are likewise of interest. The right of inducting a cleric in the corporal possession of his office or benefice belonged to the archdeacon *"de iure communi."*[49] The right of institution with relation to a benefice of free conferral belonged to the bishop alone, but during the vacancy of a see the cathedral chapter, during the time that it governed the diocese, could grant confirmation to one who had been elected to an office or who had been presented by a patron.[50] However, the right of granting institution in office could belong to others besides the bishop by reason of a special right which they enjoyed either by way of privilege or in view of a laudably established usage or custom.[51] These views of Panormitanus may well be taken as affording a substantial picture of the practice regarding installation in office up to the time of the Council of Trent (1545-1563).

In a brief summary the picture is as follows: First, both conciliar and decretal legislation made clear that the bishop alone had the right to confer spiritual authority in his diocese, whether in the appointment to a benefice of free conferral (*institutio tituli*

---

[48] *Ibid.*, nn. 4-9.

[49] *Ibid.*, n. 8.

[50] *Loc. cit.*

[51] *Panormitanus,* lib. III, tit. 7, *de institutionibus,* c. 6, n. 1.

collativa), or in the approval of the one presented by a patron, or in the confirmation given to one elected (*institutio auctorizabilis*). However, in practice this authority as vindicated by the law exclusively for bishops was sometimes disregarded by the archdeacons and lay patrons. To stamp out these abuses the Church in its law resorted to the enactment of canonical penalties, such as the intruder's deprivation of the benefice, his deposition from his clerical rank, and even his excommunication in certain designated cases.

Secondly, the rights of patrons to present candidates for office were protected within bounds. Thirdly, the act of a cleric's installation in office (*institutio corporalis*) was *de iure communi* the right of the archdeacon. However, the bishop sometimes used his superior right and granted corporal possession of the office at the same time that he bestowed the care of souls, especially in minor benefices, by giving to the candidate a ring as the symbol of the possession of his office. Delegates of the bishop such as delegated judges, could also induct clerics into the corporal possession of their office, and thus the exercise of their power by the archdeacons began to decline. Regarding the form of the installation, the decretal legislation itself seems not to have set forth any enactments. Local customs, as also today, seem to have been the guiding norm. A form quite generally employed consisted in the handing over of some symbol of the office.

Further legal developments relative to the stability of the pastoral office through the legislation of the Council of Trent were to exercise a concomitant effect also on the subject of canonical installation.

CHAPTER IV

LEGISLATION ON INSTALLATION FROM THE COUNCIL OF TRENT TO THE CODE OF CANON LAW

Article 1. Decrees of the Council of Trent Indirectly Affecting Installation

The crystallization of the legislation regarding installation had already taken place by the time of the Council of Trent (1545-1563). This is evident from the fact that, while many decrees affecting the pastoral office were passed in that Council, no specific regulations on the subject of installation were enacted. In the broad pattern of the development of the office of pastor as shaped by the Council there were, however, a number of decrees which indirectly exercised an influence relative to installation. The fact that these decrees were frequently mentioned by the authors in their discussions regarding installation seems to warrant a study of them in the present treatise.

The Council's concern for the care of souls is evident from the regulation which commanded the bishop to divide his diocese into distinct parochial areas with permanent pastors, so that the salvation of the souls committed to the bishop's and the pastor's care might be more adequately safeguarded.[1] To be sure that those who were to hold the office of parish priest would be men of high character and capabilities, the Council enacted special rules for the examination of candidates with a view to their appointment as pastors.[2] The particular session and chapter in which these rules

[1] ". . . mandat sancta synodus episcopis pro tutiori animarum eis commissarum salute, ut distincto populo in certas propriasque parochias unicuique suum perpetuum peculiaremque parochum assignent"—Conc. Trident., sess. XXIV, *de ref.*, c. 13; cf. also sess. XIV, *de ref.*, c. 9. Latin texts of this Council are taken from *Concilii Tridentini, Diariorum, Actorum, Epistularum, Tractatuum, Nova Collectio* (ed. Societas Goerresiana, 13 vols., incomplete, Friburgi Brisgoviae, 1901—). English translations are taken from Schroeder, *Canons and Decrees of the Council of Trent* (St. Louis: B. Herder Book Co., 1941).

[2] Conc. Trident., sess. XXIV, *de ref.*, c. 18; cf. Coady, *The Appointment*

were enacted furthermore required the bishop to appoint a *vicarius oeconomus* to administer the parish during its vacancy.

In an effort to eradicate the dangers of simony associable with the conferring of the office, the Council ordered bishops diligently to examine the constitutions and to heed the laudably established customs in their dioceses with regard to election, presentation, nomination, institution, confirmation or any other provision, in the admission of clerics to the possession of office either at the cathedral church or in any other benefice. The bishops were to abolish any practices in connection with the instituting of clerics in their offices and benefices if such practices gave rise to the suspicion of simony or of sordid avarice. Any offerings, deductions or payments from the fruits of the benefice or from the daily distributions, if not converted to pious uses, were branded as simoniacal.[3]

In dealing with the right of patronage the Council gave stringent regulations to determine who were legitimately entitled to this right. It insisted that candidates presented by the patrons for confirmation be also subjected to the examination which other parish priests were required to undergo. The bishop had the right to reject those who by the examiners were found not to be qualified for the parochial or other beneficial office.[4]

---

of Pastors, The Catholic University of America Canon Law Studies, n. 52 (Washington, D. C.: The Catholic University of America, 1929), pp. 33-36; Bouix, *Tractatus de Parocho,* pp. 337-340.

[3] "In pluribus ecclesiis . . . ex prava consuetudine observari intelligitur ut in electione, praesentatione, nominatione, institutione, confirmatione, collatione vel alia provisione, sive admissione ad possessionem alicuius cathedralis ecclesiae vel beneficii, canonicatuum aut praebendarum, vel partem proventuum, seu ad distributiones quotidianas, certae conditiones seu deductiones ex fructibus, solutiones, promissiones compensationesve illicitae, aut etiam quae in aliquibus ecclesiis dicuntur turnorum lucra, interponantur. Haec cum sancta synodus detestetur, mandat episcopis, ut quaecumque huiusmodi in usus pios non convertuntur, atque ingressus eos, qui simoniacae labis aut sordidae avaritiae suspicionem habent, fieri non permittant, ipsique diligenter de eorum constitutionibus sive consuetudinibus super praedictis cognoscant, et illis tantum, quas ut laudabiles probaverint, exceptis, reliquas ut pravas ac scandalosas reiiciant et aboleant."—Conc. Trident., sess. XXIV, *de ref.,* c. 14.

[4] Conc. Trident., sess. XXV, *de ref.,* c. 9; cf. also sess. XXIV, *de ref.,* c. 18.

It was also forbidden to hold more than one residential benefice at the same time.[5]

Article 2. The Profession of Faith

Of considerable importance relative to the factor of installation was the decree of the Council which required that those who were promoted to parochial benefices make a profession of faith within two months of the day of taking possession of the benefice. Besides making the profession of faith these beneficiaries were also required to promise and swear solemnly that they would persevere in their obedience to the Roman Church. The profession of faith was to be made in the presence of the bishop, or, if he be hindered, in the presence of his vicar general or *officialis*. Those who failed to make the profession of faith in the required time were to be deprived of the fruits of the benefice, and their possession of the benefice was not to be of any avail to them.[6]

The form of the profession of faith to be employed was given by Pope Pius IV (1559-1565) in his Constitution *Iniunctum Nobis,* of November 13, 1564. He ordered that this form be used in preference to all other forms, in order that there might be uniformity.[7] The use of this particular formula was regarded as so necessary that those who made the profession according to another form were required to repeat the profession of faith in the due form before the bishop at the next diocesan synod.[8]

---

[5] Conc. Trident., sess. XXIV, *de ref.* c. 17; cf. *infra,* p. 45.

[6] "Provisi etiam de beneficiis quibuscumque, curam animarum habentibus, teneantur, a die adeptae possessionis ad minus intra duos menses, in manibus ipsius episcopi vel, eo impedito, coram generali eius vicario seu officiali, orthodoxae suae fidei publicam facere professionem, et in Romanae ecclesiae obedientia se permansuros spondeant ac iurent. . . . alioquin praedicti omnes provisi, ut supra, fructus non faciant suos, nec illis possessio suffragetur."—Conc. Trident., sess. XXIV, *de ref.,* c. 12.

[7] Pius IV, const. *"Iniunctum Nobis,"* 13 nov. 1564—*Codicis Iuris Canonici Fontes* (cura Emi Petri Card. Gasparri Editi, 9 vols., Romae [postea Civitate Vaticana]: Typis Polyglottis Vaticanis, 1923-1939. Vols. VII, VIII et IX, ed. cura et studio Emi Iustiniani Card. Serédi), n. 108 (hereafter referred to as *Fontes*); cf. Canavan, *Profession of Faith,* The Catholic University of America Canon Law Studies, n. 151 (Washington, D. C.: The Catholic University of America Press, 1942), pp. 40-43.

[8] S. C. Ep. et Reg., *Vercellen.,* 21 iul. 1578—*Fontes,* n. 1335. According to the legislation of the Council of Trent diocesan synods were to be held

On another occasion the Sacred Congregation of Rites was asked whether the form of the profession of faith on the occasion of an installation in office should be the same as the form of the synodal oath which is found in the *Pontificale Romanum,*[9] and whether it should be recited in the vernacular. The response was that the decree of Session XXIV of the Council of Trent should be observed, and the profession of faith should be made in accordance with the form prescribed by Pius IV.[10]

Substantially the same formula is used today. Some additions were made by the Sacred Congregation of the Council in 1877 with regard to the dogmatic decrees of the Vatican Council concerning the primacy and infallibility of the Roman Pontiff.[11]

Article 3. Responses of the Sacred Roman Congregations

Decisions of the Sacred Roman Congregations indicate the importance attached to the profession of faith as a requirement for the full possession of offices having the care of souls. The Sacred Congregation of the Council ruled in 1782 that those who made the profession of faith after receiving their appointment, but before they were installed in corporal possession, thereby fulfilled the decree of the Council of Trent. In the same decision it also ruled that those who failed to make the profession in the required two months were to be deprived of the fruits of the benefice only from the end of the second month, since the Council had allowed that period of grace.[12] This Congregation had also ruled that a benefi-

---

annually.—Sess. XXIV, *de ref.*, c. 2.

[9] *Pontificale Romanum* (Ratisbonae, 1891), tit. *Ordo ad Synodum.* The Roman Pontifical appeared in Rome in 1485 as the *Liber Pontificalis.* It was re-edited in 1596 under Pope Clement VIII. Revised again in 1644 under Pope Urban VIII, and in 1752 under Pope Benedict XIV, the latest typical edition appeared in Rome in 1934. Cf. *Lexikon für Theologie und Kirche* (10 vols., Freiburg im Breisgau: Herder & Co. G. M. B. H. Verlagsbuchhandlung, 1930-1938), VIII (1936), 372.

[10] S. R. C., *Briocen.*, 21 iul. 1855, n. 9—*Fontes,* n. 5976; *Decreta Authentica Congregationis Sacrorum Rituum* (6 vols., Romae: Ex Typographia Polyglotta, 1898-1927), n. 3035 (hereafter referred to as *Decreta Authentica*).

[11] S. C. C., *decr.*, 20 ian. 1877—*Fontes,* n. 4236; cf. Sebastianelli, *Praelectiones Iuris Canonici* (2. ed., 3 vols., Romae, 1905), II (*De Rebus*), pp. 280-281.

[12] S. C. C., *Tirasonen.*, 20 apr., 11 maii 1782—*Fontes,* n. 3821.

ciary who was bound to make the profession of faith had to fulfill this duty even though no warning of the obligation was given.[13]

When the Sacred Congregation of Rites was asked whether a newly appointed pastor should make the profession of faith, when on the first occasion he canonically functions in his parochial ministry, in the presence of the assembled congregation in the parish church, the response was that the decree of the Council of Trent should be observed.[14]

It was permitted to receive the income of the office before making the profession of faith if there was no bad faith involved,[15] but those who neglected to make the profession of faith within two months, besides losing the income of the benefice also sacrificed all right of legal prescription in the case, and the canonical title was of no avail to them.[16]

In a decision given by the Sacred Congregation of Bishops and Regulars in 1862 there is furnished a summary of a number of interesting questions regarding installation.[17] In the Diocese of Linz, Austria, it was the custom for the dean (*Decanus ecclesiae parochialis*) to install parochial vicars regular (*Vicarii Curati Regulares*) after they had received approval from the bishop when they had been appointed to parishes which were joined with monasteries *pleno iure*. The abbot argued that the custom should be abolished, since the installation was necessary only in the case

---

[13] S. C. C., in *Tolentina,* ad cap. 1, sess. 23, *de ref.,* posit. 74—Pallottini, *Collectio Omnium Conclusionum et Resolutionum Quae in Causis Propositis apud Sacram Congregationem Cardinalium S. Concilii Tridentini Interpretum Prodierunt ab eius Institutione Anno MDLXIV ad Annum MDCCCLX, Distinctis Titulis Alphabetico Ordine per Materias Digesta* (18 vols., Romae, 1868-1895), XV, 366, n. 8 (hereafter referred to as Pallottini).

[14] S. R. C., *Briocen.,* 21 iul. 1855—*Fontes,* n. 5976; *Decreta Authentica,* n. 3035.

[15] S. C. C., *in Tolentina,* 17 apr. 1728—*Thesaurus Resolutionum Sacrae Congregationis Concilii* (167 vols., Romae, 1718-1908), IV, 174-175 (hereafter referred to simply as *Thesaurus*); Bouix, *Tractatus de Parocho,* p. 520.

[16] S. C. C., *Tirasonen.,* 20 apr. 1782—*Fontes.* n. 3821; Pallottini, XV, 158, n. 10.

[17] S. C. Ep. et Reg., *Lincien.,* 19 sept. 1862—*Fontes,* n. 1986; Bizzarri, *Collectanea in usum Secretariae Sacrae Congregationis Episcoporum et Regularium* (Romae, 1885), pp. 681-684 (hereafter cited Bizzarri).

of permanently assigned pastors who held the parish in real title. He argued that the requirement of installation did not obtain in the case of vicars regular, since they were subject to removal at the will of their religious superior and also of the bishop. He also claimed that too festive a celebration accompanied the installation ceremony, with the result that it disturbed the regular discipline of the monastery.

The Bishop of Linz insisted that the act of installation was not an investiture in the strict and proper sense, but simply a ceremony which manifested the vicar's dependence on the prelate of the monastery and on the bishop. He also claimed that the same custom prevailed in other dioceses.

In discussing the case before presenting the solution, the Sacred Congregation stated that from the law which required the approval of the bishop for the appointment of parochial vicars regular it by no means followed that it was necessary for the bishop to proceed to investiture, since no title was conceded to the vicar. It also stated that by the general rule of law no one was allowed to place himself in possession of a benefice through his own initiative and resources, and that this right pertained to the bishop or his delegate according to the prevailing law.

In solving the case the Sacred Congregation proposed the question and shaped its answer as follows:

"An, et quomodo servanda sit consuetudo in casu?"

The reply was:

"Affirmative, sublatis abusibus quoad expensas, et clamores."[18]

It seems, therefore, that the Congregation wished to uphold local customs in matters pertaining to installation.

In the presentation of the case this custom was explained as follows:

> "Decanus enim ecclesiae parochialis coram populo legit litteras, quibus Ordinarius nominato curato regimen animarum tradit, et deinde symbolis spiritualibus, quae illi consignat, scilicet stolam, librum Evangelii, claves Ecclesiae et similia, potestatem curato concessam indicat, palamque exhibet; et tandem confluenti populo Pastorem ostendendo sermonem habet."[19]

[18] *Fontes,* n. 1986; Bizzarri, pp. 681-684.

[19] *Loc. cit.*

A number of decisions of the Sacred Congregation of the Council indicate the necessity of a just title for the valid possession of a benefice. The acts of those who held a benefice without a just title were compared to acts of theft and robbery, and consequently these were compelled to restore the fruits of the benefice from the day they took unwarranted possession of the benefice.[20] Likewise those who in bad faith intruded themselves into a benefice were required to restore the income to the rightful possessor.[21]

A benefice if occupied by a cleric after his presentation by a patron, but without previous canonical institution, was still considered vacant.[22] If such an act was done in bad faith, the person was required to make restitution of the income he had obtained. But if it was done in good faith, he could lawfully retain the income he had received, for then the consideration of legal prescription mitiated in his favor.[23]

An interesting case which illustrates the nature and effect of installation was presented from the Diocese of Aquila in 1860. A certain priest, Aloysius Vespasiani, who had been a canon in the collegiate church of St. Justa, was nominated as pastor of the parochial church of the Holy Angels by its patron. The bishop gave his approval in his private chapel, and at the same time by placing a biretta upon the priest's head in a solemn ceremony with an appropriate formula gave him corporal possession of the benefice, after which the new pastor read the profession of faith.[24]

Some time later this priest decided that he wished to retain the former benefice held by him as a canon, in preference to the parochial benefice. The bishop contended that the earlier canonical benefice was relinquished when the priest received the verbal investiture in the bishop's private chapel. The priest in turn claimed

[20] S. C. C., *In Imolen., Iurispatronatus,* 3 aug. 1816—Pallottini, XV, 158, nn. 6. 10; *Thesaurus,* LXXVI, 181-186.

[21] S. C. C., *in Nullius Nonantulae Beneficii,* 30 aug. 1845—Pallottini, XV, 158, n. 7; *Thesaurus,* CV, 303-314.

[22] S. C. C., *in Neopolitana, Iurispatronatus,* 10 iun. 1848—Pallottini, XV, 158, n. 8; *Thesaurus,* CVIII, 239, 376.

[23] S. C. C., *in Suessana Bonorum,* 17 dec. 1852—Pallottini, XV, 158, n. 9; *Thesaurus,* CXI, 507.

[24] S. C. C., *Aquilana,* 22 sept. 1860—*Fontes,* n. 5189; Pallottini, XV, 158-159, nn. 12-13; *Thesaurus,* CXIX, 529-543.

that he still held the former canonical title, since he had not actually been installed by way of corporal induction in office at the seat of the parochial benefice itself.

In deciding the case the Congregation held that the investiture ceremony in the bishop's chapel was a real installation in the parochial benefice, since it included the handing over of possession by means of an appropriate symbol, the biretta, and that the nonoccurrence of this act at the seat of the parochial benefice was inconsequential to the substance and the essence of the act.[25]

An early decision of the Congregation of Bishops and Regulars in 1603 allowed a pastor to retain possession of a prior benefice until he could obtain peaceful possession of a second benefice over which there was a controversy with relation to the examination and election. He was allowed also to receive the income of both benefices, provided that he furnished whatever was the amount necessary to maintain a priest in the first benefice.[26]

The right of the archdeacon to grant installation gradually gave way to the custom which acknowledged this authority to the bishop's delegate, who was often the dean of a neighboring collegiate chapter or the rural dean.[27] A decision of the Congregation of Bishops and Regulars in the year 1890 sanctioned this practice and allowed the bishop to delegate any priests of the diocese, and this in virtue of the common law, to perform this office. It was not allowed, however, to delegate them to accept the profession of faith.[28]

It is worthy of mention here also that the penalties which were attached to lay investiture in earlier times by Popes Gregory VII (1073-1085) and Paschal II (1099-1118)[29] during the historic "Investiture Struggle" ceased with the Constitution *Apostolicae Sedis* of Pius IX (1846-1878), which was published under the date of October 12, 1869.[30] Since this document treated specifically

---

[25] *Loc. cit.*

[26] S. C. Ep. et Reg., *Bobien.,* 28 nov. 1603—*Fontes,* n. 1625.

[27] Reiffenstuel, *Ius Canonicum Universum,* lib. III, tit. 7, n. 45.

[28] S. C. Ep. et. Reg., *Apamien.,* 14 apr. 1890—*Fontes,* n. 2016; *Collectanea S. Congregationis de Propaganda Fide* (2 vols. Romae: Typographia Polyglotta S. C. de Propaganda Fide, 1907), n. 1726 (hereafter cited *Collectanea*).

[29] C. 12, 13, 18, C. XVI, q. 7; cf. *supra,* pp. 19-21.

[30] Pius IX, const., *Apostolicae Sedis,* 12 oct. 1869—*Acta Sanctae Sedis*

of *latae sententiae* penalties, the fact that no mention was made of lay investiture penalties is sufficient to indicate that they were no longer in effect.[31]

Article 4. Legislation of Provincial Councils after the Council of Trent

Because of the spreading influence of the so-called Reformation, provincial councils held after the Council of Trent were occupied largely with the extirpation of heresy and the reform of Christian morality. Besides reaffirming the doctrines and decrees of the Council of Trent, these councils enacted many particular laws concerning the pastoral office. In connection with installation the emphasis was placed upon the manifestation of orthodox faith and obedience to the Church before possession of the office was to be taken. The six Councils of Milan, held in the years 1565, 1569, 1573, 1576, 1579, and 1582, furnish an excellent illustration of this trend.

In the I Council of Milan (1565) it was decreed that all those who obtained ecclesiastical benefices had to accept each and every definition and statute of the Council of Trent, and likewise had to promise true obedience to the Roman Pontiff.[32] The bishops were requested to publish the decree in their cities, and to see to it that all complied with it within a month.

Stringent regulations were enacted as a safeguard against all occurrence of simony in the conferring of offices. It was forbidden to accept anything, even if freely offered, in this connection. No one was allowed to accept a benefice with the understanding that he would later turn it over to the one who granted the benefice or to anyone else. Bishops and inferior prelates were forbidden to reserve, at the time they conferred the benefice, any part of the income it yielded, even if it was intended that thereby some pious purpose should be served.[33] Severe penalties were attached to the

(41 vols., Romae, 1865-1908), V (1869), 287-312 (hereafter referred to with the letters *ASS*); *Fontes*, n. 552.

[31] Santi, *Praelectiones Iuris Canonici* (2. ed., 5 vols. in 2, Ratisbonae, 1892), lib. III, tit. 7, n. 26.

[32] Mansi—XXXIVa, 5-6; Hardouin, X, 637.

[33] "Interdicimus et iis, qui jus habent conferendi quaecumque beneficia ecclesiastica, seu eis providendi, aut ad ea eligendi, praesentandi, vel nomi-

violation of these decrees, and a special oath against simony was demanded of everyone before he could be admitted to the possession of a benefice.[34]

A new development was the decree which required a beneficiary to make an inventory of all the properties of the benefice within six months of taking possession of it.[35]

In the II Council of Milan (1569) similar decrees were enacted in relation to simony and the profession of faith. In addition those who thereafter obtained possession of a benefice, even though not previously advised to do so, were required to show to the ordinary within a month the title in virtue of which they could claim possession of the benefice. If they failed to do so, they were to be fined an amount equal to half of the yearly income of the benefice.[36]

The III Council of Milan (1573)[37] as also the IV Council of Milan (1576) added provisions to the decrees regarding the oath, in order to enforce residence of the beneficiary and to protect Church property from unlawful alienation.[38]

From a decree of the IV Council it seems that the previous regulations regarding the inventory and proof of title were being exploited by notaries for their personal gain. It was forbidden to accept offerings of any kind for furnishing copies, stamps, seals, etc., in witness of the taking of possession of office. An ecclesiastical notary, if he received no other income, was allowed to receive not more than one gold coin for subscribing the acts of installation.[39] It was also allowed to take simultaneous possession of all of the properties of a benefice in the place in which the church was located, so that expenses would not be multiplied.[40]

---

nandi, et eorum ministris cuiusvis generis, ne quidquam per quamvis causam eius rei gratia ab aliquo, cui ecclesiasticum beneficium quavis ratione tribuatur, ne sponte quidem datum accipiant."—Mansi, XXXIVa, 27-28.

[34] "Neminem autem vel praesentatum, vel nominatum, vel electum, vel ab inferioribus provisum prius admittant, aut instituant episcopi, quam infrascriptum jusjurandum ab eo exegerint."—*Loc. cit.*

[35] Mansi, XXXIVa, 71.

[36] Mansi, XXXIVa, 122-123.

[37] Mansi, XXXIVa, 159.

[38] Mansi, XXXIVa, 182; Hardouin, X, 806.

[39] "Plus aureo nummo ad summum ne capiat."—Mansi, XXXIVa, 241.

[40] "Ne pro beneficii ecclesiastici possessione adipiscenda, plus quam par est, impensae quis in compluribus instrumentis eo nomine conficiendis vel

The law regarding the profession of faith and the regulations previously invoked as a safeguard against simony in the conferring of office again received mention in the V Council of Milan (1579),[41] and also in the VI Council of Milan (1582).[42]

Councils held in France and Belgium during the early post-Tridentine period also show the practice of using the occasion of investiture for the sake of enforcing the reform decrees. The profession of the orthodox faith as a prime requisite was frequently mentioned.[43] This profession of faith generally included a promise of reverence and obedience to the Church as required by the Council of Trent, which promise in a very specific manner referred to the bishop and his successors.[44]

The councils frequently adverted to the requisite promise to avoid simony or anything having the appearance of simony in connection with investiture.[45] Those who received parochial bene-

---

exscribendis faciat, cum eius bona variis locis sita sunt; id propterea decernimus et declaramus liberum esse unicuique, cui beneficium aliquod collatum, aut quovis provisionis nomine datum est, et illius solum ecclesiae, altarisve, in quo beneficii titulus est, et illorum tantum eiusdem beneficii praediorum bonorumve, quae ipse maluerit, possessionem capere: modo eam capiat, tabulis publice a notario confectis."—Mansi, XXXIVa, 240.

[41] Mansi, XXXIVa, 339-448.

[42] Mansi, XXXIVa, 524.

[43] Council of Malines (1570)—Mansi, XXXIVa, 578-580; Council of Rouen (1581)—Mansi, XXXIVa, 634; Council of Bordeaux (1583)—Mansi, XXXIVa, 748; Council of Tours (1583)—Mansi, XXXIVa, 808; Council of Cambrai (1586)—Mansi, XXXIVb, 1251; Council of Toulouse (1590)—Mansi, XXXIVb, 1272; Council of Avignon (1594)—Mansi, XXXIVb, 1352; Council of Narbonne (1609)—Mansi, XXXIVb, 1480.

[44] Council of Toulouse (1590)—Mansi, XXXIVb, 1277; Council of Avignon (1594)—Mansi, XXXIVb, 1352; Council of Malines (1605)—Mansi, XXXIVb, 1461; Provincial Council of Kalocsa in Hungary (1863)—*Acta et Decreta Sacrorum Conciliorum Recentiorum, Collectio Lacensis* (7 vols., Friburgi Brisgoviae, 1870-1890), V, 635d (hereafter cited as *Coll. Lac.*); Provincial Council of Prague (1860)—*Coll. Lac.*, V, 570a.

[45] Council of Toledo (1565)—Mansi, XXXIVa, 555; Council of Rouen (1581)—Mansi, XXXIVa, 629; Council of Rheims (1583)—Mansi, XXXIVa, 709-710; Council of Bordeaux (1583)—Mansi, XXXIVa, 775-776; Council of Toulouse (1590)—Mansi, XXXIVb, 1311; Council of Avignon (1594)—Mansi, XXXIVb, 1352; Council of Narbonne (1609)—Mansi, XXXIVb, 1512; Provincial Council of Prague (1860)—*Coll. Lac.*, V, 570a.

fices were required to promise that they would show to the bishop, generally within six months, the documents showing their title to the benefice.[46] It was also required to present an inventory of the temporal goods belonging to the benefice, and to promise to protect these goods and not to alienate them without permission.[47]

It is interesting to note that the councils of the Germanic countries were generally more specific in treating of the method and manner of investiture.[48] The archdeacon, the vice-archdeacon, the rural dean and the delegate of the bishop were named as having the right to grant investiture.[49]

The complaints made by the bishops indicate that there was still occasional interference on the part of civil authorities in connection with the canonical institution and the investiture of pastors in office.[50]

Article 5. The Oath against Modernism

A new development in connection with installation came with the famous Motu Proprio, *Sacrorum Antistitum,* of Pope Pius X in 1910. In his efforts to combat the heresy of Modernism, the Pontiff ordered that, among others, parish priests after making the profession of faith were to take the oath against Modernism before taking possession of their benefices.[51]

---

[46] Council of Rouen (1581)—Mansi, XXXIVa, 634, 641, 652; Council of Toulouse (1590)—Mansi, XXXIVb, 1311; Council of Narbonne (1609)—Mansi, XXXIVb, 1512.

[47] Council of Acqua Reggio (1585)—Mansi, XXXIVb, 985; Council of Malines (1605)—Mansi, XXXIVb, 1461; Provincial Council of Prague (1860)—*Coll. Lac.*, V, 570a.

[48] Provincial Council of Vienna (1858)—*Coll. Lac.*, V, 223a; Council of Esztergom in Hungary (1858)—*Coll. Lac.*, V, 48b; Provincial Council of Prague (1860)—*Coll. Lac.*, V, 570c; Provincial Council of Kalocsa in Hungary (1863)—*Coll. Lac.*, V, 636a.

[49] Provincial Council of Vienna (1858)—*Coll. Lac.*, V, 157d; Council of Esztergom (1858)—*Coll. Lac.*, V, 48b; Provincial Council of Prague (1860)—*Coll. Lac.*, V, 557a, 570c; Provincial Council of Cologne (1860)—*Coll. Lac.*, V, 343d; Provincial Council of Kalocsa (1863)—*Coll. Lac.*, V, 633a, 636a.

[50] Conference of the Bishops of Würzburg (1848)—*Coll. Lac.*, V, 1037c and d; Conference of the Bishops of Bavaria at Munich (1850)—*Coll. Lac.*, V, 1171c.

[51] Pius X, motu propr., *Sacrorum antistitum,* 1 sept. 1910—*Fontes,* n. 689;

Several problems were presented by the wording of this decree. It stated that the oath was to be preceded by the profession of faith according to the formula of Pius IV with the additions regarding the definitions of the Vatican Council. The difficulty arose from the requirement that the prospective incumbent was to pronounce the oath before he took possession of the benefice.[52]

Previously a period of two months subsequent to the taking of possession of the benefice was allowed as the time within which the profession of faith could be made.[53]

Accordingly the Sacred Consistorial Congregation was asked whether the period of grace allowed by the Council of Trent could still be used. The Congregation presented the question to Pope Pius X, who ordered that the response should be in the negative, and that thereafter the prospective incumbent was to make the profession of faith before taking possession of the benefice.[54]

In an earlier declaration this Congregation had ruled that the bishop could delegate any priest, whether secular or religious, to receive the oath in particular cases if there was a just cause.[55] A later declaration provided that the bishop could delegate the vicar general *"generali modo"* to receive the oath, and that parish priests could take the oath before him from whom they were to obtain the possession of the benefice.[56] To the question whether newly appointed beneficiaries had to sign not only the formula of the profession of faith but also that of the oath, the Congregation answered that regarding the profession of faith nothing new was to be introduced (*nihil innovandum*), and regarding the oath the conditions of the Motu Proprio, *Sacrorum Antistitum,* were to be observed.[57]

Acta Apostolicae Sedis, Commentarium Officiale (Romae, 1909—), II (1910), 669 (hereafter referred to with the letters *AAS*); cf. Beste, *Introductio in Codicem* (2. ed., Collegeville, Minn.: St. John's Abbey Press, 1944), p. 695.

[52] ". . . ante ineundam beneficii possessionem."—*loc. cit.*

[53] *Supra,* p. 41.

[54] S. C. Consist., 1 mart. 1911—*Fontes,* n. 2080; *AAS,* III (1911), 134.

[55] S. C. Consist., declar., 25 sept. 1910, ad VIII—*Fontes,* n. 2075; *AAS,* II (1910), 740-741.

[56] S. C. Consist., declar., 25 oct. 1910, ad III, IV—*Fontes,* n. 2077; *AAS,* II (1910), 856-857.

[57] *Ibid.,* ad VII—*Fontes,* n. 2077; *AAS,* II (1910), 857.

Since no mention of the oath against Modernism was made in the new Code of Canon Law, there arose the question whether the taking of this oath was still required in the future. The Sacred Congregation of the Holy Office declared in a decree of March 22, 1918, that the oath was not mentioned in the Code because it was directed against the Modernistic errors which are of a temporary and transitory nature. However, since these errors had not ceased to spread, it ruled that the prescription as issued by Pope Pius X would remain in force until the Holy See decreed otherwise.[58]

Hence they are still in effect in the present inasmuch as no new decree to the contrary has been issued.

---

[58] S. C. S. Off., *decr.*, 22 mart. 1918—*AAS,* X (1918), 136; Bouscaren, *The Canon Law Digest* (2 vols., Milwaukee, Wis.: Bruce Publishing Co., 1934-1943), I, 50-51; Beste, *Introductio in Codicem,* p. 695.

CHAPTER V

DOCTRINE OF THE COMMENTATORS

The picture of the historical development of installation would not be complete without a study of the doctrine of the more important commentators on the decretal legislation and that which followed. The fact that there are a considerable number of commentaries on this subject is evidence that it was considered as of real importance in the body of ecclesiastical law.

It has been indicated in an earlier chapter[1] that to avoid confusion in the discussion of installation the authors found it necessary to give precise definitions of the various steps involved in the conferral of office. In general the definitions of Abbas Panormitanus were followed.[2]

The principal difficulty encountered by the commentators in discussing installation was the element which centered in the necessity of corporal institution. Indeed, the controversy continues to the present time. Before treating this question in detail, the writer proposes to deal with a few other topics which appear to claim prior attention.

Most of the authors agreed that by common law the right of granting installation belonged to the archdeacon. In support of this opinion they generally cited the decretal letter *Ad haec* of Inno-

[1] *Supra*, p. 6.

[2] *Supra*, p. 6; cf. Reiffenstuel, *Ius Canonicum Universum*, lib. III, tit. 7, nn. 2-9; Ferraris, *Prompta Bibliotheca Canonica, Iuridica, Moralis, Theologica, necnon Ascetica, Polemica, Rubristica, Historica* (9 vols., Romae, 1885-1899), IV, *Institutio seu Instituere in Beneficiis*, nn. 8-11 (hereafter cited Ferraris); Engel, *Collegium Universi Iuris Canonici* (9. ed., cum annotationibus Caspari Barthel, Beneventi, 1760), lib. III, tit. 7, nn. 4-5; Garcia, *De Beneficiis Ecclesiasticis*, pars IV, c. 1, nn. 1-12; Pirhing, *Ius Canonicum in Quinque Libros Decretalium Distributum* (Dilingae, 1674-1678), lib. III, tit. 7, n. 1; Gonzalez-Tellez, *Commentaria in Quinque Libros Decretalium* (5 vols., Venetiis, 1699), lib. III, tit. 7, c. 3; Barbosa, *Iuris Ecclesiastici Universi Libri Tres* (3 vols., Lugduni, 1660), lib. III, c. 13, nn. 5-7; Leurenius, *Forum Beneficiale* (2 vols., Venetiis, 1752), pars II, q. 6 and 7; Schmalzgrueber, *Ius Ecclesiasticum Universum* (5 vols. in 12, Romae, 1843-1845), lib. III, tit. 5, n. 40 and tit. 7, n. 1.

cent III.[3] However, there was also a quite general agreement that by custom this right came to be exercised by the bishop or his delegate. The source of this custom is generally traced to the special provision which had been made in the decretal letter *Licet episcopus* of Boniface VIII.[4]

Local customs and particular laws were regarded by all the authors as the norm for determining the manner of installation, since the general law did not prescribe any special form as of necessary use.[5] Schmalzgrueber (1663-1735) stated that there existed a great variety of customs regulating the installation of pastors. In some dioceses, he stated, the bishop or his delegate granted installation to the newly appointed pastor by leading him into the parish church, by having him kiss the altar, by handing him the keys of the church, or by executing other similar acts in the church. In other dioceses it was customary to grant investiture on some feast day when the people were present for divine services. After making the profession of faith and taking the oath of obedience, the pastor received the parochial insignia. This was called the *"investitura in spiritualibus."* After these ceremonies he was accompanied to the parish house, there to be given the keys, and to be entrusted with the accounting of the parish books. This was called the *"traditio temporalium."*[6]

Article 1. The Necessity of Corporal Institution

As has been mentioned, the question of the necessity of corporal institution was the principal difficulty regarding this subject

---

[3] C. 7, X, *de officio archidiaconi,* I, 23; *supra,* p. 29; Ferraris, s. v. *Institutio,* n. 27; Reiffenstuel, *Ius Canonicum Universum,* lib. III, tit. 7, n. 43; Engel, *Collegium Universi Iuris Canonici,* lib. III, tit. 7, n. 5; Schmalzgrueber, *Ius Ecclesiasticum Universum,* lib. III, tit. 7, n. 49; Pirhing, *Ius Canonicum in Quinque Libros Decretalium Distributum,* lib. I, tit. 23, nn. 11-12.

[4] C. 28, *de praebendis et dignitatibus,* III, 4, in VI°; *supra,* p. 32; Schmalzgrueber, *loc. cit.*; Ferraris, *ibid.,* n. 28; Engel, *loc. cit.*; Gonzalez-Tellez, *Commentarium in Quinque Libros Decretalium,* lib. III, tit. 7, c. 3, n. 2.

[5] Engel, *ibid.,* nn. 4-6; Schmalzgrueber, *ibid.,* n. 52; Ferraris, *ibid.,* n. 35; Pirhing, *Ius Canonicum in Quinque Libros Decretalium Distributum,* lib. III, tit. 7, n. 1.

[6] *Ius Ecclesiasticum Universum,* lib. III, tit. 7, n. 52.

as treated by the authors. There appeared to be a universal agreement that some form of corporal institution was necessary for the complete conferral of office.

Reiffenstuel (1642-1703), using scriptural language, intimated that no one should take unto himself an honor in the Church unless called by God as Aaron was. Likewise pastors of souls should not enter into the sheepfold of Christ except through the gate which is opened by the gatekeeper.[7] From the context of this passage it is obvious that by the gate in the metaphor was meant the canonical institution, and by the gatekeeper was meant the corporal induction or installation.

Reiffenstuel likewise stated that it would have been useless to include corporal institution in ecclesiastical legislation if anyone could, on his own authority, take possession of a benefice granted to him.[8] Santi (1830-1885) declared that the reason for installation was obvious, namely, the avoidance of confusion and the preclusion of all doubt as to the vested right of possession on the part of the beneficiary.[9]

Citing Ioannes Andreae (1272-1348) and Fagnanus (1598-1678), Reiffenstuel stated that three things are necessary for the complete canonical institution. The person who confers the office must have the power of conferring it, the recipient must be capable of receiving it, and the solemnities prescribed by the law must be observed.[10] These three things, he maintained, are necessary in general for any institution in the wide sense.[11]

The problem entailed added difficulty, however, when the authors debated whether in the act of taking possession of a benefice the corporal institution was necessary as a requirement for the validity or simply for the lawfulness of the holding of the benefice. Some authors seemed to hold in theory that it was necessary in the sense of an essential requisite, but in practice they seemed ready to regard it as necessary simply in the sense of a

---

[7] *Ius Canonicum Universum,* lib. III, tit. 7, n. 52.

[8] *Loc. cit.*

[9] *Praelectiones Iuris Canonici,* lib. III, tit. 7, n. 24.

[10] *Ius Canonicum Universum,* lib. III, tit. 7, n. 10.

[11] ". . . generatin loquendo ad quamlibet institutionem late sumptam . . . alioquin enim ex defectu unius horum, iam non foret amplius Institutio Canonica."—*ibid.,* n. 11.

prescription for lawful procedure. Others merely asserted that installation was required; they simply abstracted from all possible qualifications regarding the degree or measure in which corporal institution was necessary in the various circumstances in which the law called for it. In clarification of the debate a number of distinctions attending the manner of installation were proposed. These will be treated in the articles which follow.

Article 2. *Ius in Re* and *Ius ad Rem*

A number of authors emphasized the distinction between the *ius in re* and the *ius ad rem.* Garcia (+1645) devoted individual chapters to the study of the methods relating to the acquisition of each of these.[12] The *ius in re,* he taught, was acquired through the free conferral (*collatio*) of a benefice as soon as the conferral was accepted, even before the taking of corporal possession of the benefice had ensued.[13] The same right was also acquired through the canonical institution of one who had been presented for office by a patron, through the confirmation of one who had been elected to office, and through the admission of one for whom a postulation had been made.[14] Reiffenstuel held this same view, and indicated that he adhered to the teaching of the *Glossa ordinaria,* Covarruvias (+1577), Flaminius Parisius (+1603) and Gonzalez-Tellez (+ca. 1673).[15]

The *ius ad rem* was the right which the prospective beneficiary acquired through the act of being presented by a patron. It had this effect that, if the presentee was suitable for the office, the superior was obligated to give him canonical institution in that office.[16] Garcia listed twelve ways by which a *ius ad rem* in relation to a benefice could be acquired. Besides presentation he also mentioned election, regardless of its previous acceptance or non-acceptance by the one elected, reservation by a superior, conferral if not yet accepted, an expectative grant or concession (*gratia ex-*

---

[12] *De Beneficiis Ecclesiasticis,* pars IV, c. 2 and 3.

[13] *Ibid.,* c. 2, n. 1.

[14] *Ibid.,* n. 3.

[15] *Ius Canonicum Universum,* lib. III, tit. 7, n. 78; cf. Schmalzgrueber, *Ius Ecclesiasticum Universum,* lib. I, tit. 7, n. 6.

[16] Schmalzgrueber, *loc. cit.*

pectativa), a right of exercising an elective choice (*ius optandi*), etc.[17]

The reason for this important distinction is seen in the quite universal agreement among the authors that anyone who without a title took possession of a benefice, or unjustly injected himself into a benefice, simply did not gain canonical possession of it.[18] The same was true in the case of those who occupied a benefice by force or with violence, even though there previously existed for them the right to acquire possession of the benefice in question. The basis for this agreement in doctrine was the law as enacted in the *Liber Sextus*. That law, by way of penalty, entailed the deprivation of any rights which had been obtained on the part of persons who acted with violence or force in seeking to gain corporal possession of the benefice to which this appointment related.[19]

Article 3. Verbal and Actual Installation

Another distinction which is important in the discussion regarding the necessity of corporal institution was that which was made between verbal and actual installation. Engel (1634-1674) stated that customarily a twofold distinction was invoked in the consideration of investiture.[20] Verbal investiture was that which was accompanied exclusively with the use of words and the handing over of some particular sign or symbol of office, and actual or real investiture was that which was effected through the actual inducting of the prospective beneficiary into the possession of the benefice. The first of these, he contended, should be considered as creating simply the obligation of later granting the actual posses-

---

[17] Garcia, *De Beneficiis Ecclesiasticis,* pars IV, c. 3; cf. Reiffenstuel, *Ius Canonicum Universum,* lib. III, tit. 7, n. 75.

[18] Reiffenstuel, *ibid.,* n. 57; cf. also *ibid.,* tit. 5, n. 343; Garcia, *ibid.,* c. 2, n. 8; Engel, *Collegium Universi Iuris Canonici,* lib. III, tit. 7, n. 4; Schmalzgrueber, *Ius Ecclesiasticum Universum,* lib. III, tit. 7, n. 65.

[19] C. 18, *de praebendis et dignitatibus,* III, 4, in VI°; *supra,* p. 32; cf. Garcia, *ibid.,* n. 9; Reiffenstuel, *ibid.,* n. 59; Schmalzgrueber, *loc. cit.*; Engel, *loc. cit.*; Santi, *Praelectiones Iuris Canonici,* lib. III, tit. 7, n. 24; Rossi, *De Paroecia* (Romae: Pustet, 1923), pp. 120-123; Sebastianelli, *Praelectiones Iuris Canonici,* II (*De Rebus*), n. 227.

[20] *Collegium Universi Iuris Canonici,* lib. III, tit. 7, n. 5.

sion, or at most the permission for the beneficiary later to occupy the vacant benefice on his own authority.[21]

Reiffenstuel, basing his opinion on that of Julius Clarus (fl. 1555) and of Engel, referred to verbal investiture by designating it as an *"actio abusiva."* By this he implied that the verbal investiture reflected but a sign or symbol in token of the actual investiture. The sign or symbol frequently employed was the act by which the proper superior, with the accompaniment of an explanatory formulary, imposed a biretta on the head of the prospective beneficiary in token of his authority, and presented a ring to him in token of his perpetual incumbency in the benefice.[22]

Usually in the presence of the bishop or his vicar general, presiding in a gathering of ecclesiastics, the prospective beneficiary made the profession of faith as prescribed by the Council of Trent, and took the oath of obedience and fidelity to the bishop and his successors. After this, with appropriate words signifying the intent of the investiture, the presiding prelate imposed the biretta and presented the ring.[23]

Reiffenstuel stated further that the ceremony of verbal investiture at times was undertaken apart from any previous election for, presentation to, or conferral of office. In that event it was juridically the equivalent of a simple conferral of office (*collatio*). If the verbal investiture was preceded by any of the acts leading to an ultimate institution in office, then one had to distinguish whether this ceremony occurred in or away from the seat of the benefice. In the latter event the verbal investiture was simply the equivalent of a quasi-confirmation of the *ius in re.* It did not imply the actual granting of the corporal possession, but simply created the obligation of later granting the actual possession, or at most it connoted the grant of a permission to the appointed beneficiary to occupy the benefice on his own authority. But in the former event, that is, when the ceremony of verbal investiture occurred at the seat of the benefice itself, then it became the equivalent of a real and actual investiture, which transferred to the appointed bene-

---

[21] *Loc. cit.*

[22] *Ius Canonicum Universum,* lib. III, tit. 7, n. 46.

[23] *Ibid.,* n. 47.

ficiary the actual and corporal possession of the benefice that was to be filled through his incumbency in it.[24]

Article 4. Validity or Lawfulness

In the more important question whether the action of those who contrary to the law took possession of a benefice on their own authority was juridically invalid or simply illicit, there was no universal agreement among the authors. The specific question here to be treated concerns those who already had acquired a *ius in re.* It has already been mentioned that anyone who took possession when he enjoyed only a *ius ad rem* could not validly take possession of that right on his own authority. The same was true of anyone who forced himself into a benefice which was still legally occupied by another. If violence had been used, the offender thereby lost all right to the benefice, and became incapable also of receiving it at any later time.[25]

Garcia listed the names of the various authors, both before and during his time, who formed the two schools of thought on the question of validity and lawfulness in relation to the taking of possession of a benefice on one's own authority if one already had acquired a *ius in re* with reference to the benefice.[26] Among those who held that the unauthorized act of taking possession was invalid he listed the following: Dinus Mugellanus, who wrote about the year 1300, Lapus Tactus, the Abbot of the Monastery of St. Miniato in Florence, who wrote about the year 1320, Paulus de Liazariis (+1356), a pupil of Ioannes Andreae (+1348), who later became a professor at Bologna and Perugia, Petrus de Ancharano (+1416), also a professor at Bologna, Petrus Rebuffus (+1557), a professor at the University of Paris, and Flaminius Parisius (+1603), a professor at Rome and later the Bishop of Bitonto in the region of Apulia, Italy.[27]

It is interesting to note that the opinions of Lapus Tactus, of Paulus de Liazariis and of Petrus Ancharanus were expressed in

---

[24] *Ibid.,* n. 48.

[25] *Supra,* p. 32.

[26] *De Beneficiis Ecclesiasticis,* pars IV, c. 2, nn. 4-5.

[27] Cf. Van Hove, *Commentarium Lovaniense in Codicem Iuris Canonici* (5 tom., Mechliniae: Dessain, 1928-1945), Tom. I, vol. I, *Prolegomena* (2. ed., 1945) pp. 473-528.

connection with their treatment of the decretal *Eum qui,* in the *Liber Sextus.*[28] This decretal dealt with the case of those who either by force or unjustly occupied a benefice, and without a title to it injected themselves into its possession.

Among those who held the opposite opinion, namely, that for the holding of a benefice the act of corporal installation was necessary solely for the lawful possession of it, Garcia listed Rochus Curtius (+1495) and Diego Covarruvias (1512-1577), who together with Cardinal Ugo Buoncompagni (afterwards Pope Gregory XIII) was authorized to formulate the reform decrees of the Council of Trent.[29] He also listed Flaminius Parisius as holding this view, stating that this author was not consistent in his comments. Likewise he quoted Rebuffus as stating that the opinion which regarded the necessity of corporal installation in office as a requirement which touched the element simply of licitness in the holding of the benefice was common in practice.[30]

Garcia indicated his own opinion by stating that those who had received canonical title to a benefice were acknowledged as capable of validly administering the benefice before they had taken corporal possession of it, as long of course as the benefice was *de iure* vacant when the administration was assumed. If corporal installation were a postulate for the valid administration, so he argued, then such acts of administration would have to be recognized as the equivalent of acts of spoliation, which view however was not generally accepted in practice.[31] He likewise contended that the law of the *Liber Sextus* in the decretal *Eum qui* did not militate against this opinion, inasmuch as that decretal considered solely those who had occupied a benefice by force or unjustly, and then held possession of it without a title.[32] The same was to be said with reference to the earlier decretal *Ad aures* of Alexander III, which related to the case wherein a just and canonical title was lacking.[33]

---

[28] C. 18, *de praebendis et dignitatibus,* III, 4, in VI°; *supra,* p. 32.

[29] Cicognani, *Canon Law,* p. 392.

[30] *De Beneficiis Ecclesiasticis,* pars IV, c. 2, n. 6.

[31] *Ibid.,* n. 7.

[32] *Ibid.,* n. 9.

[33] *Ibid.,* n. 8. Cf. *Quinque Compilationes Antiquae necnon Collectio Canonum Lipsiensis* (ed. Friedberg, Lipsiae, 1882), Comp. I, lib. III, tit. 7, n. 2;

Engel (1634-1674), when quoting Covarruvias in substantiation of his position, stated that one who had received a title to a benefice (*ius in re*) could not lawfully take possession of it on his own authority. If he nevertheless unlawfully took possession of it, he was to be punished by the bishop with appropriate penalties.[34] If in taking such possession he used violence, he *ipso facto* lost all right to the benefice in question. Reiffenstuel extended the application of this principle to show that installation was necessary only from the viewpoint of lawfulness for the act. If installation were necessary from the viewpoint of validity as well, then the person considered in the earlier of these two cases should likewise lose the right to the benefice, rather than become liable merely for discretional punishment to be inflicted by the bishop.[35]

Engel stressed the distinction between verbal and actual installation. He stated that once the verbal investiture had taken place the actual induction into office at the seat of the benefice could be entrusted, as sometimes it was, to a layman.[36] But he deplored any such practice in the light of the legislation of the Council of Trent regarding the right of patronage. Yet this practice seemed to indicate that, consequent upon a verbal investiture, the further act of induction in office was not essential to the validity of the act of taking possession of the office.[37]

Reiffenstuel held that, once a person had received verbal investiture, he actually acquired from his superior whatever the latter in his power could bestow. Therefore such a person could proceed on his own authority to take possession of his benefice. Verbal investiture connoted a tacit permission for occupying the benefice which currently was *de iure* vacant. In support of this doctrine Reiffenstuel cited Rebuffus (+1557), Julius Clarus (fl. 1555), Covarruvias (+1577), Laymann (+1635) and Engel (+1674).[38]

Jaffé, n. 8884.

[34] ". . . poena saltem arbitraria ab Episcopo puniendus . . ."—*Collegium Universi Iuris Canonici,* lib. III, tit. 7, n. 4.

[35] *Ius Canonicum Universum,* lib. III, tit. 7, n. 55.

[36] *Ibid.,* nn. 5-6.

[37] Cf. Pirhing, *Ius Canonicum in Quinque Libros Decretalium Distributum,* lib. III, tit. 7, n. 3.

[38] *Ius Canonicum Universum,* lib. III, tit. 7, n. 53; cf. Ferraris, s. v., *Institutio,* n. 36.

With Laymann however he limited the application of his doctrine in such a way that, if a local custom or particular statute demanded actual or real investiture as well, then this custom was to be observed for the lawful taking of possession.[39]

Another argument which Reiffenstuel presented to indicate that one who had received a canonical title could on his own authority take possession was the fact that, although many laws had been enacted regarding installation, it was nowhere stated that the taking of corporal possession was invariably required as essential for the valid holding of the benefice.[40] He also pointed to the fact that a person who had been elected to an office could proceed to the administration of that office after he had received confirmation; if the confirmation had been given, the person no longer had to await the ceremony of his actual installation for either the valid or the licit administration of the benefice whose incumbent he actually was.[41]

Schmalzgrueber (1663-1735) expressed his opinion thus: When a prelate confers a benefice, he does so either apart from or in connection with some employed sign or symbol of the benefice conferred. If he uses the first of these methods, the beneficiary may not on his own authority take possession of even a vacant benefice. In the second case, however, the act of investiture can at the same time connote the act of institution in office. Now, if the prelate has the right of granting possession, then his act of investiture is to be understood as connoting also whatever permission is requisite for the person to take possession of the benefice even on his own authority.[42]

Later authors seem mainly to re-echo the same doctrine regarding the subject of installation. This could well be expected, for no new laws were enacted regarding it. Santi (1830-1885), for example, simply stated that it was forbidden for a cleric on his own authority to take possession of a benefice granted to him. If he rashly attempted to do this, he became liable for punishment within the free discretion of his ordinary. If he used violence to gain pos-

[39] *Ibid.*, n. 54.

[40] *Ibid.*, n. 56.

[41] *Ibid.*, n. 57.

[42] *Ius Ecclesiasticum Universum*, lib. III, tit. 7, n. 63.

session, he lost all right to the benefice.[43] Similar views were expressed by Sebastianelli (+1920)[44] and by Rossi.[45]

In concluding this article one may summarize the doctrine of the commentators as follows:

1. All the authors agreed that without a canonical title no one could validly take possession even of a vacant benefice.

2. If a person who held canonical title to a benefice used force or violence to gain possession of it on his own authority, he thereby lost all title to it.

3. If a person who had acquired a title by simple conferral, but who had not yet been granted a verbal investiture by means of some symbol of his office, took possession on his own authority he was to be punished by his superior, but he did not lose the "*ius in re.*"

4. If a person had acquired a title through verbal investiture, he then also enjoyed a tacit permission on his own authority to take possession of the benefice, unless some local custom or particular statute required also a real and actual installation in addition to the previous act of the verbal investiture.

5. Some authors from the fourteenth through the sixteenth century, however, had held that a real and actual installation was necessary for the valid possession of a benefice, even when a verbal investiture had previously been granted.

---

[43] Santi, *Praelectiones Iuris Canonici,* lib. III, tit. 7, n. 25; cf. Bouix, *Tractatus de Parocho,* p. 375.

[44] *Praelectiones Iuris Canonici,* II (*De Rebus*), n. 227.

[45] *De Paroecia,* pp. 120-123 and p. 175.

PART TWO

CANONICAL COMMENTARY

CHAPTER VI

THE DEFINITION OF TERMS

Article 1. An Explanation of Canonical Installation

According to the general concepts of canonical legislation the full conferral of an office or of a benefice is completed and has its entire effect through the corporal installation in office. This assertion is substantially correct if it is also added that there are some few offices, such as that of vicar general, the minor curial offices and those of some religious superiors, which do not require corporal installation for complete juridic effects.

The institute of canonical installation is referred to in the Code of Canon Law as *"missio in possessionem seu institutio corporalis."*[1] Authors also refer to it with such terms as *apprehensio beneficii, captio possessionis, introductio in possessionem, inductio, institutio realis, investitura, installatio, inthronizatio,* etc.[2]

Cappello defines canonical installation as the act of a competent ecclesiastical superior by which a beneficiary is accorded the actual possession of a benefice, the title to which he has already obtained by legitimate conferral.[3] Berutti gives practically the same notions, but also includes offices along with benefices when he defines installation as the act or solemnity by which a cleric is granted the real and actual possession of an office or a benefice which has been legitimately conferred upon him.[4]

From these definitions and especially from the terms used to describe canonical installation several concepts are quite clear. Installation is separate from the appointment to an office or a benefice, for the beneficiary or the officeholder to be installed must already have been appointed to that benefice or office. Likewise installation is not to be confused with presentation or nomination to office, for

---

1 Can. 1443, § 2.

2 Beste, *Introductio in Codicem,* pp. 710-711; Berutti, *Institutiones Iuris Canonici* (6 vols. in 7, Vol. II, pars I, Taurini-Romae: Marietti, 1943), Vol. II, pars I, p. 268.

3 *Summa Iuris Canonici,* II, 565.

4 *Loc. cit.*

these consist in the designation of a particular person for an office by those who enjoy the right of patronage over that office or by those who have some other right or privilege to do this. Neither is installation to be identified with confirmation in office or admission to an office, for these obtain only in the case wherein someone is elected to or postulated for an office.

Canonical installation is by no means equivalent to the conferral of office as envisioned in canon 147, although the case could possibly occur in which all of the acts prescribed in that canon could coalesce into the one act of corporal installation. This could happen if a legitimate superior proceeded to induct a cleric into the corporal possession of a vacant office of free conferral apart from any previous canonical acts which as intermediate steps lead to the eventual filling of the office.[5]

A further difficulty in the application of the terminology concerning installation in office arises from the not infrequent employment of the term *canonical institution* for the purpose of designating the *canonica provisio* which is spoken of in the canons on the conferral of office.[6] In a wide sense the word *institution* is sometimes also used as a term that includes the notion of corporal installation. More properly, however, *institutio* refers only to that form of canonical assignment of office by which an office is granted to one who has been presented by a patron, or to one who has been nominated for the office by a group or a person having that right or privilege.[7] The complications arising from the inaccurate use of terms with reference to installation were already apparent to the glossators of the early legislation relating to this canonical institute.[8]

As an aid in the solution of the problems to be met later in the discussion of the necessity of installation in office, it seems imperative to present a clear analysis of the meaning of the term *canonica provisio* with reference to ecclesiastical offices. It may be said to comprise two distinct concepts, namely, the designation of the person to receive the office and the actual concession of the

[5] Panormitanus, lib. III, tit. 7, n. 9.

[6] Cans. 147-159.

[7] Can. 148, §§ 1-2.

[8] Cf. Reg. 1, R. J., in VI°, s. v., *Beneficium; supra*, p. 34.

power of the office. The designation of the person is made in three ways: it is accomplished through the free appointment by the superior, through the nomination or presentation by a patron, or through the election or postulation by a chapter or some other electoral group. From this designation the person acquires a *ius ad rem* with reference to the office or to the benefice. The actual concession of the power of the office is achieved through the free conferral by the superior, through the institution of the one nominated by an ecclesiastic or presented by a patron, through the confirmation of the one elected, or through the admission of one who has been postulated. Through any of these acts the person acquires a *ius in re* to the office or to the benefice.[9]

While these two actions, namely, the designation of the person and the actual concession of the power of the office, are the only ones specifically mentioned in the canons on the conferral of office, there is an implicit reference to the later canons in which a third step is required before the officeholder or the beneficiary may legitimately exercise the authority of his office or of his benefice. This third step is the *missio in possessionem* or the corporal installation.[10]

It may be argued that there is special reference to this step in canon 147, § 2, which states that the concession of an ecclesiastical office must be made according to the norm of the sacred canons.[11] or again in canon 177, § 4, which states that upon the receipt of the confirmation of the competent superior the person elected to office

---

[9] It should be noted that the terminology of the *ius ad rem* and the *ius in re* is used with reference to offices as well as to benefices, and that the various ways used in the designation of the person and in the concession of authority are sometimes employed in the case of an office which is not a benefice as well as in the case of an office which is erected as a benefice. Cf. Wernz-Vidal, *Ius Canonicum* (7 vols. in 9, Tom. II [*De Personis*], 3 ed. a P. Aguirre recognita, Romae: Apud Aedes Universitatis Gregorianae, 1943), II, 190-192 and 244.

[10] Cf. can. 240, §§ 1-2 (referring to cardinals); can. 334, §§ 2-3 (referring to bishops); can. 313, §§ 1-2 (referring to apostolic administrators); can. 322, § 1 (referring to abbots); can. 293, § 2 (referring to vicars and prefects apostolic); can. 353 (referring to coadjutor bishops); can. 461 (referring to pastors); and cans. 1443-1445 (referring to beneficiaries).

[11] "*. . . ad normam sacrorum canonum facta.*"

obtains the full right to that office unless the law rules otherwise.[12] The necessity of corporal installation may certainly be called a further prescription of the law, closely relating to the *provisio canonica,* and, in the cases wherein it is prescribed, an integral part of it.

And yet, it may be asked, if corporal installation is an integral part of the conferral of office, why are there not specific regulations concerning it in the canons on the conferral of office? Wasner answers this question with several possible explanations.[13] He maintains that installation as it stands in the law today is really only the granting of possession of the temporal goods of the benefice, the spiritual office itself being conferred with the granting of the title, and possession of the benefice being necessary merely for the exercise of the power of the office. This would be a plausible argument except that there are instances of offices which are not strictly benefices and nevertheless require installation, such as that of a *vicarius actualis,* and likewise there are benefices which are offices only in a broad sense, such as that of membership in a collegiate chapter.

Wasner further states that there was some discussion in the preparation of the Code about changing the juridic effects of installation in the conferring of office by allowing the tenor of canon 148, § 1, to apply to all offices, but that inasmuch as that would have entailed many necessary changes, installation was retained with reference to those offices which have at the same time the character of a benefice.[14] He also mentions, and this seems to be the strongest argument, that installation is necessary to prevent the taking of possession of an office by private authority, especially in the case wherein the office might be vacant *de iure* but not *de facto.*[15]

From the foregoing explanations it may be concluded that the real purpose of canonical installation is to establish clearly and publicly the officeholder's or the beneficiary's right to exercise the powers of his office or his benefice, and to enjoy the fruits accru-

[12] ". . . *nisi aliud iure caveatur.*" Cf. Bouscaren-Ellis, *Canon Law* (Milwaukee: Bruce Publishing Co., 1946), pp. 123-124.

[13] Wasner, "De Institutione Corporali In Jure Canonico. Delibatio Juridico-Historica," *Jus Pontificium* (Romae, 1921-1940), XVII (1937), 133-134.

[14] *Ibid.*, p. 134.

[15] *Ibid.*, p. 133.

ing from it. Hence the necessary elements seem to be the intervention of the legitimate superior, the presentation of a proper title, and the carrying out of the proper rite or solemnity.

Article 2. The Pastoral Office and Installation

It has already been noted that the legislation concerning canonical installation is applied to many different offices. Cardinals who have been promoted to the bishopric of a suburbicarian see must receive possession of the same in the manner prescribed for other bishops, and the other cardinals must have received possession of their titular churches before they are allowed to perform the functions of local ordinaries in these churches.[16] Residential bishops receive the canonical possession of their diocese by presenting to the cathedral chapter or to the board of diocesan consultors the apostolic letter of appointment.[17] Similar legislation is provided for apostolic administrators,[18] for coadjutor bishops,[19] for vicars and prefects apostolic,[20] and for abbots and prelates *nullius*.[21] The manner of the installation of pastors[22] is regulated in the same way as that which is prescribed for appointees to benefices in general.[23] It is the purpose of this study to treat only of the canonical installation of pastors.

It happens, however, that the rights and obligations of a pastor are conferred by the general law upon a number of vicars who have various positions with respect to a parish. Canon 451, § 2, lists others who come in law under the name of pastors and are held equal to them in all parochial rights and duties. Among these are quasi-pastors, those who are in charge of quasi-parishes where the territory has not yet been divided into canonical parishes, and other parochial vicars if they are vested with the full parochial charge of the parish during the time of their office.

Hence it seems advisable to give a more detailed study to these various offices and their relationship to canonical installation.

---

16 Can. 240, §§ 1-2.

17 Can. 334, § 3.

18 Can. 313, §§ 1-2.

19 Can. 353, §§ 1-3.

20 Can. 293, § 2.

21 Can. 322, § 1.

22 Can. 461.

23 Cans. 1443-1445.

A. *Pastors* (Parochi)

In canonical legislation the concept of a pastor is expressed by the term *parochus.* There are those who maintain that it is improper to render this term with the word *pastor,* since in the strict sense the title of pastor, comprising the offices of teacher, sanctifier, and judge or ruler, belongs rather to the bishops as the successors of the Apostles.[24] More properly the term *parochus* is rendered with the expression *parish priest.* However, in the United States the latter term is more commonly used for the sake of indicating all priests engaged in parochial work as apart from those engaged in teaching, as chaplains, or in other priestly work not connected with a parish. The concept of pastor is commonly understood to coincide with the term *parochus.* Hence in this study the word *pastor* is used where perhaps more technically one might use the expression *parish priest.*

The Code defines a pastor as the individual priest or as the moral person to whom a parish has been given in title with the care of souls to be exercised under the authority of the local ordinary.[25]

Four elements should be noted in this definition. The pastor must be an individual priest—a layman cannot be appointed a pastor—or a moral person, such as a collegiate chapter, a monastery or a religious body. In this latter case the moral person holds the title of pastor as a permanently established beneficiary, but an individual priest must be appointed to administer the parish as the actual vicar or pastoral incumbent. The parish must be given *in title,* i.e., the priest who is the pastor must be given possession of the parish through a legitimate cause. He must have incumbent on him the care of souls (*cura animarum*). The bishop may indeed restrict the execution of certain matters to himself, such as the absolution from reserved sins or the exemption of some parishioners from the pastor's authority, since the final element in the pastoral office consists in the exercise of this office under the authority of the local ordinary. The bishop may not, however, restrict a pastor's authority in such an arbitrary manner and to

---

[24] Bouix, *Tractatus de Parocho,* pp. 142-160; Augustine, *A Commentary on the New Code of Canon Law,* II, 511.

[25] Can. 451, § 1.

such an extent as to reduce his power to naught and thus impair his effective work.[26]

A study of the above-mentioned elements of the character of the pastoral office is of practical importance, especially since it has been maintained by some that parish priests in the United States are not *parochi* in the strict canonical sense.[27] It should be noted here that the II Plenary Council of Baltimore in 1866 stated that at that time there were no strictly canonical parishes in the United States, but that it was the wish of the Council that they should be gradually introduced, especially in the larger cities, so that the discipline in this country might be brought into conformity with the universal law of the Church.[28] The III Plenary Council in 1884 repeated the decrees of the II Council[29] and then enacted legislation providing for the establishment of irremovable rectors.[30] Earlier, however, the Council had stated that there were as yet no canonically erected parishes.[31]

Even after the United States was removed from the jurisdiction of the Sacred Congregation for the Propagation of the Faith in 1909, and after the promulgation of the Code of Canon Law in 1918, there were those who held that parishes in this country were not strict canonical parishes, either because they had no fixed territorial limits or because they were not formally erected as required by the Code. These questions are now definitely answered through the various responses of the Sacred Congregations.

---

[26] Beste, *Introductio in Codicem*, p. 285; Ramstein, *A Manual of Canon Law* (Hoboken, N. J.: Terminal Printing and Publishing Co., 1947), pp. 262-263.

[27] Cf. Augustine, *A Commentary on the New Code of Canon Law*, II, 512-513; Donnellan, *The Obligation of the* MISSA PRO POPULO, The Catholic University of America Canon Law Studies, n. 155 (Washington, D. C.: The Catholic University of America Press, 1942), pp. 37-41 and 68-73.

[28] *Concilii Plenarii Baltimorensis II, in Ecclesia Metropolitana Baltimorensi, a die VII ad diem XXI Octobris, A.D. MDCCCLXVI, Habiti, et a Sede Apostolica Recogniti, Acta et Decreta* (ed. altera, Baltimorae: Joannes Murphy, 1894), nn. 123-125.

[29] *Acta et Decreta Concilii Plenarii Baltimorensis III, A.D. MDCCCLXXXIV* (Baltimorae: Typis Joannes Murphy Sociorum, 1886), n. 32.

[30] *Ibid.*, n. 33.

[31] *Ibid.*, n. 24.

The Apostolic Delegate, in a letter to the Bishops of the United States on November 10, 1922, stated that he had submitted certain questions to the Pontifical Commission for the Authentic Interpretation of the Canons of the Code regarding the status of parishes in this country. The reply of the Commission indicated that it was not necessary for the ordinary to issue a formal decree declaring explicitly that a certain district was erected into a parish in order that it might be considered a true canonical parish. The President of the Commission also added that a parish was always an ecclesiastical benefice according to the norm of canon 1411, 5°, if it had the proper endowment, or, even if lacking such endowment, if it had been erected with the provision that the necessary revenues would be obtained from other sources.[32]

In summarizing the import of this response, the Apostolic Delegate stated in his letter that it was evident that all parishes of the United States having the three necessary qualifications, *viz.,* a resident pastor, an endowment or other sources of revenue, and proper boundaries, were not only parishes in the strict canonical sense, but ecclesiastical benefices as well.[33]

Regarding the matter of parish boundaries the writer of "Studies and Conferences" in *The Ecclesiastical Review* rightly pointed out that, though there may still exist some cases in which parish boundaries are not formally defined, in most cases the boundaries observed by the respective pastors have been informally approved by the local ordinary by his manner of appointing pastors to these parishes, etc. "Thus it has come to pass that all or very nearly all parishes in these United States actually have boundaries," he stated.[34]

---

[32] Bouscaren, *Canon Law Digest,* I, 150. Canon 1409 defines an ecclesiastical benefice as a juridical entity, permanently constituted or erected by the competent ecclesiastical authority, and consisting in a sacred office which accords the right to receive the revenue accruing from the endowment of such office.

[33] *Ibid.,* p. 151; Woywod, *A Practical Commentary on the Code of Canon Law* (7. ed., revised by Callistus Smith, 2 vols., New York: Joseph F. Wagner, Inc. 1945), I, 84.

[34] "Parishes Without Boundaries," *The Ecclesiastical Review* (Philadelphia, 1889-1943; Washington, 1944—. From Vol. I [1889] to Vol. XXXII [1904] and after Vol. CIX [1943], *The American Ecclesiastical Review*),

From this brief summary of the nature of parishes and the pastoral office it seems evident that pastors in the United States, as elsewhere, are obligated by the law of the installation of pastors both by the provisions of canon 461 as true canonical pastors and also by the provisions of canons 1443 and 1444 as the appointees to an ecclesiastic benefice.

B. *Quasi-pastors* (QUASI-PAROCHI)

The establishment of quasi-parishes is provided for in canon 216 in the same manner as provision is made for the erection of canonical parishes. Paragraph 2 of that canon states that, where it can conveniently be done, vicariates and prefectures apostolic should be divided into distinct territorial sections with a proper church in the same manner as a diocese is divided into parishes. Paragraph 3 adds that, if a proper rector is assigned to this district, he is called a quasi-pastor. In canonical legislation these come under the name of pastors and are held equal to pastors in all parochial rights and duties.[35] Hence the law of installation seems to apply to them as well as to pastors.

Since the promulgation of the Code of Canon Law there have been several Instructions from the Sacred Roman Congregations which serve to clarify certain questions regarding quasi-parishes and quasi-pastors. A Declaration of the Sacred Consistorial Congregation stated that the divisions of a diocese were to be known as *parishes,* the expression *quasi-parish* or *mission* being reserved for those parts into which vicariates and prefectures apostolic are divided for the care of souls.[36] This Declaration definitely settled the argument of some pastors in the United States who maintained

---

LXXXIII (1930), 392 (hereafter cited *ER* and *AER* respectively). Cf. also *ER, LXXXIX* (1933), 628-630, and *ER,* LXXXII (1930), 425; Ramstein, *A Manual of Canon Law,* pp. 264-265.

[35] Can. 451, § 2, 1°.

[36] S. C. Consist., declaratio, 1 aug. 1919—*AAS,* XI (1919), 346; Bouscaren, *Canon Law Digest,* I, 146-147; *Periodica de Re Morali, Liturgica* (Brugis, 1905-1936; Romae, 1937—. 8 vols., from 1905 to 1919, *Periodica de Religiosis et Missionariis;* 7 vols., from 1920 to 1927, *Periodica de Re Canonica et Morali Utili praesertim Religiosis et Missionariis*), X (1922), 57-58 (hereafter cited as *Periodica*); Maroto, "De Missa pro Populo," *Apollinaris* (Romae, 1928—), VI (1933), 421-431.

that they were only quasi-pastors, inasmuch as their parishes had never been canonically erected according to the legislation of the Code.[37]

An Instruction of the Sacred Congregation for the Propagation of the Faith to vicars and prefects apostolic, given on July 25, 1920, has a special bearing on the present problem. After admonishing the vicars and prefects to divide their territories into distinct parts, each having its own population, its own church, and its own pastor, according to canon 216, § 2, the Sacred Congregation went on to describe the manner of the erection of a quasi-parish, and set forth the rights and duties of quasi-pastors as given in the Code.[38]

Number 6 of this Introduction is as follows:

> "As soon as the quasi-parish is erected, the rights and duties of the quasi-pastor as set down in the Code go into effect (especially canons 451, § 2, 1°; 454, § 4; 456; 459; 461; 1356; 306; 462; and the following)."[39]

For the present purpose it is important to note that it is canon 461 which states that pastors are to take possession of their parishes according to the manner prescribed in canons 1443 and 1444.

From this brief presentation of the nature of quasi-parishes and quasi-pastors it seems evident that the law of installation is definitely binding upon quasi-pastors. Canons 216, § 2, and 451, § 2, 1°, as well as the later Instructions of the Sacred Roman Congregations show that the office of quasi-pastors is for all practical purposes the same as the office of pastors, except that because of the missionary character of their work quasi-pastors are exempted from a few of the obligations of pastors in that on a lesser number of occasions are they obliged to apply the *Missa pro populo.*[40] In far the greater number of cases they are governed by the same norms as pastors, and specifically they are subject to the law of installation in office as stated in the Instruction of the

---

[37] Donnellan, *The Obligation of the* MISSA PRO POPULO, pp. 69-70; *ER,* LX (1919), 182-183.

[38] S. C. de Prop. Fide, instr., 25 iul. 1920—*AAS,* XII (1920), 331; Bouscaren, *Canon Law Digest,* I, 147-148; *Periodica,* X (1922), 203.

[39] *Loc. cit.*

[40] Can. 466, § 1.

Sacred Congregation. It is obvious, of course, that because of the missionary conditions of their work, the just cause for dispensing from this law would be present more frequently than in the case of pastors.

C. *Acting Vicars* (VICARII ACTUALES)

When the pastor of a parish is a moral person, as permitted in canon 451, the moral person has the care of souls solely in title, and not by way of active administration.[41] The actual care of souls must be exercised by a parochial vicar constituted by the moral body with the approval of the ordinary. The vicar thus constituted is presented to the ordinary who must grant to him canonical institution if he is found to be properly qualified.[42] These vicars are variously known as acting vicars, as vicars entrusted with the parochial care (*vicarii curati*), as vicars regular if they are members of the regular clergy, as vicars religious if they belong to a religious congregation, etc.

In studying the obligations of these vicars in the matter of canonical installation, it seems mandatory to review the nature of the union of a parish with a moral person. A parish may be united with a moral body *pleno iure,* i.e., the moral body becomes the pastor in full and rightful title both in temporal and in spiritual matters. A parish may also be united *quoad temporalia tantum,* i.e., the moral body becomes entitled to the revenue of the parish, but the care of souls is given to a secular priest who receives a compensation for his services from the moral body.[43] This latter union is sometimes designated as a union effected *semi-pleno iure* or *minus pleno iure.*

Besides these two forms of the incorporation of a parish with a moral body there is also a third, sometimes called a *plenissimo iure* effected union. This type of incorporation occurs in the case of an abbacy or prelacy *nullius* in which the parish is entirely removed from the territory of the local episcopal ordinary and placed under the direction of an abbot or a prelate *nullius.*[44] A special

[41] Can. 452, § 2.
[42] Can. 471, §§ 1-2.
[43] Can. 1425, §§ 1-2.
[44] Cans. 319-328.

type of quasi-union seems to be contemplated in certain canons of the Code which speak of a parish given or entrusted to religious communities.[45] Some, however, maintain that canon 456 merely speaks in generic terms of either of the two earlier mentioned types of the union of parishes with a moral body.[46]

It hardly seems necessary to give a detailed analysis of the technical nature of the office held by the vicars in each of these cases in order to determine whether or not they are subject to the law of installation. Not many of the authors discuss this particular point, and those who do are by no means in universal agreement.

Canon 471, § 4, states that to the vicar exclusively belongs the care of souls with all the rights and duties of pastors as granted in the common law and according to the approved diocesan statutes and laudable customs. Hence it seems that the necessity of their installation is a matter which applies to them as well as to pastors. It may be argued that this particular canon speaks only of parishes which are united *pleno iure* with a religious house, a capitular church or some other moral person,[47] but this does not seem to imply that this canon is applicable exclusively to parishes if they are *pleno iure* incorporated with a moral person. The general norms as here established are applicable both in the cases of parishes which are *semi-pleno iure* incorporated with a moral person, and apparently also of parishes which are merely entrusted to religious for the exercise of the pastoral care.[48]

The general principle that parochial vicars come in law under the name of and are held equal to pastors in all parochial rights and duties if they have full parochial charge of the parish during the time of their office is stated in canon 451, § 2, 2°. Hence it seems logical to insist that unless the contrary is stated in the

---

[45] ". . . paroecias religiosis concreditas . . ."—Can. 456. Cf. Bouscaren-Ellis, *Canon Law,* p. 197; Bastnagel, *The Appointment of Parochial Adjutants and Assistants,* p. 158.

[46] Augustine, *A Commentary on the New Code of Canon Law,* II, 525.

[47] "Si paroecia pleno iure fuerit unita domui religiosae, ecclesiae capitulari vel alii personae morali . . ."—Can. 471, § 1.

[48] Beste, *Introductio in Codicem,* p. 287; Bouscaren-Ellis, *Canon Law,* p. 197.

general law, or unless the nature of their office obviously exempts them, these vicars must follow the prescriptions enacted for pastors, and among them the provision which necessitates the installation in office.

The authors who held that acting vicars are not held to the law of installation base their opinion on the premise that these vicars in reality are without the possession of a parochial benefice, since the benefice is held by the moral person which is constituted as the pastor in title.[49] According to this opinion the benefice in reality never becomes vacant as long as the moral body remains the pastor in title, and accordingly the vicar receives the care of souls from the moment that he is approved by the local ordinary.

But, as Goyeneche remarks, this statement seems to be made rather arbitrarily, since a parish which is entrusted to religious becomes vacant in the same manner as secular parishes, namely, through the death, removal, resignation, etc., of the parochial vicar.[50] As evidence of this assertion one may point to canon 472, §§ 1-2, in which the question of the filling of a vacant parish is dealt with. These paragraphs make no distinction between a secular and a religious parish.

Again, while the acting vicar may indeed not possess a parochial benefice, he nonetheless does have a true ecclesiastical office in the strict sense.[51] Since, therefore, acting vicars are made equal to pastors, especially with regard to the office which they hold, though not with regard to the possession of the benefice, and since in law

---

[49] Cf. Fanfani, *De Iure Parochorum* (Taurini-Romae: Marietti, 1924), n. 96 A; Schaaf, "Corporal Installation of Pastors," *ER*, XCI (1934), 620 in footnote 2; Vermeersch-Creusen, *Epitome Iuris Canonici* (6. ed., 3 vols., Mechliniae-Romae: H. Dessain, 1937-1946), II (1940), 543. It is interesting to note that the opinion of Vermeersch-Creusen seems to be less certain in the 6th edition than in the earlier editions. The 2nd edition (1924), I, 282, has "*'installatione' non indiget*" whereas the 6th edition states "*'installatione' indigere non videtur.*"

[50] Goyeneche, "An Canon 461 Applicandus Sit Parochis Religiosis," *Commentarium pro Religiosis* (Romae, 1919—), VI (1925), 485.

[51] An ecclesiastical office in the strict sense signifies a permanently established position created either by the divine or the ecclesiastical law, conferred according to the rule of the sacred canons, and entailing some participation at least in ecclesiastical power, whether of orders or jurisdiction.—Can. 145, § 1.

they come under and are governed by the same regulations as pastors, there seems to be no reason why they should not be held, just as pastors are, to the law of canonical installation in the receiving of the jurisdiction and of the care of souls in their office according to the norms of canon 461.

Blat also maintains this position,[52] and appeals to a decision of the Sacred Congregation of Bishops and Regulars in 1862 as the basis for his opinion. In the Diocese of Linz, Austria, it was the custom for the dean to install parochial vicars regular after they had received approval from the ordinary, when they had been named to parishes which were joined with the monasteries *pleno iure*. The abbot argued that the custom should be abolished because of abuses incident to the occasion of the installation, and because he felt that the requirements of installation did not apply to vicars regular. The Sacred Congregation, without deciding the juridical question of the necessity of installation in this case, ruled that the custom should be observed.[53]

It is interesting to note that in at least one diocese where the installation of vicars religious is required the authority to preside at the granting of possession is accorded to the religious superior or to one of the *"digniores"* among the members of the religious community as designated by the superior to act as the delegate of the bishop.[54]

Before the conclusion of this article it should be made clear that, while the arguments here presented are largely those offered for the necessity of installation in the case of vicars religious in parishes united *pleno iure* to the religious body, it is the opinion of the present writer that they have force as well in the case of acting vicars of parishes united *plenissimo iure* or *semi-pleno iure* or in parishes merely entrusted (*concreditae*) to a moral person.

---

[52] Blat, *Commentarium Textus Codicis Iuris Canonici* (5 vols. in 7, Romae: Collegio "Angelico," 1921-1927), Lib. III, *De Rebus,* Partes II-VI (1923), n. 345 (hereafter cited *De Rebus*).

[53] S. C. Ep. et Reg., *Lincien.,* 19 sept. 1862—*Fontes,* n. 1986. Cf. *supra,* pp. 67-69.

[54] *Constitutiones Dioceseos Sinus Viridis Quae in Synodo Diocesana Quarta Latae et Promulgatae Fuerunt* (Pulaski, Wisc.: Typis Franciscanae Typographiae, 1921), p. 16, n. 53.

In each case the vicar holds and office, if not always a benefice, which is made equal to the office of pastor, and accordingly is governed in its rights and obligations as is the office of pastor.

D. *Administrators* (VICARII OECONOMI)

The administrator or vicar econome of a parish is governed by the rules of canons 472 and 473. He is the priest appointed to take charge of a vacant parish during its vacancy. He enjoys the same rights and duties as a pastor in those things which concern the care of souls. He must, however, do nothing that can prove prejudicial to the rights of the incoming pastor or also of the parochial benefice itself.[55] The temporary nature of his office and the fact that he does not possess the parochial benefice in title seem clearly to indicate that he is not bound by the law of installation. His office ceases when the new pastor legitimately takes possession of the parish.[56]

It may be argued, as in the case of acting vicars, that an administrator also comes under the provisions of canon 451, § 1, 2°, and is, therefore, equal to pastors in all parochial rights and obligations, and hence also in the obligations which point to the need of installation in office. It is, indeed, true that administrators come under this classification, for they possess ordinary power,[57] but their office is only temporary in character whereas the acting vicar's office is one which in and of itself is of permanent duration, even though he is removable, if he be a vicar regular or a vicar religious, *ad nutum* either of the religious superior or of the local ordinary. It could happen that an administrator will hold office over a considerably extended period of time, even longer perhaps than the average tenure of acting vicars, but the practice in some smaller dioceses of naming a young priest in his first pastoral incumbency as an administrator rather than as a pastor, and of leaving him in that status for an extended period of time, hardly seems justifiable in law.

Finally, in contradistinction to the office of the acting vicar is the fact that an administrator's authority is definitely limited to

---

[55] Can. 473, § 1.

[56] Vermeersch-Creusen, *Epitome Iuris Canonici,* I, 291.

[57] Cappello, *Summa Iuris Canonici,* II, 17.

those things which pertain to the care of souls, and that only for the time of the vacancy of the parish. He is likewise admonished not to do anything that would prejudice the rights of the new pastor.[58] From the nature of his office, therefore, it seems that an administrator is not obliged to follow the law of installation before assuming his office in the vacant parish.

E. *Substitute Vicars* (Vicarii Substituti)

What has been said concerning administrators and the law of installation is true to an even greater extent in the case of substitute vicars. Appointment of these vicars is required in two instances, namely, to take charge of a parish during the absence of a pastor who will be away from his parish for more than a week,[59] and to take charge of the parish whose pastor has been removed by judicial process, during the time his appeal is pending with the Holy See.[60] The substitute vicar takes the place of the pastor in all things which pertain to the care of souls, unless the local ordinary or the pastor place restrictions upon his power.[61]

In ordinary circumstances, therefore, the substitute vicar falls under the classification of canon 451, § 2, 2°, and he enjoys ordinary power.[62] From the very nature of his office, however, it is evident that he is not subject to the law of installation, since it is of a purely temporary nature and his power can be restricted either by the ordinary or by the pastor.

F. *Adjutant Vicars* (Vicarii Adiutores)

The adjutant vicar is the vicar given to a pastor who through old age, mental debility, incompetence, blindness, or other similar permanent causes as deriving from his own person, is incapable of discharging his duties properly.[63] To determine the adjutant

[58] Can. 473, § 1.

[59] Can. 465, §§ 4-5.

[60] Can. 1923, § 2.

[61] Can. 474; Vermeersch-Creusen, *Epitome Iuris Canonici,* I, 292-293.

[62] Cappello, *Summa Iuris Canonici,* II, 17 and 110; Cappello, "De Vicario Substituto," *Periodica,* XIX (1930), 1-10; Claeys-Bouuaert, "De Vicariis Substitutis," *Jus Pontificium,* VII (1927), 72-81.

[63] Can. 475, § 1.

vicar's rights and duties two cases must be considered. If he takes the place of the pastor in all things, he has all the rights and duties of a pastor, with the exception of the obligation of the *Missa pro populo*; if, however, he supplies in only a part of the pastoral duties, his rights and obligations must be determined from his letter of appointment.[64]

The second case mentioned presents no problem for this study, for in that case the adjutant vicar can evidently not be held to the law of installation, since he does not hold a benefice and since moreover it is questionable whether he exercises more than a merely delegated power. In the first case, however, in which the vicar takes the place of the pastor in all things, he exercises ordinary power and falls under the classification of a pastor according to the norms of canon 451, § 2, 2°.[65] Nonetheless even in that case the adjutant vicar seems not to be subject to the law of installation in office because of the temporary nature of his office, and above all because of the fact that the pastor still remains in possession of the parish.

It could be argued that in view of the parallelism with the office of coadjutor bishop, who is obliged to take possession of his office in a formal manner,[66] the adjutant vicar should be similarly obligated. The obligation of the coadjutor bishop, however, arises from the fact either that he is appointed with the right of succession and automatically becomes the ordinary upon the vacancy of the see,[67] or that he is appointed as coadjutor to the see itself, in which case his office continues even after the vacancy of the see.[68] An adjutant vicar, on the contrary, may not be appointed with the right of succession except by the Holy See,[69] and his office becomes vacant as soon as the pastoral office becomes vacant.

---

[64] Can. 475, § 2.

[65] Vermeersch-Creusen, *Epitome Iuris Canonici,* I, 293; Cappello, *Summa Iuris Canonici,* II, 112.

[66] Can. 353, §§ 1-3.

[67] Can. 355, § 1.

[68] Can. 355, § 3.

[69] Can. 1433; Cappello, *ibid.,* in footnote; Beste, *Introductio in Codicem,* p. 300; Bastnagel, *The Appointment of Parochial Adjutants and Assistants,* pp. 177-185.

G. *Assistant Pastors* (Vicarii Cooperatores)

If the pastor alone cannot take care of all the work of the parish because of the large number of souls in the parish or for other objective reasons, the ordinary may assign to him one or more parochial vicars, known in the law as *vicarii cooperatores,* and commonly called assistant pastors or curates.[70] The contention of some that an assistant pastor's office in the United States is a canonical benefice in the strict sense seems to be without sufficient foundation.[71] Canon 477, § 2, indicates that it is possible for the office of assistant pastor to be established as a true canonical benefice, and this is apparently done in some countries of Europe. This seems, however, to be the exception rather than the rule in this country.[72] Likewise the opinion that his authority evinces an ordinary rather than a delegated power does not seem to be solidly founded.[73]

In view of the nature of his office, therefore, it seems certain that the assistant pastor is not subject to the law of installation, unless his office is also established as a true canonical benefice. In this latter case he would be required to receive formal possession of his benefice according to the norm of canons 1443 and 1444.

---

[70] Can. 476, § 1.

[71] Cf. *ER,* LXXVII (1927), 74-79; *ibid.,* 306-312.

[72] Woywod, *A Practical Commentary on the Code of Canon Law,* I, 174; Beste, *Introductio in Codicem,* p. 302; Bastnagel, *The Appointment of Parochial Adjutants and Assistants,* p. 139.

[73] Cappello, *Summa Iuris Canonici,* II, 114-116; Coronata, *Institutiones Iuris Canonici,* I, n. 492; Vermeersch-Creusen, *Epitome Iuris Canonici,* I, 294-295; Beste, *ibid.,* p. 301; Bastnagel, *ibid.,* pp. 141-145; De Meester, *Juris Canonici et Juris Canonico-Civilis Compendium* (nova ed., 3 vols. in 4, Brugis: Descleé, De Brouwer, 1921-1928), II, n. 881.

CHAPTER VII

THE NECESSITY OF INSTALLATION

It is a long-standing principle of canonical legislation that an ecclesiastical benefice cannot be obtained without the intervention of the competent ecclesiastical authority. The first of the *Regulae Juris* included in the *Liber Sextus* of Boniface VIII (1294-1303) explicitly enunciated this principle when it stated that an ecclesiastical benefice could not licitly be obtained without canonical institution.[1] The intense and bitter so-called Investiture Struggle between the Germanic kings and the papacy involved principally the defense of this doctrine of the rights of the Church in the canonical provisions for ecclesiastical offices and benefices.[2] The principle became more or less firmly established with the issuance of decretal letters on the subject, especially by Popes Alexander III (1159-1181) and Innocent III (1198-1216).[3]

The Code of Canon Law embodies this doctrine and broadens the principle to the extent that an ecclesiastical office cannot be *validly* obtained without the canonical *provisio*.[4] This canonical *provisio* is understood to be the conferral of an ecclesiastical office by the competent ecclesiastical authority, made in accordance with the norms of the sacred canons.[5]

It has already been shown that canonical installation or corporal induction into office, while not the equivalent to or the essential part of this canonical *provisio*, is nonetheless an integral part of it. Three elements were noted in this definition, namely, the designation of the person to receive the office, the actual conces-

---

[1] "Beneficium ecclesiasticum non potest licite sine institutione canonica obtineri."—Reg. 1, R. J., in VI°.

[2] *Supra*, pp. 17-24.

[3] *Supra*, pp. 26-29.

[4] "Officium ecclesiasticum nequit sine provisione canonica valide obtineri." —Can. 147, § 1.

[5] "Nomine *canonicae provisionis* venit concessio officii ecclesiastici a competente auctoritate ecclesiastica ad normam canonum facta."—Can. 147, § 2.

sion of the power of the office, and the corporal induction into the possession of the office.[6]

The latter element, i.e., the corporal induction into the possession of the office, or the canonical installation, does not occur in all cases of the conferral of office, since there are some offices which do not require this corporal induction, such as the office of vicar general. There can be little doubt, however, that it is meant to be included in the conferral of offices which also have the character of a benefice. Canon 146 specifically states that in reference to offices which come under the name of benefices, not only the canons on the conferral of office are to be observed, but also the prescriptions of the canons on ecclesiastical benefices as contained in Book III, Part V, of the Code.[7]

Among these canons on ecclesiastical benefices canons 1443 to 1445 inclusive treat specifically of the necessity, manner and time of the *missio in possessionem,* or the canonical installation in a benefice. Canon 1443 states that no one shall on his own authority take possession of a benefice conferred upon him. Paragraph 2 of the canon gives the authority to grant possession in the case of non-consistorial benefices to the local ordinary, who may also delegate another ecclesiastic to perform this function. Canon 1444 specifies that the canonical installation is to be carried out in the manner prescribed by particular legislation or by legitimate local custom. It also gives the ordinary the authority to dispense from this manner or rite for a just cause, in which case the dispensation takes the place of the formal installation. Canon 1445 allows the taking of possession of a benefice by means of a proxy who must have a special mandate to perform this function.

It has been mentioned previously that the office of pastor is a benefice in the true canonical sense.[8] An ecclesiastical benefice, it will be recalled, is a juridical entity, permanently constituted or erected by the competent ecclesiastical authority, and consisting of a sacred office and the right to receive the revenue accruing

---

[6] *Supra,* pp. 68-69.

[7] "De beneficialibus officiis in specie, praeter canones qui sequuntur, custodiantur insuper praescripta can. 1409 seqq."—Can. 146.

[8] *Supra,* p. 74. Cf. Letter of the Apostolic Delegate to the Bishops of the United States—Bouscaren, *Canon Law Digest,* I, 150.

from the endowment of this office.[9] The endowment may consist either of goods owned by the benefice itself, or of definite and obligatory payments of some family or moral person, or of the voluntary offerings of the faithful, provided there is a proper assurance of a definite income, or of so-called stole fees, or finally of choral distributions.[10] As soon, therefore, as a parish has been properly erected and a provision has been made for a definite income for the incumbent pastor, there can be little doubt that the pastor's office is a true canonical benefice, and that accordingly the pastor is obliged to take possession of his office in the manner prescribed for the incumbent of a benefice.

As if to set aside all possible doubt in this matter, canon 461 states explicitly that the pastor receives the care of souls from the moment he has taken possession of his parish in the manner prescribed by canons 1443 to 1445. Canon 1095, § 1, 1°, which treats of the pastor's right to assist at marriage, also mentions that this right obtains only from the day of the taking of canonical possession of the parish in the manner prescribed in canon 1444, § 1. Another important reference to installation is found in canon 2394, which inflicts severe penalties upon those who take possession of an ecclesiastical benefice or office by their own authority.

Several reasons are at once apparent for the detailed provisions of the canons already mentioned with reference to the installation of pastors. The pastor, when he takes office, assumes many and serious obligations both in the guidance of the souls committed to his care and also in the administration of the benefice itself. It is natural, therefore, that the moment of his acceptance of these obligations should be precisely marked and set apart with certain solemnities emphasizing the nature of these responsibilities. The parishioners, likewise, are obliged to support their pastor not only with financial assistance but also through respect, reverence and obedience to his ministrations. The rite of installation, if carried out with proper solemnity, is well calculated to impress these things upon the minds of the parishioners. It is an important occa-

---

[9] Can. 1409. Cf. Cappello, *Summa Iuris Canonici,* II, 539-544; Beste, *Introductio in Codicem,* pp. 695-698.

[10] Can. 1410.

sion on which the rights and duties of the pastor may be presented dramatically to the people, and it gives them also the opportunity to know the training and qualifications which the pastor brings with him in assuming these responsibilities.

Of greater juridical import is the necessity of establishing beyond the possibility of doubt the rightful possessor of the pastor's jurisdiction in cases in which that fact may be open to dispute. The practice of the Apostolic Datary and the decisions of the Supreme Apostolic Signatura in cases of disputed possession clearly emphasize the importance of the proper installation in office.[11]

It is interesting to notice a number of the characteristics of the law concerning installation which clearly indicate the importance attached to it. The intervention of the proper ecclesiastical authority is always necessary. In the case of non-consistorial benefices this authority is reserved to the ordinary. If the installation is to be performed by another, he must be delegated by the ordinary. This delegate may not be a layman; he must be an ecclesiastic. If the installation does not take place, a dispensation must be obtained from the ordinary. This dispensation must be express and in writing. The profession of faith is required either prior to or in the act of installation. If a proxy is to be used for the rite, he must have a special mandate to perform this function.[12] The profession of faith, however, cannot be made through a proxy.[13] Finally, severe penalties are to be inflicted upon those who violate the law requiring installation in office.[14]

It can hardly be denied, then, that the canonical installation of pastors is an important and necessary step in the proper delineation of the pastoral office, and hence to disregard entirely the prescriptions of the canons as mentioned certainly manifests a lack of appreciation and understanding of the intent and purpose of canonical legislation.

---

[11] Cf. Suprema Signatura, decisio, 27 iun. 1918—*AAS*, X (1918), 391-393.

[12] Cans. 1443-1445. Cf. Wasner, "De Institutione Corporali In Jure Canonico. Delibatio Juridico-Historica," *Jus Pontificium*, XVII (1937), 136.

[13] Can. 1407.

[14] Cans. 2394-2395.

Article 1. Necessity for Validity or for Lawfulness

In view of the obvious importance attached to the canonical legislation concerning the installation of pastors, the question naturally arisis: Is canonical installation necessary for the validity of the pastor's acts, or is it necessary only for the lawfulness of the exercise of his office?

The majority of the accepted authors writing on the Code speaks in more or less emphatic terms in stating the necessity of canonical installation without, however, touching directly the question as to whether it is necessary for the validity of the pastor's acts, or only for their lawfulness or licitness. Various expressions used by these authors indicate the importance which they attach to installation, but from these expressions it is impossible to attribute to them either an opinion which explicitly postulates, or an opinion which positively precludes, installation as a factor for the validity of the pastor's acts. A few examples will illustrate this point.

Vermeersch-Creusen states: "*Prohibetur ne quis propria auctoritate possessionem beneficii capiat. Requiritur igitur missio in possessionem . . .*"[15] Wernz (1842-1914)-Vidal (1868-1939) use the expression: "*. . . collatarius . . . in actualem autem possessionem officii . . . ordinarie nequaquam per apprehensionem propria auctoritate factam, sed per introductionem a competente Superiore ecclesiastico peractam immitti debet.*"[16] Augustine (1872-1943) simply stated that no one shall take possession of a benefice conferred upon him, on his own authority, or before he has made the profession of faith.[17] Pistocchi speaks of installation in these words: "*Inhibetur possessio corporalis propria auctoritate, etsi praecesserit tituli collatio. Facilis exinde haberetur abusuum occasio . . .*"[18]

In this group of authors the following may also be included: Ayrinhac (1867-1930),[19] Badii (1884-1938),[20] Blat,[21] Cocchi,[22]

---

[15] *Epitome Iuris Canonici,* II, 542.

[16] *Ius Canonicum,* II, 374.

[17] *A Commentary on the New Code of Canon Law,* VI, 521.

[18] *De Re Beneficiali* (Taurini: Marietti, 1928), p. 222.

[19] *Administrative Legislation in the New Code of Canon Law* (New York: Longmans, Green and Co., 1930), pp. 344-345.

[20] *Institutiones Iuris Canonici* (2 vols., Florentiae: Libreria Editrice Fior-

Ferreres (1861-1936),[23] Prümmer (1866-1931),[24] Raus (1881-1943),[25] Rossi,[26] Sipos,[27] and others. To evaluate properly the various expressions used by these authors it is necessary to bear in mind that, when a certain act is strongly prohibited or forbidden, it does not necessarily follow that the action, if nonetheless performed, is therefore invalid.[28] If this principle is borne in mind, it is apparent that the authors cited above can hardly be alleged as favoring one opinion or the other in this matter.

Those authors who hold that corporal installation in office is necessary for the validity of the pastor's acts are very explicit in their statements. Fanfani states: *"Si autem paroecia sit saecularis, immissio novi parochi in possessione paroeciae semper requiritur, ut quis munia parochialia valide et licite exercere valeat."*[29] Berutti admits that canon 1443, § 1, contains neither an expressly nor an equivalently invalidating clause which would require canonical installation for the validity of the possession of a benefice, but he maintains that in the case of pastors canon 461 expressly requires the canonical installation for the validity of the pastor's parochial actions.[30] Coronata also agrees that the canons on corporal installation, considered in terms of the wording of the canons, do not contain an invalidating or disqualifying law, but he holds that the penalties stated in canon 2394 postulate these canons as enacting

---

entina, 1921-1922), II, n. 561.

21 *De Rebus,* pp. 427-429.

22 *Commentarium in Codicem Iuris Canonici* (8 vols. in 5, Vol. VI [Lib. III, *De Rebus,* Partes IV-VI], 4. ed. recognita, Torino: Marietti, 1947) VI, 201.

23 *Institutiones Canonicae* (ed. altera, 2 vols., Barcinone: Eugenius Subirana, 1920), II, 176-177.

24 *Manuale Iuris Canonici* (5. ed., Friburgi Brisgoviae: Herder and Co., 1927), p. 517.

25 *Institutiones Canonicae* (ed. altera, Parisiis: Typis Emmanuelis Vitte, 1931), p. 219.

26 *De Paroecia,* n. 178, pp. 175-176.

27 *Enchiridion Iuris Canonici* (4. ed., Pécs: Ex Typographia "Haladas R. T.," 1940), p. 781.

28 Cicognani, *Canon Law,* p. 560.

29 *De Iure Parochorum,* n. 96, p. 89.

30 *Institutiones Iuris Canonici,* Vol. II, pars I, p. 270.

an invalidating law.[31] Beste,[32] Cappello[33] and Park[34] also hold that the requirements of canonical installation are necessary for the validity of the pastor's actions. Bouscaren-Ellis insist that the taking of possession canonically may be required for the validity of official acts,[35] but they seem to feel that this requirement can be fulfilled if the bishop, in the decree appointing the pastor, designates a day on which he is to enter into possession of the parish.[36]

Before consideration be given to the arguments proposed by these authors, mention should likewise be made of those writers who consider the regulations of canonical installation as necessary only for the lawfulness or licitness of the subsequent actions. Ramstein clearly holds this opinion when he says: "Where formal installations are not observed, . . . the appointment becomes effective from the first moment of the actual exercise of the office."[37]

In describing the three parts of canonical *provisio,* namely, the designation of the person, the concession of the authority of the office, and the introduction into the possession of the office or the benefice, Chelodi (1880-1922) made this significant statement: *"Primus actus tribuit ius ad rem, alter ius in re, tertius non est essentialis et interdum omittitur."*[38] In a footnote he stated further that this third step *"habet tamen momentum processuale, quia per eum tituli accedit possessio."*[39]

Maroto gives the same division of the three steps in *canonical provision.* He states that the *provisio* is substantially accomplished by the second act (i.e., the concession of the power of office) which is often not distinguished from the first (i.e., the designation of the person), and that the third step (i.e., introduction into posses-

---

[31] *Institutiones Iuris Canonici,* II, 391.

[32] *Introductio in Codicem,* p. 711.

[33] *Summa Iuris Canonici,* II, 36 and 566.

[34] "The Necessity of Installation of Pastors," *The Homiletic and Pastoral Review* (New York: Joseph F. Wagner, Inc., 1900—), XXXV (1935), 579-592 (hereafter cited *HPR*).

[35] *Canon Law,* pp. 124, 201.

[36] *Ibid.,* p. 202.

[37] *A Manual of Canon Law,* p. 268.

[38] *Ius Canonicum de Personis* (3. ed., curavit P. Ciprotti, Trento: Libreria Moderna Editrice, 1942), p. 214.

[39] *Ibid.,* footnote 3.

sion of the office or the benefice) is not always necessary from the very nature of things and is sometimes dispensed with.[40]

Beneditti maintains that the omission of the solemnities of formal installation does not prevent a pastor from exercising the powers of his office if he has received from the bishop or his delegate the document conferring the benefice.[41] Schaaf (1883-1946) admitted that the appointment alone does not suffice to give actual possession of the parish to the appointee, but he contended that no formal ceremony of taking possession is necessary. He suggested that a mere decree supplementing the appointment by actually placing the new pastor in possession of the parish will suffice for the validity of the installation.[42]

The examination of the various opinions of the authors makes it obvious that the problem under consideration is one not hastily to be settled. For a better understanding of it a brief study of the interpretation of invalidating (*irritantes*) and disqualifying (*inhabilitantes*) laws will be helpful.[43] An invalidating law is one that renders invalid certain acts which, by the natural law and the general principles of positive or human law, would otherwise be valid.[44] Thus, for example, a marriage which is not performed in the presence of the proper pastor, etc., is an invalid marriage because of the invalidating effect of canon 1094. A disqualifying law is one that renders a person incapable of performing certain acts.[45] Thus a man cannot enter a valid marriage before the completion of his sixteenth year because of the disqualifying effect of canon 1067.

Canon 11 states that only those laws are to be considered as invalidating or disqualifying which expressly or equivalently state that an action is null and void, or that a person is incapacitated from acting. The reason for this prescription of law is obvious,

---

[40] "Tertius vero ex ipsa rerum natura non esset necessarius ea aliquando dispensatur . . ."—*Institutiones Iuris Canonici* (2 vols., Vol. I, 3. ed., 1921, Madrid: Editorial del Corazón de Maria, 1919-1921), I, 686-687.

[41] "Presa di Possesso," *Perfice Munus!* (Torino, 1926—), IV (1929), 365.

[42] *ER*, XCI (1934), 622.

[43] Cf. Roelker, "The Interpretation of Invalidating Laws," *The Jurist* (Washington, D. C., 1941—), III (1943), 364-403.

[44] Cicognani, *Canon Law*, p. 558; Beste, *Introductio in Codicem*, p. 66.

[45] *Loc. cit.*

since invalidating and disqualifying laws by their nature and because of their severity are odious, and accordingly no laws should have these effects unless they are clearly stated in the wording of the law.[46] Hence it is without question, as has been stated earlier, that a law which prohibits a certain action does not necessarily invalidate that action if it is performed in violation of the law.

A problem arises, however, in the determination of what constitute *expressly* or *equivalently* invalidating expressions or characteristics. On this point the authors are by no means in universal agreement.[47] Some authors interpret the word *expresse* to mean the same as *explicite,* and the word *aequivalenter* to mean the same as *implicite.*[48] This interpretation hardly seems satisfactory since it may be pointed out that the command of a law can be *expressly* stated either in an explicit or in an implicit manner.[49]

Other authors give a somewhat different interpretation of canon 11. They hold that a law is expressly invalidating or disqualifying when it states in clear and precise words that the act is null or that the person is disqualified from performing a certain act; it is an equivalently invalidating law when a terminology is used which has the same significance without being directly stated or when words of the same importance are used.[50] As Coronata observes,[51] it is

---

[46] "Odia restringi, et favores convenit ampliari."—Reg. 15, R. J., in VI°.

[47] Cf. Roelker, "art. cit." *The Jurist,* III (1943), 391; Park, "art. cit.," *HPR,* XXXV, 583; Van Hove, *Commentarium Lovaniense in Codicem Iuris Canonici,* Vol. I, tom. 2, *De Legibus Ecclesiasticis* (1930), pp. 167-168.

[48] Blat, *Commentarium Textus Iuris Canonici,* Lib. I, *Normae Generales* (1921), p. 84; Berutti, *Institutiones Iuris Canonici,* Vol. I, *Normae Generales* (1936), pp. 75-76; Ojetti, *Commentarium in Codicem Iuris Canonici* (4 vols., Vol. I, *Normae Generales* [1927], Romae: Apud Aedes Universitatis Gregorianae, 1927-1931), I, 99. Cf. Van Hove, *loc. cit.*; Coronata, *Institutiones Iuris Canonici,* I, 35.

[49] E. g., the expressions *"invalide admittuntur"* in can. 542, 1°, *"ad validitatem requiritur"* in can. 572, § 1, *"ut valeat"* in can. 555, § 1, etc., are expressly invalidating phrases stated in an explicit manner; in the expressions *"effectum non sortitur"* in can. 116, *"nullum habet iuridicum effectum"* in can. 162, § 5, *"ut quis sit patrinus"* in can. 765, etc., the invalidating character of the law is expressly stated but in an implicit or indirect manner.

[50] Beste, *Introductio in Codicem,* p. 67; Cappello, *Summa Iuris Canonici,* I, 73-74; Cicognani, *Canon Law,* p. 560; Van Hove, *De Legibus Ecclesiasticis,* p. 168; Vermeersch-Creusen, *Epitome Iuris Canonici,* I, 74.

[51] *Institutiones Iuris Canonici,* I, 35.

not always clear in this opinion which laws are expressly invalidating and which are equivalently invalidating since some of these authors classify as expressly invalidating those expressions which others call equivalently invalidating. Hence the opinion seems more acceptable which holds that a law is expressly invalidating or disqualifying only when the invalidating or disqualifying effect is stated either in precise and clear words or in words having the same import.

Regardless of which of these opinions is held the question of express invalidation presents no great difficulty in the present case, since a law which states directly or unmistakably that an act must be performed in a certain manner under pain of nullity or invalidity is certainly an invalidating law.

The explanation of an equivalently invalidating law is not as simple. To be equivalent means to have the same or equal effect or force. Hence a law which, while not stating so directly, is worded in such a way as to render an act invalid when it is performed contrary to the law is an equivalently invalidating law. Some authors speak of this as indirect invalidation as distinguished from direct or express invalidation.[52] This phraseology, while perhaps acceptable, does not adequately solve the question, for it may be asked to what degree or to what extent one is to accept this indirection as establishing the presence of an invalidating character in a law.

To obviate this difficulty some authors, as has been noted, hold that the law must contain a clause with practically the same meaning or significance as *expresse.*[53] Others hold the opinion, which appears to be more acceptable, that a law can also be equivalently invalidating if it assigns certain formalities or solemnities in the performance of an act. If the substantial formalities are neglected, the act will be invalid.[54]

Again the difficulty arises in determining which formalities are

[52] Cf. Roelker, "art. cit.," *The Jurist,* III (1943), 391.

[53] Toso, *Ad Codicem Iuris Canonici Commentaria Minora* (5 vols., Romae: Marietti, 1920-1927), I, 28. Cf. Van Hove, *loc. cit.*

[54] Coronata, *Institutiones Iuris Canonici,* I, 35-36; Cance, *Le Code de Droit Canonique* (7. ed., 3 vols., Paris: Librarie LeCoffre, 1946), I, n. 40, p. 48; Cocchi, *Commentarium in Codicem Iuris Canonici,* I, 36; Cicognani, *Canon Law,* p. 560; Maroto, *Institutiones Iuris Canonici,* I, n. 225.

substantial and which are merely accidental to an act. Roelker describes the emphasis which Suarez (1548-1617) placed upon the distinction between a form specified by law in the actual concession of power and the form also specified by law but presupposing the actual concession of power.[55] D'Annibale (1815-1892) tried to establish a simple criterion for determining the substantial form of an act when he stated that it generally calls for the intervention of a specified public authority or the necessity of drawing up public documents according to law.[56]

While these and similar distinctions and criteria may be helpful in forming conclusions with regard to equivalently nullifying laws, it seems advisable to resort in each case to the various rules of the general interpretation of law, and to consider as equivalently invalidating only those laws which require certain forms or solemnities as a *"conditio sine qua non"* for the validity of the act.[57] This course seems the more advisable in view of canon 15, which states that all laws, including invalidating and disqualifying laws, lose their force in a *dubium iuris.*[58]

In the light of the foregoing considerations concerning invalidating laws, it is clear that the law regarding installation of pastors does not contain any explicitly invalidating clauses either in canon 461 or in canons 1443 to 1445, by which this canon is governed.[59] Those authors who hold that installation in office is necessary for the validity of the pastor's actions maintain that the law does, however, contain an equivalently invalidating character because of its connection with various other canons in the Code. Park emphasizes especially the fact that installation is a part of the *canonica provisio* and as such is necessary for the validity of the pastor's office by virtue of canon 147, § 1.[60]

He rightly contends that installation is an integral part of canonical provision, as has been explained,[61] but his conclusion that

---

[55] Roelker, "art. cit." The Jurist, III (1943), 394.

[56] *Summula Theologiae Moralis* (3. ed., 3 vols., Romae, 1892), I, n. 213.

[57] Cf. cans. 18 and 1680.

[58] Cf. Woywod, *A Practical Commentary on the Code of Canon Law,* I, 10-11.

[59] Schaaf, *ER,* XCI (1934), 623.

[60] "Art. cit.," *HPR,* XXXV (1935), 580-585.

[61] *Supra,* p. 70.

it is, therefore, necessary for the validity of the pastor's office seems to be an undue extension of the meaning of an equivalently invalidating clause. For the reason simply that installation is an *integral* part of canonical provision, it does not follow that it is an *essential* part, or a substantial form, the omission of which would constitute an equivalent invalidation. If this were true, one could argue that every formula of law concerning canonical provision points to a necessary element for its validity.[62] It may be objected that to call installation an integral part of canonical provision, though not an essential part, is a mere quibbling over words, but it cannot be denied that there is a considerable difference between the two. An arm is an integral part of the human body, but it is not an essential part.

Consequently when Park says, "it is sound interpretation to conclude that the three acts which collectively make canonical provision are separately necessary for its validity,"[63] his argument, at least in the opinion of the writer, loses its force. In his support he cites the axiom: *Ubi lex non distinguit, nec nostrum est distinguere.* The writer contends that the law makes a definite distinction between the various parts of canonical provision and their substantial importance.

In support of this contention it may be pointed out that the chapter of the Code which treats of canonical provision[64] devotes separate articles to the various ways of the designation of the person and to the actual granting of authority, which are the essential parts of canonical provision. If canonical installation were to be considered of equal importance with these two steps, then it seems that an article on this subject should also have been included in this particular chapter.[65]

---

[62] E. g., canon 159, which states that the appointment to any office is to be made in writing.

[63] *Ibid.*, p. 584.

[64] Lib. II, tit. IV, cap. I.

[65] Cf. Wasner, *Jus Pontificium,* XVII (1937), 133-135. After showing that installation no longer has any juridical importance in the case of the Roman Pontiff, Wasner states: "In provisione aliorum officiorum superius dictorum, evolutio iuridica in Codice Iuris Canonici expressa, quasi media via anceps stat. Conceptus provisionis institutionem corporalem tamquam

Park also draws an argument in his support from canon 6, 2° and 3°, which require that those canons which re-state former laws must be interpreted in accordance with the accepted import of these laws, and hence the interpretations accepted by the approved authors are to be followed. However, he admits that the authors before the Code do not always agree whether installation under the pre-Code law was necessary for validity or only for licitness.[66] He calls upon statements of Reiffenstuel (1642-1703), which show that he considered installation as a very necessary part of canonical provision, but it can hardly be said that Reiffenstuel thought of this necessity as required for the validity of the concession of office.

In an earlier part of this treatise[67] it has been shown that Reiffenstuel felt strongly that corporal installation was necessary for the full concession of office as envisioned in the law.[68] He regarded the practice of so-called verbal installation as an *"actio abusiva,"* i.e., a mere token of real or actual installation.[69] He likewise held that an intruder, i.e., one who attempted to take possession of an office without having a *ius in re, ipso iure* lost all right to the office.[70] One who, though possessing a *ius in re,* used violence in taking possessionof an office, *ipso facto* lost his right to the office.[71] Yet Reiffenstuel used this very case as an illustration to show that installation was necessary only for licitness, since in similar circumstances wherein no violence occurred the offender was to be punished with appropriate penalties, but did not lose the *ius in re.*[72] He, indeed, held that, if a local custom or particular statute demanded actual or real investiture, this custom was to be observed for the lawful taking of possession.[73] His opinion, however, is

---

actum iuridico effectu praeditum excludit, práctice tamen usque redit in provisionibus plurium officiorum." Cf. also Chelodi, *Ius Canonicum de Personis,* p. 214.

[66] *Ibid.,* p. 583.

[67] *Supra,* pp. 55-57.

[68] *Ius Canonicum Universum,* lib. III, tit. 7, nn. 9 and 11.

[69] *Ibid.,* n. 46.

[70] *Ibid.,* n. 52.

[71] *Ibid.,* n. 59.

[72] *Ibid.,* n. 55.

[73] *Ibid.,* n. 54.

summed up in his statement that, although many laws had been enacted regarding installation, it was nowhere stated that the taking of corporal possession was invariably required as essential for the valid holding of a benefice.[74]

Other arguments presented by the authors in proof of their contention that the installation of pastors in office is necessary for the validity of subsequent actions are drawn from canons 334, 1095, § 1, and 2394. It is proposed that if by virtue of canon 334 canonical installation is necessary for the validity of the possession of an office in the case of residential bishops, as is readily admitted, then by virtue of canons 461 and 1443 it should also be regarded as necessary in the case of pastors.[75]

There are, however, several reasons which militate against this argument as deriving from the factor of parallelism. The office of a pastor can hardly be compared to the office of a residential bishop any more than can the bishop's office be compared to the office of the Roman Pontiff. In the case of the Roman Pontiff no one argues that the formal ceremonies of coronation have any juridic effect. If the suggested proposition were a valid argument, it could similarly be stated that the bishop's installation would be necessary only for licitness. Moreover, in reference to residential bishops a specific form is given in detail for the installation proper.

The bishop must present his apostolic letters of appointment to the cathedral chapter in the presence of the secretary of the chapter or of the chancellor of the curia, who must make an entry of the fact into the records of the diocese. Concerning pastors the form which the installation is to take is left to particular legislation or legitimate local custom. It is the writer's contention that in the case of bishops a specific and substantial form is required, and hence it constitutes an essential and therefore necessary element for the validity, whereas in the case of pastors the form is less specific and very indefinite, and hence it cannot be considered as a substantial form which is required for validity. It may, indeed, be admitted that it could become for pastors also a substantial form, necessary for validity, if particular legislation or local cus-

[74] *Ibid.*, n. 56.

[75] Park, "art. cit.," *HPR*, XXXV (1935), 585.

tom were to make it such. This is in accord with the teaching of Reiffenstuel, as cited above.[76]

It is maintained by the stricter opinion that the parallelism between the office of a residential bishop and the office of a pastor is clearly indicated in canon 1095, § 1, 1°,[77] and this canon is also cited as proof by itself of the necessity of the installation of a pastor for the validity of his acts. With reference to this asserted parallelism it is, indeed, true that both pastors and local ordinaries can validly assist at marriage only within the respective limitations as set by canons 334, § 3, and 1444, § 1. It does not follow, however, that the taking of canonical possession of their benefices is a matter of identical import in each case, for canon 1095, § 1, 1°, makes particular reference to special canons governing each case respectively.[78]

It is, indeed, true that the pastor as well as the bishop must be in valid possession of his benefice before he can validly assist at marriages,[79] but it does not necessarily follow that the formal taking of possession of the benefice is therefore necessary for the bishop and for the pastor in the same manner for the valid possession of his benefice. That question must be judged on the basis of canon 334, § 3, and canon 1444, § 1, respectively, and not on the basis of canon 1095. This latter canon merely states that the pastor and the bishop can validly assist at marriages only from the day on which they have taken possession of their benefice without judging the question of the necessity of the taking of possession of the benefice through formal installation.

Canon 1095, § 1, 1°, in addition contains this phrase *"vel initi officii."* There can be no doubt that this phrase contemplates primarily the case of those local ordinaries who do not have a benefice,

---

[76] *Supra,* p. 97.

[77] "Parochus et loci Ordinarius valide matrimonio assistunt: 1° A die tantummodo adeptae canonicae possessionis beneficii ad normam can. 334, § 3, 1444, § 1, vel initi officii, . . ." Cf. Park, *loc. cit.*

[78] ". . . ad normam can. 334, § 3, 1444, § 1 . . ."

[79] Coronata, *Institutiones Iuris Canonici de Sacramentis* (3 vols., Taurini-Romae: Marietti, 1943-1946), III (1946), 762; Cappello, *Tractatus Canonico-Moralis de Sacramentis* (3 vols. in 5, Vol. III, 3. ed., Taurinorum Augustae-Romae: Apud Marietti et Aedes Universitatis Gregorianae, 1933), III, n. 661, 1°.

such as the vicar general, and also those wh o in law take the place of the pastor, such as the adjutant vicar. These have the right to assist at marriage from the time that they have entered upon the exercise of their office. Is it not possible for this phrase to be applied also to a pastor who, even though illicitly, has not followed the letter of the law as enacted in canon 1444?[80]

Since the phrase *"initi officii"* is nowhere defined in law, the commentators give little explanation of it.[81] The presence of this phrase in canon 1095, § 1, 1°, seems to the writer adequately to protect the validity of the assistance at marriage when performed by a pastor who may have taken possession of his parish without a formal installation, so that it appears needless to resort to the juridical factor of common error in the presence of which according to canon 209 the act would be assured of validity.

Finally, those authors who hold that installation is necessary for the validity of the pastor's acts cite the penalties inflicted upon usurpers in office as pointing equivalently to the invalidating character of the law which requires the fact of installation.[82] In the

---

[80] Cf. Augustine, *A Commentary on the New Code of Canon Law,* V, 276. He states, "The pastor, in the United States, is supposed, and justly so, to have the title of parish-priest after he has received his appointment to a pastorate. However, our text says *initi officii,* which means actual entrance upon office. A pastor may enter upon his office by merely taking possession of the parsonage in an informal way, or formally with the usual ceremonies." Cf. De Becker, *Praelectiones Canonicae de Matrimonio* (ed. nova, Louvain: Establiss. Fr. Ceuterick, 1931), p. 136, "Quare, in praxi, attendendum est ad leges particulares, consuetudines probatas ex quibus iudicandum erit de installatione rite peracta seu *de inito officio,* cum nulla, in iure communi, existat formula sacramentalis ad hoc praescripta." (The italics are those of the writer.)

[81] Cf. Woywod, *A Practical Commentary on the Code of Canon Law,* I, 666; Cappello, *Tractatus Canonico-Moralis de Sacramentis,* III, n. 661; Coronata, *Institutiones Iuris Canonici de Sacramentis,* III, 762-763; De Becker, *Praelectiones Canonicae de Matrimonio,* p. 136.

[82] "Qui beneficium, officium vel dignitatem ecclesiasticam propria auctoritate occupaverit vel, ad ea electus, praesentatus, nominatus in eorundem possessionem vel regimen seu administrationem sese ingesserit, antequam necessarias litteras confirmationis vel institutionis acceperit easque illis ostenderit, quibus de iure debet: 1° Sit ipso iure ad eadem inhabilis et praeterea ab Ordinario pro gravitate culpae puniatur; 2° Per suspensionem, privationem beneficii, officii, dignitatis antea obtentae et, si res ferat, etiam per

mind of the writer this seems to be the strongest argument in favor of their opinion. It does not, however, appear to present an insurmountable difficulty to the opposite opinion which holds that installation is necessary only for the licitness of the pastor's acts. It must be remembered that laws which state a penalty, or which restrict the free exercise of one's rights, must be interpreted in a strict sense;[83] in other words, the binding force of the penalty must be clearly demonstrated in accordance with the ancient rule of law: *Odia restringi et favores convenit ampliari.*[84]

In the light of this principle the phrase *"propria auctoritate occupaverit"* bears further examination. In the long list of indicated sources as cited by Cardinal Gasparri in the footnote to canon 2394 one notes the almost exclusive emphasis that is placed on the penalties inflicted in former times upon those who presumed to occupy a benefice or an office by force or by violence, or upon those who accepted a benefice from the hands of a layman without receiving the title from the proper ecclesiastical authority, or upon those who proceeded to assume the administration of an office while possessing only a *ius ad rem* and not a *ius in re* with relation to the benefice. In fact, the cited references do not point to a single case in which the person possessed a clear and undisputed *ius in re* to the benefice.[85]

---

depositionem, cogatur a beneficii, officii, dignitatis occupatione eorumque regimine vel administratione statim, monitione praemissa, recedere; 3° Capitula vero, conventus aliique omnes ad quos spectat, huiusmodi electos, praesentatos vel nominatos ante litterarum exhibitionem admittentes, ipso facto a iure eligendi, nominandi vel praesentandi suspensi maneant ad beneplacitum Sedis Apostolicae."—Can. 2394. Cf. Coronata, *Institutiones Iuris Canonici,* II, 391; Park, "art. cit.," *HPR,* XXXV (1935), 585-586; Fanfani, *De Iure Parochorum,* p. 91, n. 100.

[83] Cans. 19 and 2219.

[84] Reg. 15, R. J., in VI°.

[85] To understand the force of this argument it should be recalled that the *ius ad rem* arises from the designation of the person for the office or benefice either through the free appoinment by the superior, through the nomination or presentation by a patron, or through the election or postulation by a chapter or some other electoral group. The *ius in re* arises from the concession of the power of the office through the free conferral by the superior, through the institution of the one nominated by an ecclesiastic or presented by a patron, through the confirmation of the one elected, or through the admission of one who has been postulated. Cf. *supra,* pp. 68-69.

It should also be noted that the phrase "*propria auctoritate occupare*" is used commonly in connection with the idea of taking hold of a benefice with force or violence, or with other unjust means.[86]

Thus it seems within the bounds of an orthodox interpretation to limit the disqualifying effect of canon 2394 in regard to installation to the cases in which a person attempts to occupy a benefice without a proper title, or with the use of force or of violence. This interpretation apparently is followed by a number of authors who speak of the disqualifying penalty for those who use violence in taking possession of office, but who moderate the penalty for those who peacefully occupy a benefice, even by their own authority, provided that in good faith they thought themselves to possess a *ius in re* to the benefice.[87] This view is also expressed by the authors before the Code.[88]

In conclusion, then, it may be said that the installation of pastors in office is an integral part of canonical provision, and, as such, should be faithfully observed. It cannot, however, be said that it is absolutely necessary for the validity of the pastor's acts, for (1) the law nowhere contains an expressly invalidating or disqualifying character as required by canon 11, and (2) the law likewise does not contain an equivalently disqualifying character: (a) either by virtue of its connection with canon 147, § 1, since installation is only an integral, but not a substantial, part or essential formality to be observed in canonical provision; (b) or by virtue of canon 1095, § 1, 1°, since this law also provides for the valid assistance at marriage without installation; (c) or by comparison with the installation of residential bishops, as required in canon 334, § 3, since these offices cannot be adequately compared in this matter, and also because the formalities in one case are very specific and in the other case indefinite; (d) or, finally, in consequence of the penalties prescribed in canon 2394, since these penalties, if strictly interpreted, concern rather those who take possession of a benefice

[86] E. g., c. 18, *de praebendis et dignitatibus,* III, 4, in VI°.

[87] Cf. Rossi, *De Paroecia,* p. 175, n. 178; Wernz-Vidal, *Ius Canonicum,* II, 374.

[88] Reiffenstuel, *Ius Canonicum Universum,* lib. III, tit. 7, n. 54; Garcia, *De Beneficiis Ecclesiasticis,* pars IV, c. 2, n. 6; Engel, *Collegium Universi Iuris Canonici,* lib. III, tit. 7, nn. 4-9; cf. *Supra,* pp. 59-63.

without a proper title (*ius in re*), or through the use of force or of violence.

This opinion seems also to be justified in the light of the principle stated in canon 15, namely, that invalidating and disqualifying laws lose their force *in dubio iuris*. The contention that there actually exists a *dubium iuris* in this law seems justified in the fact that a number of reputable authors may be cited as not supporting the law's invalidating or disqualifying force as outlined above.

Finally, it must nevertheless be admitted that particular legislation or legitimate local custom, as occasioned in consequence of the circumstances of a particular locality, can specify that the formalities of the installation of pastors are substantial formalities, and thus they could become essential for the valid taking of possession of the parochial benefice and the consequent valid exercise of the pastor's office.

It may be argued that this latter proposal would give to the local ordinary the power to make an invalidating law in a matter in which the general law of the Church in The Code of Canon Law has already established a definite norm.[89] The answer to this difficulty seems clear in that the law of the Code in the matter of the installation of pastors specifically gives the power to the local ordinary to legislate concerning installation when it states that installation in a benefice is to be carried out in the manner specified by particular law or by legitimate custom.[90] The bishop can in turn enforce his law by means of an invalidating clause if he so desires.[91] He can establish certain formalities which must be fulfilled before he will recognize an act as valid. He has the power to appoint pastors as well as the power to grant to them the possession of their benefice.[92] It seems logical therefore that he may require certain formalities before he will consider his appointment or his granting of possession of a parish to a pastor as valid.

---

[89] For a fuller discussion of the power of the bishop to enact invalidating laws cf. Roelker, "The Power to Enact Invalidating Laws," *The Jurist*, III (1943), 231-257.

[90] Can. 1444, § 1.

[91] Roelker, "art. cit.," *The Jurist*, III (1943), 238-240.

[92] Cans. 455, § 1, and 1443, § 2.

Article 2. Dispensation from the Law of Installation

It is easy to understand that in certain circumstances it would be difficult, if not impossible, to carry out the details of the legislation concerning the installation of pastors in office. This difficulty is anticipated in the law itself, which gives the local ordinary the power to dispense from the manner and rite of installation if there is a just cause. The law further states that in this case the dispensation itself takes the place of the formal installation.[93] Four characteristics should be noted in the law: 1) a just cause is required for the granting of the dispensation; 2) the grant must be made expressly; 3) it must likewise be made in writing; and 4) when it is thus conceded it takes the place of installation and has the same effect.

1. The general norms to be observed in the granting of dispensations give an indication of what is meant by a "just" cause.[94] The cause is just and reasonable if a due proportion and balance exists between the gravity of the law from which a dispensation is requested and the amount of hardship which the observance of the law would otherwise entail.[95] Thus the dispensation from certain laws requires a *"iusta causa,"*[96] a *"gravis causa,"*[97] a *"causa legitima,"*[98] a *"causa peculiaris,"*[99] a *"iusta et gravis causa,"*[100] etc. Michiels gives many other illustrations from the canons to show what is to be understood by a just and reasonable cause in relation to the law from which a dispensation is granted.[101]

It would be difficult, if not impossible, to determine the various

---

[93] ". . . nisi iusta ex causa Ordinarius ab eo modo seu ritu expresse in scriptis dispensaverit; quo in casu haec dispensatio locum tenet captae possessionis."—Can. 1444, § 1.

[94] "A lege ecclesiastica ne dispensetur sine iusta et rationabili causa, habita ratione gravitatis legis a qua dispensatur . . ."—Can. 84, § 1.

[95] Ramstein, *A Manual of Canon Law,* p. 120; cf. Cicognani, *Canon Law,* pp. 852-855; Michiels, *Normae Generales Iuris Canonici* (2 vols., Lublin, Polonia: Universitas Catholica, 1929), II, 498-513.

[96] E.g., cans. 998, § 1; 1119; 1245, § 1; 1313; 1444, § 1.

[97] E.g., can. 972, § 1.

[98] E.g., can. 1028, § 1.

[99] E.g., Can. 1245, § 2.

[100] E.g., can. 1061, § 1, 1°.

[101] *Ibid.,* p. 506.

causes which, because of peculiar circumstances, might be considered as just causes for the granting of a dispensation from the law of the installation of pastors in office. The danger of causing factions or quarrels among the people, the fact that such difficulties have existed during the previous pastorate and might arise again through a public ceremony of installation, the difficulties of travel because of distance or because of the poor accessibility of the place, the hardships of inclement weather, the lack of a suitable church for this public ceremony in the case of a newly-organized parish, objections on the part of civil authorities, or the danger of causing a civil disturbance are but a few of the causes which may be mentioned. It should be emphasized, however, that a *just* cause is required for the validity of the dispensation, since the law states that a dispensation granted by one inferior to the legislator himself is illicit and invalid if granted without a just cause.[102] In a case of doubt as to the sufficiency of the cause, the dispensation may be licitly requested and both licitly and validly granted.[103]

The mere fact that neither local custom nor particular legislation prescribes a special rite or manner of installation to be followed does not seem to be a sufficient cause for granting the dispensation, since in these circumstances the law seems to place the burden upon the local ordinary to establish such a manner. Hence the practice, prevalent in some dioceses, of granting a dispensation in each and every case hardly seems justifiable.

2. The dispensation, if granted, must be *expressly made.*[104] An *express* dispensation is one that is explicitly or directly stated in words or in writing. It is in opposition to a *tacit* dispensation which is implicitly known from the superior's manner of acting or is contained in some other action.[105] It may be argued that if the dispensation is implicitly granted it is an express dispensation because it arises from an express action of the superior. In this

---

[102] Can. 84, § 1. It is hardly necessary to enter here into a discussion of the controversy concerning the validity of a dispensation which is granted when in reality a just cause does not exist. Cf. Michiels, *op. cit.*, II, 507-511.

[103] Can. 84, § 2.

[104] Can. 1444, § 1.

[105] E.g., can. 1053. Cf. Cappello, *Summa Iuris Canonici,* I, 127; Coronata, *Institutiones Iuris Canonici,* I, 119; Cicognani, *Canon Law,* p. 831; Beste, *Introductio in Codicem,* p. 126.

understanding of terms a tacit dispensation would be identical with a presumed dispensation. In the strict terminology of the law this latter seems not to be any dispensation at all, but rather a dissimulation or mere toleration.[106] Michiels, however, points out that the essential elements of a dispensation are the will of the legislator to dispense and, in the case of one inferior to the legislator, the actual existence of a just cause.[107]

In the case of the installation of pastors, however, a tacit dispensation in the sense of a presumed dispensation cannot be admitted, since the law specifically states that the dispensation must be express and in writing.[108] Accordingly, as Park insists, the bishop's letter which simply appoints a priest as pastor of a certain parish cannot be considered as tantamount to a dispensation.[109] Even if the letter were to name a certain date on which the appointment takes effect, or on which the new pastor should begin his ministry in the parish, it does not seem that this can be considered as a dispensation from the law of installation. In this latter instance there could certainly be a reasonable presumption of a tacit dispensation, but, as has been stated, the law in this matter requires an express dispensation.

3. The reason for which the law requires that the dispensation should be in writing is obvious. The dispensation itself then becomes the official document attesting to the valid taking of possession of the pastoral office. This formality is, therefore, important in order to avoid difficulties at a later time. It does not seem, however, that the dispensation must be in writing to be valid.[110]

4. As has already been mentioned, the dispensation when granted takes the place of the installation of the pastor in his parish. Accordingly all the juridical effects resulting from the act of installation in office may be applied from the moment that the dispensation is granted. These effects are discussed in a separate chapter.[111]

---

[106] Cf. Coronata, *Institutiones Iuris Canonici,* I, 119, in footnote 5.

[107] *Normae Generales Iuris Canonici,* II, 458-460.

[108] ". . . nisi . . . expresse in scriptis dispensaverit . . ."—Can. 1444, § 1.

[109] "Art. cit.," *HPR,* XXXV (1935), 588.

[110] Cappello, *Summa Iuris Canonici,* II, 567.

[111] *Infra,* pp. 138-174.

Article 3. Customs Contrary to the Law of Installation

In the United States it is sometimes stated that the custom of omitting the installation of pastors in office has existed for a sufficient length of time to set aside the force of the law in this country.[112] Indeed, it is true that there is no special statute nor any particular legislation on this subject which applies to the entire country, since no mention is made of the installation of pastors in the provincial or plenary Councils of Baltimore.[113] It cannot be said, however, that there exists a universal custom which derogates the law for the entire country.

From a questionnaire which was submitted to the chancery officials of the United States in November, 1947,—to which a response was received from more than 80% of the archdioceses and dioceses in this country—it was learned that at least 42 archdioceses and dioceses, or approximately one-third of the dioceses in the country, have a strictly formal and public ceremony for the installation of pastors, as prescribed by synodal or extra-synodal legislation. Besides these, nine archdioceses and dioceses have an informal procedure which is carried out privately or by a decree of the ordinary. Another ten dioceses which do not have a prescribed form, though an occasional formal ceremony is held, nonetheless have the general practice of granting an explicit, written dispensation from installation at the time of the appointment of the pastor.[114] In a further considerable number of dioceses it was indicated that a tacit dispensation, sometimes in the sense of an implicit dispensation and sometimes in the sense of a presumed dispensation, from the law of installation is understood, either because the letter of appointment of a pastor contains an effective date for the beginning of the ministry in the parish, or because other similar indications have been given by the ordinary, or because nothing whatever is said concerning installation and the general presumption, ap-

---

[112] Cf. Park, *loc. cit.*

[113] Woywod, *A Practical Commentary on the Code of Canon Law,* I, 166.

[114] This practice does not seem to be justified, since it can hardly be admitted that a just cause for the dispensation exists in every such case. Cf. *supra,* p. 104.

parently sanctioned by the ordinary, concludes that a dispensation is granted.[115]

Thus it is readily clear that the number of dioceses in which no reference is made to the law of installation of pastors is by far a minority of the total number of dioceses in the country. Hence there can be no question of a custom contrary to the law of installation in the entire country. Surely no such custom exists in those dioceses which have a prescribed form of installation or an informal procedure. It likewise does not seem possible to acknowledge the existence of such a custom in those dioceses which have an occasional formal ceremony of installation, or in those dioceses which have the practice of granting an explicit dispensation from the law of installation, since these acts constitute a recognition of the binding force of the law.

To determine the possibility of the existence of a contrary custom in those dioceses which make no reference to the law of installation of pastors, it is necessary to understand the essential elements required for the existence of a legitimate custom contrary to the law (*contra legem*). Such a custom must be reasonable and endowed with the juridical element of legal prescription through a continuous and uninterrupted usage of forty years. If the law contains a clause forbidding contrary customs in the future, only a reasonable custom that is either immemorial or of a hundred years' standing can obtain the force of law.[116] The Code gives only a negative definition of a reasonable custom when it states that a custom which is expressly reproved in the law is an unreasonable custom.[117]

The laws governing the installation of pastors do not contain any clauses prohibiting contrary future customs. Therefore a custom of forty years' standing would be sufficient to derogate this law. It must also be admitted that such a custom would be a

[115] Neither does this practice seem acceptable, since the law specifically requires an express and written dispensation. Cf. *supra*, pp. 105-106.

[116] ". . . neque iuri ecclesiastico praeiudicium affert, nisi fuerit rationabilis et legitime per annos quadraginto continuos et completos praescripta; contra legem vero ecclesiasticam quae clausulam contineatur futuras consuetudines prohibentem, sola praescribere potest rationabilis consuetudo centenaria aut immemorabilis."—Can. 27, § 1.

[117] Can. 27, § 2.

reasonable custom in the legal sense of that term, since it is not such as to undermine any fundamental discipline of the Church.[118]

It should be noted, however, that by virtue of canon 5 all immemorial customs, both local and universal, which existed as contrary to the canons of the Code, when it became binding law, were abolished, even if the Code did not explicitly disapprove of them. But if they were not explicitly reprobated by the Code, then the continuance of immemorial and centenary customs could be tolerated by the ordinary if he felt that they could not be prudently abolished because of unfavorable local circumstances and the tenacious traditions current among the people. Ordinary contrary customs, i.e., other than immemorial or centenary customs, were unconditionally suppressed unless the Code explicitly stated otherwise.[119]

An immemorial custom contrary to the law of installation was not unconditionally abrogated by the Code, but there seems to be little cause to feel that it could not prudently be abolished, and hence, unless in a given case its continuance was nevertheless tolerated by the ordinary, it is evident that such a custom was entirely eliminated by the contrary law of the Code. Inasmuch as the requisite time for the establishing of a similar custom since the advent of the Code has not yet elapsed, it is difficult to understand how such a custom can be in effect at this time. This view is emphatically stated by Cappello[120] and Park.[121]

It may be granted that in a particular locality such a custom could lawfully exist, if at the time of the advent of the Code it was already an immemorial custom, and in addition the ordinary deemed that he could not prudently abolish it in view of unfavorable local or personal circumstances as then extant, though it is difficult to see what these circumstances may have been.

Some may perhaps contend that an existing contrary custom could not have been an immemorial contrary custom for the simple reason that parishes in the strict sense did not exist in the United

---

[118] Cf. Beste, *Introductio in Codicem,* p. 93.

[119] Coronata, *Institutiones Iuris Canonici,* I, 7-10.

[120] *Summa Iuris Canonici,* II, 566; also in *Periodica,* XVIII (1929), 148*-149*.

[121] "Art. cit.," *HPR,* XXXV (1935), 588.

States until January 1, 1909, when the Church in this country was removed from the jurisdiction of the Sacred Congregation for the Propagation of the Faith and placed under the general legislation of the Church in all things, or, as others have insisted, until the advent of the Code in 1918.[122]

These objections, however, are not admissible. First of all, an immemorial custom could exist as a custom contrary to the law of the Code when the latter became binding law, even apart from the consideration whether from time immemorial the custom had always existed as *contrary to the law.* For the principle in canon 5 applies not only to customs which from time immemorial were contrary to the law and in addition stand in opposition to the Code as well, but also to such customs which, regardless of their earlier juridical status, existed as immemorial customs that opposed the newly enacted law of the Code. Furthermore, even if one were to admit the validity of the asserted contentions, there did exist at least quasi-parishes, in 1909 as well as in 1918, and in either assumption quasi-pastors as well as pastors would have been bound by the law of installation in office.[123]

In the view of this writer, then, unless an immemorial custom existed in 1918, whether contrary to the law at that time or not, became then contrary to the law when the present Code came into effect, and was continued later by way of legitimate toleration, there cannot presently exist in this country any contrary custom which derogates from the law that requires the installation of pastors in office.

Article 4. Penalties for Unlawful Occupation of the Pastoral Office

The importance of the pastoral office obviously dictates the necessity of penal sanctions against those who unlawfully occupy that office. The penalties which especially concern violations in the matter of installation in office are found in the following canons:

Canon 2394.—Qui beneficium, officium vel dignitatem ecclesiasticam propria auctoritate occupaverit vel, ad ea electus, praesentatus, nominatus in eorundem possessionem vel regi-

---

[122] Cf. *supra*, pp. 73-75.

[123] Cf. *supra*, pp. 75-77.

men seu administrationem sese ingesserit, antequam necessarias litteras confirmationis vel institutionis acceperit easque illis ostenderit, quibus de iure debet:

1° Sit ipso iure ad eadem inhabilis et praeterea ab Ordinario pro gravitate culpae puniatur;

2° Per suspensionem, privationem beneficii, officii, dignitatis antea obtentae et, si res ferat, etiam per depositionem, cogatur a beneficii, officii, dignitatis occupatione eorumque regimine vel administratione statim, monitione praemissa, recedere;

3° Capitula vero, conventus aliique omnes ad quos spectat, huiusmodi electos, praesentatos vel nominatos ante litterarum exhibitionem admittentes, ipso facto a iure eligendi, nominandi vel praesentandi suspensi maneant ad beneplacitum Sedis Apostolicae.

Canon 2395.—Qui scienter acceptat collationem officii, beneficii vel dignitatis de iure non vacantis et patiatur se in eius possessionem immitti, sit ipso facto inhabilis ad illa postea assequenda aliisque poenis pro modo culpae puniatur.

Canon 2396.—Clericus, qui assecutus pacificem possessionem officii vel beneficii cum priore incompatibilis, prius quoque retinere praesumpserit contra praescriptum can. 156, 1439, utroque privatus ipso iure existat.

It is immediately apparent that the most severe penalty is contained in canon 2394, 1°. The penalty there enacted is a *latae sententiae* penalty which makes the pastor who unlawfully occupies his office *ipso iure* disqualified from holding that office. It is, therefore, at least an equivalently invalidating or disqualifying law. If it is to be applied in its full measure to all those who violate the laws of installation in office, it seems unduly severe when related to the fact that no greater, but simply the same, penalty is in store for the other more serious delicts of which the law simultaneously takes cognizance. It would immediately follow that a great number of pastors, especially in the United States, would be disqualified from holding their office, and would in reality be only putative pastors. The validity of their many actions could only be upheld on the basis of common error according to the norms of canon 209. This would appear to entail such a sweeping and far-reaching application of that principle as could hardly have been intended by the legislator. It would seem to reduce the law to an absurdity.

It must be admitted that the great majority of authors seems to accept the view that any substantial violation of the law of installation in office is subject to the full penalty enacted in canon 2394, 1°. It should be noted, however, that very few of these authors offer a detailed explanation of the law. Many simply state the words of the canon without discussing its full application.[124]

Those authors who insist more specifically that the full penalty of disqualification is to be applied to those who violate the laws of installation in office include the following: Coronata,[125] Eichmann (1870-1945),[126] Augustine,[127] Cocchi,[128] Pistocchi,[129] Wernz-Vidal,[130] and others. The statements of these authors, however, do not necessarily imply that this penalty ensues automatically in every case.

All authors are agreed that the purpose of this penalty is to prevent acts of intrusion or usurpation.[131] There are, indeed, a number of acts which might constitute such intrusion or usurpation.[132] This is indicated by the number and the variety of the pre-Code

[124] Ayrinhac-Lydon, *Penal Legislation in the New Code of Canon Law* (New York: Benzinger Brothers, Inc., 1944), p. 310; Blat, *Commentarium Textus Codicis Iuris Canonici,* V, 309-310; Bouscaren-Ellis, *Canon Law,* p. 875; Cance, *Le Code de Droit Canonique,* III, 432 and 434; De Meester, *Juris Canonici et Juris Canonico-Civilis Compendium,* Tom. III, pars II, p. 285, n. 1897; Fanfani, *De Iure Parochorum,* pp. 91-92; Prümmer, *Manuale Iuris Canonici,* p. 693; Raus, *Institutiones Canonicae,* pp. 728 and 731; Rossi, *De Paroecia,* pp. 175-176; Salucci, *Diritto Penale* (2 vols., Subiaco: Tipografia dei Monasteri, 1926-1930), II, 361-362; Sipos, *Enchiridion Iuris Canonici,* pp. 781 and 1018; Woywod, *A Practical Commentary on the Code of Canon Law,* II, 524.

[125] *Institutiones Iuris Canonici,* IV, 670-673.

[126] *Lehrbuch des Kirchenrechts* (2. ed., Paderborn: Druck und Verlag von Ferdinand Schöningh, 1926), p. 751; *Das Strafrecht des* CODEX IURIS CANONICI (Paderborn: Druck und Verlag von Ferdinand Schöningh, 1920), n. 102, pp. 225-227.

[127] *A Commentary on the New Code of Canon Law,* VIII, 494-496.

[128] *Commentarium in Codicem Iuris Canonici,* VIII, 386-387.

[129] *De Re Beneficiali,* pp. 222-223; *I Canoni Penali del Codice Ecclesiastico* (Torino-Roma: Marietti, 1925), pp. 335-339.

[130] *Ius Canonicum,* VII, 594-596.

[131] Cf. Wernz-Vidal, *Ius Canonicum,* VII, 595. "Arcere periculum intrusionis est res summe necessarium ad publicum bonum, unde delicta in hac materia specialem habent gravitatem."

[132] Cf. Maroto, *Institutiones Iuris Canonici,* I, 684-685.

laws which had a bearing on the matter treated in canon 2394. Reference to these laws is made by Gasparri in his footnote to this canon.

An act of intrusion is committed by one who as a result of his hostility or by means of captivity forces a pastor to leave or to be absent from his parish and thereupon assumes possession of it.[133] This case is partially covered by canon 2395, which forbids anyone knowingly to accept an office or to be placed in possession of an office which is not *de iure* vacant. The same effect of intrusion obtains when one unjustly or with force occupies a benefice which is not vacant either *de facto* or *de iure*. It should be noted that a benefice is vacant *de facto* when no one holds actual possession of it; it is vacant *de iure* when no one holds legal title to it. Accordingly, when a benefice is not vacant *de facto,* an act of intrusion could still occur even though the intruder possessed a valid title to the benefice.[134]

An obvious act of intrusion or usurpation is the acceptance of an office or benefice from the hands of a lay or civil authority, or even from any ecclesiastical authority other than the one who has a right to grant the title or the possession of the benefice or office.[135] It is also a usurpation of authority if one who has been elected to an office, or if one who has been presented or nominated for an office, presumes to administer that office before having received the confirmation of his election, presentation or nomination from the competent ecclesiastical authority. Such a person would have only a *ius ad rem* and not a *ius in re* to the office or benefice.[136] Even though a person lawfully possessed a *ius in re* to an office or benefice, he would nonetheless be an intruder if he proceeded to

---

[133] C. 42, C. VII, q. 1; Leo X (in Conc. Lateranen. V), const. *Regimini universalis,* 4 maii 1515, § 11—*Fontes,* n. 66.

[134] C. 18, *de praebendis et dignitatibus,* III, 4, in VI°.

[135] Cc. 11-17, 19, C. XVI, q. 7; c. 3, X, *de institutionibus,* III, 7; c. 4, 21, X, *de iure patronatus,* III, 38; Pius IX, ep. encycl. *Etsi multa,* 21 nov. 1873—*Fontes,* n. 566; Pius IX, ep. *Quod nunquam,* 5 febr. 1875—*Fontes,* n. 568; S. C. C., decr. 30 apr. 1873, nn. I, II—*Fontes,* n. 4225.

[136] C. 7, X, *de consuetudine,* I, 4; c. 17, 23, X, *de electione et electi potestate,* I, 6; c. 5, *de electione et electi potestate,* I, 6, in VI°; Pius IX, const. *Romanus Pontifex,* 28 aug. 1873—*Fontes,* n. 565; Clemens XI, const. *In supremo,* 24 aug. 1709, § 3—*Fontes,* n. 266.

administer the office or the benefice without first presenting his letters of confirmation or appointment to those who are entitled to examine these letters; the same would be true if he entered upon the administration of the office or the benefice before carrying out certain formalities in the taking of possession of the office or the benefice as specified by the competent authority.[137] These latter cases could occur on the part of bishops, apostolic administrators, vicars and prefects apostolic, and abbots and prelates *nullius,* who did not present their apostolic letter of appointment to the proper authorities, as prescribed in the canons, before assuming the administration of their respective offices.[138]

A pastor would also be guilty of these acts of intrusion if he failed to observe the formalities of installation as prescribed in a particular diocese in consequence of a legitimate local custom (i.e., not merely a local usage, but a legitimately established custom of forty years' duration which requires these formalities for the valid possession of a parochial benefice) or as the result of particular legislation (i.e., a synodal or extra-synodal statute requiring these formalities for the valid possession).

It does not seem, however, that a pastor could be guilty of acts of intrusion or usurpation if, upon having received his letter of appointment, and accordingly possessing a clear title or *ius in re* to the benefice, he proceeded to occupy the benefice when in reality no special formalities of taking possession were required by legitimate local custom or by particular legislation. It is hardly justifiable to consider him to be guilty of intrusion or usurpation solely on the basis of the law as enacted in canons 461 and 1443, since these canons do not point to any specific form to be observed in the taking of possession of a benefice or of a parish.

Augustine obviously admits the validity of this assertion even though he makes the statement that the penalty applies to violations of the law of canon 1443. Yet he says, "In our country the in-

---

[137] Iulius II, const. *Romani Pontificis,* 28 iul. 1505—*Fontes,* n. 62; c. 1, *de electione,* I, 3, in Extravag. com.; Paulus IV, const. *Incumbentia,* 1 nov. 1557, §§ 2, 8—*Fontes,* n. 91.

[138] Can. 334, § 3, for residential bishops; can. 313, §§ 1-2, for apostolic administrators; can. 293, § 2, for vicar and prefects apostolic; can. 322, § 1, for abbots and prelates *nullius.*

stallation of pastors is not always performed; and, consequently, this canon does not concern pastors in dioceses where this formality is usually omitted."[139] Wernz-Vidal admit that the delict of those who when they have a canonical title take possession of a benefice on their own authority, independently of the superior, is a less grave delict, but they apparently consider such persons liable for the fully penalty because of the possible danger of intrusion.[140] It should be noted, however, that in discussing the necessity of installation these authors apparently hold a milder view.[141] Rossi, who insists strongly on the application of the penalty of canon 2394, likewise allows for a milder interpretation.[142]

Chelodi applied the phrase "*propria auctoritate occupare*" only to the act of taking possession of a benefice by force or with the use of violence, or without a proper title, or without the presentation of the letters of appointment to the proper authorities.[143] This is a far more lenient opinion than is expressed by most authors. It is, indeed, more in accord with the principles of the interpretation of penal laws than is the opinion of those who hold that every violation of the law of installation entails the *latae sententiae* penalty of disqualification.[144] It seems, however, to be in accord with

---

[139] *A Commentary on the New Code of Canon Law,* VIII, 495.

[140] "Minus grave est delictum illius, qui iam titulum canonicum habet officii, beneficii, dignitatis, si, independenter a Superiore, ipse propria auctoritate occupat beneficii possessionem. Id posset facere intrusus, qui titulo carens illum falso allegaret; quare occupatio propria auctoritate facta per se induceret periculum intrusionis."—*Ius Canonicum,* VII, 595.

[141] "Quodsi clericus, obtenta institutione collativa tituli, absque ulla institutione corporali possessionem officii sibi collati et etiam de facto vacantis propria auctoritate contra praxim receptam capiat, a Superiore ecclesiastico competente optimo iure condigna poena castigari potest."—*Ius Canonicum,* II, 374.

[142] "Quim imo si quis clericus, habita tituli collatoria institutione vel libera collatione, ausus fuisset (contra praxim quae iam communiter invaluerat) sua propria auctoritate, absque corporali institutione, officii sumere possessionem, condigna poena debebat a superiore castigari."—*De Paroecia,* p. 175.

[143] *Ius Canonicum de Delictis et Poenis et de Iudiciis Criminalibus* (5. ed. a P. Ciprotti recognita et aucta, Trento: Libreria Moderna Editrice, 1943), pp. 154-156.

[144] "In poenis benignior est interpretatio facienda"—Can. 2219, § 1; cf. also can. 19.

canonical equity and orthodox interpretation to apply this phrase also to pastors who neglect a specific formality required for the validity of possession of their parochial benefice by legitimate local custom or by particular legislation. It seems entirely reasonable to call them "intruders" in their office unless they have observed these specific formalities, and hence the full penalty of disqualification should apply to them.

This middle view seems more in harmony with the legislation before the Code. It has already been noted that not a single piece of legislation cited in the footnote to canon 2394 by Gasparri concerned the violation of the law of installation in office by one who, having a proper canonical title, peacefully occupied a vacant benefice on his own authority, unless it was specifically required that certain formalities be observed. This was likewise the opinion of the commentators before the Code, as is evident from the teachings of Garcia (+1645),[145] Engel (ca. 1634-1674),[146] Reiffenstuel (1642-1703),[147] Bouix (1808-1870),[148] and Santi (1830-1885).[149]

Though a pastor who violates the laws concerning installation in office may not necessarily be subject to the *latae sententiae* penalty of disqualification for that office, as has been indicated, it does not follow that he may not be punished in other ways according to the gravity of his offense. For the canon specifically states that besides the *latae sententiae* penalty he may be punished by the ordinary according to the gravity of his guilt.[150]

In conclusion, then, the penalties for the violation of the laws concerning the installation of pastors in office may be summarized as follows:

1) *Ipso iure* disqualified from holding the parochial benefice and also subject to punishment by the ordinary according to the gravity of their offense are those (a) who take possession of a vacant parish by their own authority without a proper canonical title;

---

[145] *De Beneficiis Ecclesiasticis,* pars IV, c. 2, nn. 6-11.

[146] *Collegium Universi Iuris Canonici,* lib. III, tit. 7, n. 4.

[147] *Ius Canonicum Universum,* lib. III, tit. 7, nn. 52-58.

[148] *Tractatus de Parocho,* p. 375.

[149] *Praelectiones Iuris Canonici,* lib. III, tit. 7, n. 25.

[150] Can. 2394, 1°.

(b) who, having been elected, presented or nominated to a pastorate, take possession of a vacant parish or proceed to administer it before they have received their letters of confirmation and presented them to the competent authorities; (c) who, though having a proper canonical title with a *ius in re* in relation to the benefice, use force or violence to gain possession of a parish which is vacant *de iure,* but not vacant *de facto*; (d) who, though having a proper canonical title with a *ius in re* to the benefice, take possession of a parish which is vacant both *de iure* and *de facto,* but who fail to observe the specific formalities which are required for the validity of the possession of the benefice, either by local custom or by particular legislation.[151]

2) Those guilty of the delicts mentioned above are upon previous warning to be compelled to withdraw from their occupancy of the benefice and their administration of it. This is to be accomplished by means of a suspension, by means of a deprivation of the benefice previously obtained by them, or even by means of a deposition, if the gravity of the offense justifies it.[152]

3) Those who knowingly (*scienter*) accept an appointment to a parish which is not *de iure* vacant, and allow themselves to be inducted into possession of the parish, are automatically (*ipso facto*) disqualified from obtaining it later, and are also to be punished with other penalties according to the gravity of their delict.[153]

4) Those who, having obtained peaceful possession of a parish, presume to retain possession of a previously-obtained, incompatible benefice are automatically (*ipso iure*) deprived of both benefices.[154]

5) Those who, though having a proper canonical title with a *ius in re* to the benefice, take possession, without the consent of the ordinary or superior, of a parochial benefice which is vacant both *de iure* and *de facto* are subject to punishment by the ordinary according to the gravity of their guilt. This applies in the case in which no special formalities are required by legitimate local custom or by particular legislation for the valid possession of the

[151] Can. 2394, 1°.
[152] Can. 2394, 2°.
[153] Can. 2395.
[154] Can. 2396.

parochial benefice though a certain form may be required for licit possession. These pastors are not subject, however, to the automatic penalty of disqualification from holding possession of the parochial benefice.[155]

[155] Can. 2394, 1°.

CHAPTER VIII

THE MANNER OF CANONICAL INSTALLATION

While a uniformity of practice in the more essential matters of ecclesiastical discipline is a goal constantly to be fostered, the Church wisely leaves room for the expression of the various legitimate and praiseworthy local traditions in the less important affairs of ecclesiastical legislation. That fact is verified with reference to the manner that is prescribed for the installation of pastors in office. In the case of non-consistorial benefices the manner or rite of installation is to be carried out according to the prescriptions accepted by particular legislation or legitimate local custom.[1]

Hence it is to be expected that neither the *Ceremonial of Bishops,* nor the *Roman Pontifical,* nor the *Roman Ritual* contains any formula, or even any suggestions of a form to be used in the installation of pastors.[2] In his recent treatise on the *Roman Pontifical,* Nabuco includes a section on pontifical functions which are not to be found either in the *Roman Pontifical* or in the *Roman Ritual.* In this section he suggests a general order to be followed in the corporal installation of pastors.[3] Many excellent forms of installation are to be found in the synodal books of various dioceses.[4] Sev-

[1] Can. 1444, § 1.

[2] Cf. Hanrahan, "The Induction of Parish Priests," *The Clergy Review* (London, 1931—), IX (1939), 338-340.

[3] *Pontificalis Romani Expositio Juridico-Practica* (3 vols., Petropoli, Brasilia: Sumptibus Editora Vozes Ltda., 1945), III, 414-415.

[4] E.g., *Statuta Archidiocesis Sancti Francisci Lata ac Promulgata ab Exmo ac Revmo Ioanne J. Mitty, Archiepiscopo Santi Francisci in Synodo Diocesana Secunda* (San Francisco, Calif.: The Monitor Publishing Co., 1936), pp. 134-136; *Synodus Dioecesana Fargensis Prima iuxta Canones Sacros et Decreta Conciliorum Baltimorensium in Ecclesia Cathedrali Stae, Mariae Virginis ab Exmo ac Revmo Aloisio J. Muench, S. T. D., Episcopo Fargensi; Diebus XXIX et XXX Septembris A. D. MCMXLI Habita* (Milwaukee, Wis.: Bruce Publishing Co., 1941), pp. 203-207; *Statuta Archidioeceseos Indianapolitanae Lata ac Promulgata ab Exmo ac Revmo. Paulo Schulte, D. D., Archiepiscopo Indianapolitano in Synodo Archidioecesana (I) Septima Die 21 Mensis Maii 1947 Habita* (Indianapolis, Ind.: Standard Printing Co., 1947), pp. 112-113; *Synodus Dioecesana Omahensis Quarta*

eral of the authors also furnish examples of complete ceremonials that are in use or may be used for this solemnity.[5] Rebuffus (1487-1557), in his work *Praxis Beneficiorum,* incorporated a typical notary's report of the installation ceremony at that time.[6]

An examination of these various forms of installation indicates that a wide variety of symbolical acts may be adapted for this solemnity.

Article 1. The Rite of Installation

The primary purpose of the rite of installation is to acknowledge by means of a public act that the new pastor has received a legitimate title to the parochial benefice in question, and to signify by means of an external solemnity that he is given the actual peaceful possession of the benefice with all of its corresponding rights and obligations. In view of this purpose certain elements are to be desired in every installation rite.

Wernz-Vidal emphasize the importance of determining the fact that the benefice is at least *de iure* vacant.[7] This may prerequire the citation of the one who is alleged to have lost the title to the benefice, or it may demand the previous institution of a juridical action against the one who may be *de facto* in possession of the benefice in a case of a disputed title. If the fact of the loss of the title is public information, the citation of the party does not seem necessary.[8]

Difficulties of this nature do not commonly arise in this country, but in a number of dioceses it is customary to require that the previous pastor, or the administrator who had been appointed according to the provisions of canon 472, be present at the installation ceremony. Some caution is especially advisable in the transfer of pastors when a number of pastors are transferred at the same time. Care must be taken to preclude the possibility of a pastor's

(Omaha, Nebraska: Typis Burkley Envelope and Printing Co., 1934), pp. 169-170.

[5] Rossi, *De Paroecia,* pp. 182-185, n. 182; Biccari, "Preso di Possesso," *Perfice Munus!* III (1928), 542-543.

[6] Lib. I, cap. XXIII, n. 14, as quoted by Hanrahan, "art. cit.," *The Clergy Review,* IX (1939), 338.

[7] *Ius Canonicum,* II, 375.

[8] *Loc. cit.*

taking possession of a parish which is not yet vacant *de iure*. This difficulty is sometimes obviated in that the incumbent pastor is requested to resign his pastorate, and is then given an appointment as a temporary administrator until the new pastor takes possession of the parish, or until he himself is installed in his new parish.

In this connection it should be pointed out that the actual granting of possession is to be considered as being complete from the moment of the completion of the installation ceremony according to the provisions of canon 34, § 2. This fact is deduced from canon 461, which states that the pastor obtains the *cura animarum* from the moment of taking possession of the parochial benefice.[9] Hence any parochial functions performed by the new pastor even immediately before the installation ceremony would be illicit, and in some circumstances also invalid. Actions performed by him immediately after the ceremony would be both licit and valid.

Since the time of the actually effected granting of possession of the benefice must be computed from the very moment at which the possession was granted (*de momento*), the reason for some caution in the case of the transfer of a number of pastors at the same time is evident. Unless some provision is made, as has been mentioned, the parish does not become vacant *de iure* until the incumbent pastor has actually taken possession of his new parish and thereby has relinquished all right to the title which he previously held.

After the determination of the fact that the parish is vacant *de iure,* the next important element in the rite of installation is the recognition of the true and valid title held by the new pastor. This requires the intervention of the ecclesiastical authority in the person of the installing officer. In the case of non-consistorial benefices this authority is the local ordinary, who however may delegate another ecclesiastic to perform this function.[10]

At this point a consideration of the possible participation of the laity in the installation ceremony is of importance. It is obvious that a layman cannot exercise the authority of an installing officer. This follows both from the fact that the law specifically requires

[9] Cappello, *Summa Iuris Canonici,* II, 36.

[10] Can. 1443, § 2.

that the delegate be an ecclesiastic, and also from the more fundamental reason that a layman may not exercise any ecclesiastical jurisdictional authority, which is chiefly spiritual in its nature.[11] However, it may be advisable to have at least a representative of the laity as a witness to the installation ceremony in view of the acknowledged civil effects of this act in those localities in which the parish is not recognized as a moral person unless it is incorporated according to the manner prescribed by the civil law. In some dioceses either the lay members of the parish corporation or the parish trustees are required to sign the document drawn up by the ecclesiastical notary in attestation of the act of installation. However, these possible difficulties should more properly be obviated by means of a careful wording of the articles of incorporation.

The question of the general participation of the members of the congregation by their presence at the installation ceremony is one which provokes many arguments. While there is no juridic necessity for the presence of the laity at the installation ceremony, it cannot be denied that many benefits can be derived from their attendance if the symbolical rite is performed in such a manner as to educate the faithful in the sacred character of the duties and obligations of the pastoral office, and in the corresponding obligation of the faithful to support their pastor in his ministry.

The various rites of installation in common usage in this country may be divided into formal installation or informal (or perhaps more properly, less formal) installation on the basis of the public or private solemnity.[12] In a considerable number of dioceses the public solemnity is required; in other dioceses it is customary to have the installation rite conducted privately, either in the parish rectory, or in the bishop's residence, or in the diocesan chancery office. In some instances it is the practice to have both a private granting of possession and a public presentation of the new pastor to the congregation.

Authors on this subject sometimes refer to the presence of the faithful at the installation ceremony, but it is nowhere insisted upon

---

[11] Coronata, *Institutiones Iuris Canonici,* II, 392; Rossi, *De Paroecia,* p. 177.

[12] Cf. *infra,* Appendix I and II, pp. 177-181.

as of necessity.[13] Sipos states that in Hungary it is customary for the induction into possession to consist of two parts, namely, the verbal investiture which is attended to by the ordinary in the curial palace, and the real or actual installation, which is conducted in the presence of the congregation. This latter, he says, has no juridical effect.[14] That this practice was evidently observed in Czechoslovakia also is learned from a decision of the Sacred Congregation of the Council in response to a question from the Archdiocese of Olomouc. This question asked in effect which of the two parts of the act of installation was to be considered as connoting the actual moment of the granting of possession to the benefice. The reply of the Sacred Congregation stated that the act which gave the pastor the unrestricted right to exercise the powers connected with his office was to be so considered.[15] This was interpreted in the diocesan reviews of the time as meaning that the investiture, or the first part of the ceremony described above, connoted the real taking of possession of the parochial office.[16]

Writers before the promulgation of the Code frequently distinguished between verbal and real (actual) investiture, and also between the investiture which was conducted in the place of the benefice (*in re praesenti*) and that which was conducted away from the benefice (*in re absenti*).[17] It will be remembered that Reiffenstuel referred to the so-called verbal investiture as an "*actio abusiva,*" and apparently did not approve of this method.[18] What-

---

[13] Rossi, *De Paroecia*, pp. 182-184; Biccari, "Presa di Possesso," *Perfice Munus!*, III (1928), 542; Sipos, *Enchiridion Iuris Canonici*, p. 781.

[14] *Loc. cit.*

[15] "Nomine possessionis hic intelligi illum actum, qui sive institutio corporalis, sive inthronizatio, sive installatio, sive aliter nuncupetur, tamen semper id efficit, ut institutus in beneficium exinde adipiscatur liberum exercitium potestatis, suo officio adnexae." S. C. C., *Olomucen.*, 4 iul. 1908—"Über den Sinn 'adepta possessio' in Ehedekret 'Ne temere' vom 2, Aug. 1907," *Archiv für katholisches Kirchenrecht* (Innsbruck, 1857-1861; Mainz, 1862—), LXXXIX (1909), 327-329.

[16] Cf. "De die qua parochus existimandus sit adeptus esse possessionem beneficii, vel officium invisse ut matrimoniis in paroecia valide assistat," *Periodica*, V (1913), 184, n. 427A.

[17] Cf. *supra*, pp. 57-58.

[18] *Ius Canonicum Universum*, lib. III, tit. 7, n. 46. Cf. Coronata, *Institutiones Iuris Canonici*, II, 391, who holds that a verbal investiture when con-

ever may be said for the practice of having the faithful present at the installation ceremony, it is clear that this is not essential to the installation rite.

After the recognition of the valid title to the benefice as held by the new pastor, the next important step is the symbolical act which signifies the actual granting and acceptance of the possession of the parochial benefice. It is particularly on this point that a great variety of procedures is followed. Any number of very simple or very formal symbols may be used. The bestowal either of the biretta or of the stole, or in former times also of the ring, the handing over of the keys of the church or of the tabernacle, the transfer of the parish records, the kissing of the altar, the inspection of the confessional, of the baptistery, of the holy oils, of the sacred vessels, of the pulpit, etc., are some of the many symbolical actions employed as the signs or tokens with which to signify the actual granting of possession of the parochial benefice.

In discussing the quality of the act necessary to signify the taking of possession, Leurenius listed five considerations: 1) the reasonable customs and particular statutes of a locality must be observed or otherwise the action can be annulled; 2) if the benefice has a proper church or altar, the ceremony ought to be held there; 3) a simple act such as the kissing of the altar or the touching of the door of the church is sufficient to signify the acceptance of possession; 4) if one is impeded from taking possession, the mere visual inspection of the church is sufficient, provided that the notary makes a notation of the reason for the use of this act, but this procedure is generally not approved by the law; 5) if there is no church, the granting of possession of the principal property of the benefice is sufficient.[19]

Finally, it is important that a public document should be drawn up in attestation to the fact that the installation ceremony has taken place.[20] This record, if properly signed and sealed, will suffice as proof for the fact of real possession in a case of dispute. For this reason it is customary to require that a copy of this document be

---

ducted away from the benefice is not sufficient unless it is equivalent to a dispensation from installation.

[19] *Forum Beneficiale,* pars II, sec. III, cap. 4, q. 804.

[20] Cf. *infra,* Appendix III, pp. ....

sent to the chancery office within a specified period of time, and that a second copy be kept among the parish records. It should also be noted here that the new pastor is obliged to make the profession of faith and to take the oath against Modernism, either before or in the act of installation.[21] It is also possible for him to make use of a proxy in the ceremony of installation, if this be necessary,[22] but the profession of faith cannot be made through a proxy.[23] These latter provisions will be discussed in separate articles.

It seems, then, that a fitting ceremony of installation should include the making of the profession of faith and the taking of the oath against Modernism, unless these acts have been performed previously, and should furthermore evince the determination of the fact that the parochial benefice is vacant *de iure,* the recognition of the title to possession by the legitimate authority, a symbolical act that signifies the granting and the acceptance of the actual possession, and the drawing up of a public document in attestation of these facts. Other but less important elements to be reckoned with are the following: the place of the ceremony, the participation of lay witnesses, the presence of the faithful, etc.

In view of these considerations it is difficult to see how on the part of the ordinary, the mere designation of a day on which the new pastor is to enter into the possession of the parish can be considered as sufficient to take the place of installation, as is suggested by Bouscaren-Ellis.[24] The use simply of a decree which supplements the letter of appointment by actually placing the new pastor in possession of the parish, as is suggested by Schaaf, likewise seems inadequate.[25] It can readily be admitted that such procedures would allow the new pastor to take possession of the parish without fear of incurring the penalties prescribed for the violation of the laws concerning installation in office, but they can hardly be considered to take the place of what the law, as it stands, intends to be a rite or manner of installation in office.

---

[21] Can. 1443, § 1.

[22] Can. 1445.

[23] Can. 1407.

[24] *Canon Law,* p. 202.

[25] "Art. cit.," *ER,* XCI (1934), 622.

Article 2. The Installing Officer

In general whoever has the right to confer a benefice or an office has also the right to grant the actual possession of the benefice or the office, either personally or through a delegate.[26] Hence the granting of possession in the case of non-consistorial benefices is the right of the local ordinary, who may delegate another ecclesiastic to perform this function.[27]

The general authority given to the ordinary in this matter seems also to include the right to grant possession of a non-consistorial benefice even when it is conferred by the Holy See, unless other provisions are specified in the letter of appointment.[28] D'Angelo (1885-1930) discussed the practice of the Apostolic Datary in such cases. He insisted that the ordinary may not assume this right in virtue of canon 1443, § 2, if, in the bull of appointment, another ecclesiastic is specifically named for the exercise of this authority. The ordinary may not even substitute himself in place of his own vicar general; though the two juridically constitute one official person, yet physically the two exist as distinct and separate persons.[29]

Cappello says that the vicar general does not share the authority which is given to the episcopal local ordinary in canon 1443, § 2, unless he has received a special mandate for that purpose.[30] The reason offered for this opinion is the fact that the vicar general does not have the basic authority to confer the title to a parochial benefice unless he possesses a special mandate.[31] However, since installation in office is in reality only an integral part, and usually not an essential part of the canonical provision, the lack of authority to confer the title does not seem to imply a consequent lack of authority for presiding over the act of installation.

During the vacancy of the diocese the vicar capitular or the diocesan administrator may freely confer the actual possession of

---

26 Cappello, *Summa Iuris Canonici,* II, 565.

27 Can. 1443, § 2.

28 Vermeersch-Creusen, *Epitome Iuris Canonici,* II, 542; Fanfani, *De Iure Parochorum,* p. 90; Pistocchi, *De Re Beneficiali,* p. 227.

29 "De Possessione Beneficii," *Apollinaris,* I (1928), 411-415.

30 *Summa Iuris Canonici,* II, 565.

31 Cans. 1432, § 2; 455, § 3.

a benefice in cases in which the candidate for the parochial benefice is elected by the members of a collegiate moral person, presented by a patron, or nominated by someone who possesses that right.[32] If the see has been vacant for more than a year, then the vicar or administrator may also exercise this authority in the parishes for which he himself has freely appointed a pastor.[33] It seems, moreover, that he may likewise officiate at the installation of a pastor who was already appointed but not yet installed when the see became vacant. This is quite logical in view of the fact that through his appointment the new pastor had already obtained a *ius in re* with reference to the benefice.

In former times the archdeacon had ordinary power to grant possession of an office or a benefice. This right was sometimes abused through the fact that the archdeacon began to assume also the authority to grant the title to the benefice. Because of these abuses the bishops began to exercise this office themselves, and the authority of the archdeacon gradually disappeared.[34]

In many dioceses today it is customary to give a general delegation of the authority to officiate at the installation of pastors to the rural dean.[35] The ordinary may of course substitute another ecclesiastic, or he may exercise the office himself in particular cases. In some cases this authority is delegated to the parochial administrator who had been appointed under the provisions of canon 472, or to the previous pastor. It should be noted that the delegate's authority is limited to the act of installation. He does not have authority to correct any possible mistakes if the title to the benefice has been granted illicitly. Neither does he have authority to institute action against one who may unlawfully occupy a benefice.[36]

This delegation of authority may not be given to a layman. This is evident from the fact that the law explicitly states "*alium* ECCLESIASTICUM virum,"[37] as well as from the more fundamental

[32] Can. 455, § 2, 2°.

[33] Can. 455, § 2, 3°.

[34] Cf. *supra*, pp. 28ff.

[35] Beste, *Introductio in Codicem*, p. 711; Cappello, *Summa Iuris Canonici*, II, 566.

[36] Pistocchi, *De Re Beneficiali*, p. 227.

[37] Can. 1443, § 2.

reason that a layman cannot exercise jurisdiction in the Church. It is, however, possible that a layman could be given authority to grant possession of a benefice by virtue of an apostolic indult, though this is not commonly done.[38]

It hardly seems necessary to state that the granting of possession to a benefice must be performed *gratis* and without the intervention of simony. This is easily deduced from canon 1441, which forbids as simoniacal any deductions from the revenue of the benefice, or any compensations or payments to the one who confers the benefice, to the patron, or to any others. These restrictions have application primarily with reference to the granting of the title to the benefice, but they are also applicable to the act of installation in office.[39] The giving of an offering to the installing officer and the acceptance of it by him in compensation for the expenses incurred by travelling to the place of the benefice do not give rise to any act of simony, since the Holy See frequently allows the imposition of a tax to cover the expenses involved in the execution of a rescript. However, the Sacred Congregation of the Council did reject the statute of a provincial council which had allowed a stipend to be given from the benefice in question to the examiners in the *concursus* in consideration of their extra duty.[40]

Article 3. The Time of Installation

If a formal ceremony of installation is used, it is frequently conducted in connection with some other sacred function, such as the celebration of Mass, the observance of a solemn *Te Deum*, or the giving of Benediction with the Blessed Sacrament. Of far greater importance is the time within which the newly appointed pastor must be actually installed in the parish. This time is to be specified by the ordinary. If the pastor fails to take possession within the time determined, the ordinary may declare the benefice

[38] Rossi, *De Paroecia,* p. 177; Beste, *Introductio in Codicem,* p. 711; Wernz-Vidal, *Ius Canonicum,* II, 374.

[39] Cf. Fanfani, *De Iure Parochorum,* p. 90; Wernz-Vidal, *Ius Canonicum,* II, 375; Coronata, *Institutiones Iuris Canonici,* II, 8-13.

[40] Related by Romani, "De Beneficiis Paroecialibus Conferendis," *Ius Pontificium,* XIII (1933), 178.

to be vacant in accordance with the terms of canon 188, 2°, unless a just impediment has prevented the appointee from being installed.[41]

The law gives no special indication to guide the ordinary in defining the time for the taking of possession of a parochial benefice. A bishop is required by law to receive episcopal consecration within three months, and to be installed within four months, from the time he receives the apostolic letters of appointment.[42] Canon 155 prescribes that the conferring of offices which have become vacant should not be deferred beyond six months, unless the law makes a special provision for a longer period. In the case of a vacant parish the ordinary may defer the appointment of a new pastor if in his prudent judgment this seems advisable because of particular circumstances.[43]

As soon as the time has been set within which the installation must take place, the law enacted in canon 188, 2°, becomes applicable. This canon states that an office shall by tacit renunciation become vacant *ipso facto,* apart from all need of any further declaration, if a cleric who has obtained the title to an office neglects to take possession of the office within the time prescribed by the ordinary. However, in the case of a parochial benefice it seems that there is need for a declaration of the vacancy by the ordinary.[44]

Woywod maintained that the force of canon 188, § 2, takes effect automatically, and that the declaration of the ordinary is thereupon necessary, not indeed for the sake of effecting the vacancy of the benefice, but solely with a view to serving notice of the vacancy, so that others may apply for the title.[45] Rossi also seems to hold this view when he says that the ordinary must declare the vacancy.[46]

Such a result would obviously restrict the authority of the ordinary once he had set a time for the installation, and it would seem to work an undue hardship upon an appointee who might be unable to take possession of his benefice within the required time because of a reasonable impediment. This opinion, therefore, seems

---

41 Can. 1444, § 2.

42 Can. 333.

43 Can. 458.

44 ". . . beneficium vacare declaret ad norman can. 188, 2°."—Can. 1444, § 2.

45 "Law of the Code on Benefices," *HPR,* XXIX (1929), 387.

46 ". . . paroeciam debet declarare vacantem . . ."—*De Paroecia,* p. 178.

too severe. It seems more reasonable to hold that the ordinary must, indeed, declare the benefice to be vacant before he proceeds to make a new appointment to the benefice, but that he is not obliged to do so if he does not wish to reject the previous appointee. Cappello apparently inclines to this view when he says that the sentence is "*mere declaratoria.*" He explains this remark by stating that it must first be determined that the ordinary set the time definitely, that the time has actually elapsed, and that there was no justifiable impediment to prevent the taking of possession.[47] This is in accord with his opinion that the ordinary may, if he so chooses, prolong the time which has been set.[48]

The period of time allowed for the taking of possession of a benefice is set, not as a duration which lapses despite concomitant hindrances, but as a duration which lapses only when hindrances are not present, for a just impediment serves as an excuse from the fulfillment of the obligation within the stated time.[49] Such impediments could result from the sickness of the appointee, the difficulties of travel, the quarrels and dissensions among the people, the interference from the civil authorities, etc.[50] Another cause for delay could follow from the fact that the title to the benefice is being contested. If an action of this nature is pending, or if there has been interposed an appeal which has a suspensive effect, then the installation may not take place.[51]

It has already been mentioned that the appointee may avail himself of the use of a proxy if there is a good reason, or that he may also request a dispensation from the rite of installation. However, he is not obliged to adopt either of these methods, even though he will not be able to take possession of the benefice within the determined time, provided always that there is a just impediment in warrant of the delay.

Finally, it should be noted that the duration of the time allowed for the installation is to be computed in accordance with the prin-

[47] *Summa Iuris Canonici*, II, 567.

[48] *Loc. cit.*

[49] ". . . nisi iustum obstiterit impedimentum . . ."—Can. 1444, § 2; cf. also can. 35.

[50] Cappello, *loc. cit.*

[51] Coronata, *Institutiones Iuris Canonici*, II, 892; Wernz-Vidal, *Ius Canonicum*, II, 375.

ciples for the computation of time as outlined in canons 32 to 35, according as one or the other principle finds application in the case. It is debated whether or not the ordinary may prolong the time for the installation once it has been determined. The more common opinion is that he may do so for any good reason.[52]

Article 4. The Profession of Faith

Because of the nature of his office it is easily understood that either before installation or in the act of installation the newly appointed pastor is obliged to make the profession of faith.[53] This requirement dates from the time of the Council of Trent.[54] The formula to be used for this profession of faith is substantially the same as that given by Pope Pius IV in his Constitution *Iniunctum nobis,* with some additions which were made by the Sacred Congregation of the Council in 1877 with regard to the dogmatic decrees of the Vatican Council.[55]

The profession of faith is to be made before the ordinary or his delegate.[56] The fact that the vicar general is listed in this canon in the same group with pastors and others who are obliged to make the profession of faith before the ordinary or his delegate does not preclude him from accepting the profession of faith from a pastor since it is nowhere intimated that the vicar general needs a special mandate to perform this function.[57]

The ordinary may delegate any cleric to accept the profession

---

[52] Cappello, *Summa Iuris Canonici,* II, 567.

[53] Cans. 461; 1406, § 1, 7°; § 1; cf. Canavan, *Profession of Faith,* pp. 79-84.

[54] Sess. XXIV, *de ref.,* c. 12; cf. *supra,* pp. 41-42.

[55] S. C. C., decr., 20 ian. 1877—*Fontes,* n. 4236. This formula can be found in the beginning of most editions of the Code of Canon Law, and also in the *Addenda* of some editions of the *Roman Ritual.* Cf. *Rituale Romanum Pauli V Pontificis Maximi Jussu Editum Aliorumque Pontificum Cura Recognitum atque Auctoritate Sanctissimi D. N. Pii Papae XI ad Normam Codicis Iuris Canonici Accommodatum* (ed. iuxta typicam, Romae-Tornaci-Parisiis: Desclée et Socii, 1927), pp. (58)-(61); also Denzinger, *Enchiridion Symbolorum Definitionum et Declarationum de Rebus Fidei et Morum* (ed. 18-20, a C. Bannwart denuo compositum, iteratis curis edidit J. Umberg, Friburgi Brisgoviae: Herder and Co., 1932), nn. 994-1000 (hereafter referred to as *Enchiridion Symbolorum*).

[56] Can. 1407, 7°.

[57] Canavan, *Profession of Faith,* p. 84.

of faith. It is naturally more becoming that the cleric who is to receive the profession of faith from a pastor be a priest, although that arrangement is not absolutely necessary. Specifically stated is the fact that a lay person may not be delegated to perform this function, since it connotes an act of spiritual jurisdiction.[58] If the rural dean or some other ecclesiastic is given a general delegation of authority to officiate at the installation of pastors, as is done in many places, then it is also advisable that he be given delegation to accept the profession of faith. If, however, the sharing of this second delegation has been neglected, it seems that the delegate who is to officiate at the installation may nevertheless accept the profession of faith, since the law directly allows this profession to accompany the act of installation and to form part of the employed ceremony.[59] In this case the concession of the delegation to officiate at the installation certainly could be interpreted as including the further faculty to receive the profession of faith.[60]

It should be noted that the profession of faith may not be made through a proxy or a procurator.[61] This restriction applies even though a procurator will be used for the act of installation. The use of a proxy for the profession of faith was a matter of debate in former times.[62] Some authors held that it was permissible to make use of a proxy in view specifically of the two Rules of Law, namely, *Potest quis per alium, quod potest facere per seipsum,*[63] and, *Qui facit per alium, est perinde, ac si faciat per seipsum.*[64] But the Sacred Congregation of the Council rendered repeated decisions which declared that the use of a proxy could not be allowed, and that the profession, if made by a proxy, could not be accepted.[65] The present law leaves no doubt in the matter.

[58] Can. 1407; cf. Coronata, *Institutiones Iuris Canonici,* II, 349; Canavan, *op. cit.,* p. 56.

[59] ". . . ante possessionem aut in ipso possessionis capiendae actu . . ."—Can. 461.

[60] Cf. can. 66, § 3.

[61] Can. 1407.

[62] Cf. Canavan, *op. cit.,* p. 55.

[63] Reg. 68, R. J., in VI°.

[64] Reg. 72, R. J., in VI°.

[65] S. C. C., *Panormitana,* mense maio 1586—*Fontes,* n. 2167; S. C. C., *Valentina,* 5 febr. 1610—*Fontes,* n. 2387; S. C. C., *Cathacen.,* 26 ian., 9 febr. 1726—*Fontes,* n. 3310; cf. Raia, *De Parochis* (Roma: Desclée, 1921),

The sworn profession of faith should also be signed and retained as a public document. Usually it is returned to the chancery office. This is especially advisable in view of the penalties which are attached to the failure to make this profession.[66] It does not seem, however, that the failure to sign the document would nullify the profession.[67]

Although the making of the profession of faith is a grave and personal obligation for the newly appointed pastor, and indeed remains so until the obligation is fulfilled,[68] the failure to make the profession of faith does not affect the validity of the pastoral functions.[69] Neither canon 461 nor canon 1443, § 1, sets it down as a condition *sine qua non* for the valid taking of possession of the parochial benefice. One who fails to make the profession of faith may, however, be deprived of his benefice if he is warned to supply for his neglect within a stated time, and thereupon wantonly fails to do so.[70] Thus it seems implicitly indicated that the taking of possession without the profession of faith, though it be illicit, yet is not invalid, for if the pastor could not take possession of the benefice validly when the profession of faith has been omitted, why should the law through a threatened penalty contemplate a deprivation of the benefice in consequence of the continued neglect to supply for this omission? Likewise the canon allows for a just impediment to excuse from the delict.

A further penalty as enacted in canon 2403 is not as easily understood. This canon requires that one who fails to make the profession of faith is not allowed to receive the income from his

---

p. 55; Pistocchi, *De Re Beneficiali,* p. 225; Canavan, *Profession of Faith,* p. 43.

[66] Can. 2403.

[67] D'Angelo, "De Professione Fidei," *Apollinaris,* I (1928), 416.

[68] Coronata, *Institutiones Iuris Canonici,* II, 351; Canavan, *op. cit.,* p. 105.

[69] Goyeneche, "An Valida Sint necne Acta a Superiore Maiore Posita, Qui necdum Fidei Professionem Emisit?" *Commentarium pro Religiosis,* XIII (1932), 265; *ibid.,* XVIII (1937), 96; Koudelka, *Pastors, Their Rights and Duties According to the New Code of Canon Law,* The Catholic University of America Canon Law Studies, n. 11 (Washington, D. C.: The Catholic University of America, 1921), p. 30; Bicarri, "Giuramento e Possesso," *Perfice Munus!,* III (1928), 541; Canavan, *loc. cit.*

[70] Can. 2403.

benefice.[71] It is debated whether this penalty applies immediately from the time that he takes possession of the benefice, or only from the time that he has received a warning to supply for his neglect. It seems to apply only from the time that the negligent pastor may be declared contumacious. According to the wording of the canon the forfeiture of the revenue would then be in effect when the warning has not been heeded during the allotted time for compliance with it.[72]

The difficulty lies in the interpretation of the word *"interim."* Those who hold the stricter view maintain that the word contemplates the entire period of time which has elapsed from the moment when possession of the benefice was obtained. This seems to be too severe, for thus the law would in its effects practically become the equivalent of a disqualifying law. It should also be noted that in the structure of the canon this word takes its place only after mention has been made of the warning and of the declaration of contumacy that follows. Hence the more lenient view seems to offer the more acceptable interpretation.

In conclusion it should be noted that the law expressly reprobates all contrary customs that would adversely affect the legislation concerning the mandatory profession of faith.[73] Hence even an immemorial or a centenary custom of omitting the profession of faith could never succeed in supplanting the law which so incontestably, once and for all, makes the profession of faith an absolutely mandatory act for the pastor's personal performance.

Article 5. The Oath against Modernism

The Code of Canon Law makes no mention of the obligation of taking the oath against Modernism. This obligation was originally imposed by Pope Pius X for the purpose of counteracting the evils

---

[71] ". . . nec interim beneficii, officii, dignitatis, muneris fructus facit suos."

[72] Cf. D'Angelo, "art. cit.," *Apollinaris,* I (1928), 416; Bicarri, "art. cit.," *Perfice Munus!,* III (1928), 541; Canavan, *op. cit.,* pp. 109-110; Coronata, *Institutiones Iuris Canonici,* IV, 678; Chelodi, *Ius Poenale,* p. 157; Augustine, *A Commentary on the New Code of Canon Law,* VIII, 504; *contra,* Eichmann, *Däs Strafrecht des* Codex Iuris Canonici, p. 231; idem, *Lehrbuch des Kirchenrechts,* p. 753.

[73] Can. 1408; cf. Canavan, *op. cit.,* pp. 101-103.

resulting from the spread of this heresy.[74] This omission in the Code created some doubt as to whether this obligation was still in effect. Accordingly a question was proposed to the Sacred Congregation of the Holy Office on March 20, 1918, and the Sacred Congregation issued a decree on the subject two days later. The decree indicated that the oath was not mentioned in the Code since the errors of Modernism against which it was directed are of a temporary and transitory nature. However, since these errors had not ceased to spread, the decree indicated that the obligation imposed by Pope Pius X was to remain in force until the Holy See decreed otherwise.[75]

No specific penalties are imposed upon one who refuses to take the required oath, but the offender is to be reported to the Sacred Congregation of the Holy Office, which will then upon an investigation of the matter take such measures as may be called for.[76]

Because of the character of the oath against Modernism, dealing as it does with matters of faith and morals, practically the same regulations are urged in the manner of taking the oath as are stipulated for making the profession of faith. The oath must be taken before the local ordinary or his delegate, and the use of a proxy or a procurator to fulfil this obligation is forbidden. Likewise the oath should be signed, and a copy should be kept in the diocesan archives.[77]

The formula for the taking of this oath remains the same as that given by Pope Pius X.[78]

Article 6. Installation by Proxy

It has already been mentioned at different times that one may take possession of a benefice by means of a proxy or a procurator.[79]

[74] Pius X, motu propr., *Sacrorum antistitum,* 1 sept. 1910—*Fontes,* n. 689; *AAS,* II (1910), 669; cf. Canavan, *Profession of Faith,* pp. 111-114; *supra,* pp. 50-52.

[75] S. C. S. Off., decr., 22 mart. 1918—*AAS,* X (1918), 136; Bouscaren, *Canon Law Digest,* I, 50-51.

[76] Beste, *Introductio in Codicem,* p. 695; Canavan, *op. cit.,* p. 110.

[77] Cf. Coronata, *Institutiones Iuris Canonici,* II, 352-353.

[78] *AAS,* II (1910), 669. It may also be found in Denzinger, *Enchiridion Symbolorum,* nn. 2145-2147, and in some editions of the *Rituale Romanum,* pp. (61)-(64).

[79] Can. 1445.

This concession of the law is in accord with the early legislation of the Decretals[80] and the general principles of the Rules of Law of the *Liber Sextus: Potest quis per alium, quod potest facere per seipsum,* and *Qui facit per alium, est perinde, ac si faciat per seipsum.*[81]

Ferreres mentioned that in Spain residential bishops generally take possession of their benefices by means of a proxy, and then at a later time make a solemn entrance into the diocese.[82] In the installation of pastors any reasonable cause will permit the use of a proxy. Such a cause could be verified in the need for taking immediate possession of a benefice in order to take care of urgent matters of administration, or to avoid possible opposition from factions in the parish or from the civil authorities. The reason need not be of equal gravity with the just cause that is postulated for the granting of a dispensation from the installation itself. Blat mentions that the appointee must be physically absent from the place of the benefice before he can licitly make use of a proxy.[83]

It is of course obvious that the proxy or procurator acquires no rights for himself in relation to the benefice because of the act of installation, but it is advisable that this should be stated in the mandate which authorizes him to act as a proxy.[84] It seems that if the installation is performed by means of a proxy, it must be subsequently ratified or acknowledged by the newly appointed pastor before the loss of any rights to a previously-held, but simultaneously incompatible benefice can be urged against him.[85] The basis for this opinion is the fact that acquired rights are always protected in law until it is shown that these rights are surrendered.

The procurator who acts in the place of a pastor for the act of installation must have a special mandate to perform this function. Both conditions are essential for the validity of his act, that, is, there must be a mandate, and it must have been issued specifically for the purpose of the act of installation. A general mandate to

[80] C. 24, X, *de praebendis et dignitatibus,* III, 5; c. 17, *de praebendis et dignitatibus,* III, 4, in VI°.

[81] Reg. 68, 72, R. J., in VI°.

[82] *Institutiones Canonicae,* II, 432.

[83] *De Rebus,* p. 429, n. 346.

[84] Cocchi, *Commentarium in Codicem Iuris Canonici,* VI, 203.

[85] Cocchi, *loc. cit.*; Santi, *Praelectiones Iuris Canonici,* lib. III, tit. 7, n. 27.

act for the pastor as a procurator in all things will not suffice for the validity of the act of installation.[86]

Since the act which the procurator performs in this case concerns the fundamental functions of the pastoral office, it is entirely fitting that the procurator should not be a layman, but should rather be a priest. However, this is not of absolute necessity, for the procurator in this instance does not participate in an act of jurisdiction, as in the case of the delegated installing officer, nor does he act in a matter of faith and morals, as in the case of the profession of faith.[87]

It is, of course, understood that the proxy, whether he be a layman or a cleric, cannot be allowed to make the profession of faith for the pastor. This act invariably remains a personal obligation, the fulfillment of which rests exclusively with the newly appointed pastor.[88]

---

[86] Cappello, *Summa Iuris Canonici,* II, 567; Pistocchi, *De Re Beneficiali,* p. 232.

[87] Cf. Rossi, *De Paroecia,* p. 179; Wernz-Vidal, *Ius Canonicum,* II, 375; Coronata, *Institutiones Iuris Canonici,* II, 392; Fanfani, *De Iure Parochorum,* p. 90; *contra,* Beste, *Introductio in Codicem,* p. 711: Blat, *De Rebus,* p. 430; Cappello, *Summa Iuris Canonici,* II, 567, who also seems to incline to this view.

[88] Cf. *supra,* pp. 131-134.

CHAPTER IX

THE JURIDICAL CONSEQUENCES OF INSTALLATION

When the act of installation has been completed, the beneficiary begins to enjoy all of the temporal and spiritual rights attached to his benefice.[1] At that moment also the pastor obtains the care of the souls belonging to his parochial benefice.[2] For a pastor, then, the act of installation is an important function, for at that time he accepts not only the general rights and obligations of the holder of a benefice, but he also receives and accepts the many special rights as well as the serious duties which ecclesiastical legislation bestows upon pastors.

It is immediately apparent that a complete discussion and commentary upon the manifold rights and duties of pastors is beyond the scope of this treatise. In a discussion of the installation of pastors, however, it is necessary to give at least a broad outline of the juridical consequences of that act.

The more important consequences or effects of the installation of pastors may be grouped under six general headings. 1) The pastor assumes the obligation of the *cura animarum,* or the care of the souls, as well as the corresponding rights or prerogatives accorded that charge. 2) He becomes entitled to the income or revenue of the parochial benefice. 3) He accepts the obligation to administer the temporal properties belonging to the parish. 4) His act of acceptance of the parish implies the tacit renunciation of any incompatible benefice which he may have held previously. 5) The act of installation, properly performed, gives the pastor the right to the presumption of the law that he is in actual possession of the parochial benefice, and anyone who wishes to contest the pastor's right to possession is under certain restrictions in the petitorial action which he must institute. 6) Proper installation in office also entitles the pastor to the right of legal prescription which

[1] Can. 1472.

[2] Can. 461.

will give to him the actual possession of the parochial benefice after three years of peaceful possession, even though in reality his title to that possession may have been invalid. These points will be discussed in fuller detail in separate articles.

It should be pointed out that these consequences invariably follow from the proper completion of the canonical act of filling the pastoral office through the act of installation. They may also arise, though improperly, through the taking of possession of the parochial benefice without canonical installation in those cases in which this latter act is not required for the valid completion of canonical filling of an office, for it has been shown that installation is an integral part of the canonical act of instituting an incumbent in office, though not necessarily an essential part which is required for the validity of the possession of the parochial benefice.[3]

Article 1. The Rights and Obligations of the *Cura Animarum*

It has been mentioned that by taking legitimate possession of his benefice a beneficiary becomes entitled to enjoy the temporal and spiritual rights connected with his benefice.[4] With the acceptance of these rights there arises also the obligation of faithfully fulfilling the duties peculiar to the benefice.[5] In the case of pastors the particular spiritual rights and duties of the parochial benefice are summed up in the phrase *cura animarum,* or the care of souls. Canon 461 states that the pastor obtains the care of souls from the moment of taking possession of the parish. Canon 464, § 1, emphasizes the fact that the pastor is obliged to exercise the care of souls from the very nature of his office, and that this power extends over all of his parishioners. unless they are legitimately exempted from his authority.[6]

This power which the pastor exercises over his parishioners is, therefore, ordinary power, since it is connected with his office.[7] Hence the bishop may not arbitrarily take away or limit the pastor's

[3] Cf. *supra,* pp. 95-97.

[4] Can. 1472.

[5] Can. 1475.

[6] "Parochus ex officio tenetur curam animarum exercere in omnes suos paroecianos, qui non sint legitime exempti."

[7] Cf. can. 197, § 1.

authority in such a manner as to destroy the effectiveness of his ministry. At the same time the pastor's authority can only be called by the title of real *jurisdiction* in the broadest sense of that term, since it has many limitations and can only be exercised under the authority of the bishop.[8] It remains, nonetheless, ordinary power, and accordingly it may be delegated by the pastor to another priest[9] within the limitations expressed in the law.[10]

The authority of the pastor extends over all those who have a domicile or quasi-domicile within the territorial limits of the parish, unless they are legitimately exempted. It also includes those who do not have a parochial domicile or quasi-domicile in any place, but who actually reside in the territory of the parish.[11] For a just and grave reason, however, the bishop may exempt a religious community or a pious institution within the territory from the authority of the pastor in certain matters, even though these are minus such exemption in the common law of the Church.[12] This exemption, however, is different from the privilege of exemption accorded to certain religious by the Holy See[13] or by the common law.[14] Seminaries also are exempted from the jurisdiction of the pastor,[15] and certain exemptions are extended to religious by the common law.[16] It is likewise possible that some persons within the limits of the parish may be exempted from the authority of the pastor by the establishment of parishes on the basis of language or of nationality, or in consideration of the rite to which these persons may belong.[17]

---

[8] Can. 451, § 1. Cf. Wernz-Vidal, *Ius Canonicum,* II, pp. 926-928, n. 730. For a complete discussion of the nature of the pastoral authority cf. Victor a Jesu Maria (Tirado), *De Iurisdictionis Acceptione in Iure Ecclestiastico* (Romae: Soc. Tip. A. Manuzio, 1940), pp. 205-222.

[9] Cf. can. 199, § 1.

[10] E.g., the pastor may not delegate *ex officio* the authority to hear confessions. Cf. can. 874, § 1; P. C. I., declaratio, 16 oct. 1919, n. 3—*AAS,* XI (1919), 477; Bouscaren, *Canon Law Digest,* I, 410-411.

[11] Cans. 94, §§ 1-3; 464, §§ 1-2.

[12] Can. 464, § 2.

[13] Can. 500, §§ 1-3.

[14] Can. 615.

[15] Can. 1368.

[16] Can. 514, §§ 1-4.

[17] Cf. Coronata, *Institutiones Iuris Canonici,* I, 563-565; Ciesluk, *National*

It is difficult to state briefly the scope of the pastor's rights and duties as implied in the granting of the care of souls. Some of these rights are strictly parochial, i.e., they belong to the pastor in such a way that another priest may not exercise them without the permission of the pastor.[18] Others of these rights are indeed parochial rights, but not exclusively to such an extent that they may not be exercised by another priest, e.g., preaching, certain blessings, etc.[19] It should be noted that in a question concerning parochial rights the presumption is in favor of the pastor, and any authorization for infringement upon these rights must be proved.[20]

More properly the rights and duties of a pastor in relation to the care of souls should be discussed separately. Since, however, a right implies a corresponding duty, it will be sufficient for the purposes of this treatise to group them together in the following broad categories: 1) the profession of faith; 2) the obligation of residence; 3) the *Missa pro populo*; 4) the preaching of the word of God; 5) the celebration of the divine offices; 6) the administration of the sacraments; 7) the task of pastoral vigilance; 8) the care of the sick, of the poor and the destitute; 9) the providing of religious education; and 10) the care of the parish records.

1. Since the pastor is the teacher and leader of the faithful, it is obvious that the orthodoxy of his faith must be beyond question. His obligation to make a profession of faith arises both from the acceptance of his benefice and his office. It is a personal obligation, and it cannot be fulfilled through a procurator.[21]

2. The faithful fulfillment of the pastoral duties requires not only the material but also the formal, personal presence of the pastor in his parish.[22] The law of residence requires the pastor to

---

Parishes in the United States, The Catholic University of America Canon Law Studies, n. 190 (Washington, D. C.: The Catholic University of America Press, 1944), pp. 52-61.

[18] Cf., e.g., can. 462.

[19] Cf. Cappello, *Summa Iuris Canonici,* II, 41.

[20] *Ibid.,* p. 42.

[21] Cans. 461; 1443, § 1; 1406, 7°; 1407; cf. *supra,* pp. 131-134.

[22] Concerning the nature of this obligation cf. Fanfani, *De Iure Parochorum,* p. 126; Reilly, *Residence of Pastors,* The Catholic University of America Canon Law Studies, n. 97 (Washington, D. C.: The Catholic University of America, 1935), pp. 35-36, 22-27.

live continuously, day and night, in the parochial residence which should be near the parish church. For a just reason the ordinary may allow the pastor to live outside of his parish, provided that the distance from the parish church is not too great.[23] Augustine gives a number of examples to illustrate the gravity of the cause required if it is to exist as a factor that suffices rightfully as excusing from the law of residence.[24]

The law allows the pastor, with the permission of the ordinary, to have a two months' vacation during each year, and also allows the time necessary for the making of an annual retreat. It provides for the occasions on which the pastor may be obliged to leave his parish unexpectedly because of urgent reasons, and also states the provisions which he must make to take care of the needs of the faithful during his absence.[25]

Severe penalties are inflicted upon a pastor who is absent from his parish unlawfully either because he lacks the required permission or because he overstays the limits of time permitted to him. He is *ipso facto* deprived of the income of his benefice for the time of his unlawful absence, and he is obliged to hand over the proportionate amount of the income to the ordinary, who will distribute it to the church, to other pious institutions or to the poor.[26] If the pastr continues his unlawful absence, he may also be deprived of his benefice, but a special procedure must be carried out for the effecting of his removal in accordance with the law.[27] If the unlawfully absent pastor fails to respond to the admonition of the ordinary, as required in the special procedure referred to above, the parish may be declared vacant *ipso iure* by reason of tacit renunciation.[28]

---

[23] Can. 465, § 1; cf. Reilly, *op. cit.*, pp. 36-37.

[24] *A Commentary on the New Code of Canon Law,* II, 547.

[25] Can. 465, §§ 2-6; cf. Coronata, *Institutiones Iuris Canonici,* I, 583-584; Fanfani, *De Iure Parochorum,* pp. 127-130; Augustine, *A Commentary on the New Code of Canon Law,* II, 546-549; Cappello, *Summa Iuris Canonici,* II, 70-72; Reilly, *Residence of Pastors,* pp. 40-43.

[26] Can. 2381, 1°. Cf. Woywod, *A Practical Commentary on the Code of Canon Law,* II, 517.

[27] Cans. 2381, 2°; 2168-2175. Cf. Koudelka, *Pastors, Their Rights and Duties According to the New Code of Canon Law,* pp. 38-41; Coronata, *Institutiones Iuris Canonici,* III, 534-541.

[28] Cans. 2169; 188, 8°. Cf. McDevitt, *The Renunciation of an Ecclesiastical*

3. The pastor is bound by divine law to offer sacrifice for his flock. From the time of taking possession of his office he is obliged by ecclesiastical law to offer the *Missa pro populo* on all Sundays and on all feast days of precept, including also those which have been suppressed.[29] This is a personal obligation which is routed in justice, and hence it endures as an obligation until its performance has been completed.[30] It cannot be performed by another unless the pastor is lawfully impeded from saying the Mass, either on the day prescribed or because of his absence from the parish.[31]

4. The obligation of preaching the word of God is committed in a special manner to the bishop for the entire diocese.[32] In fulfilling this obligation he must call upon pastors and others to assist him.[33] Accordingly the pastor by reason of his office is commissioned to exercise the ministry of preaching to his people.[34] This is a personal obligation, and hence it cannot be habitually satisfied through a substitute, but it is not so strictly personal in nature that the pastor may not enlist the aid of others in fulfilling this duty.[35] The pastor is specifically required to preach a homily on Sundays and holy days of obligation,[36] and he is likewise required to give a catechetical instruction to the faithful on these days at a time best suited for the attendance of the faithful.[37]

The obligation of conducting catechetical instructions is a most serious duty of the pastor,[38] and, if necessary, he must enlist the

---

Office, The Catholic University of America Canon Law Studies, n. 218 (Washington, D. C.: The Catholic University of America Press, 1946), pp. 150-154.

[29] Cans. 466, § 1; 339, § 1. Cf. Donnellan, *The Obligation of the* MISSA PRO POPULO, pp. 66-67 (concerning pastors), 78-85 (concerning the days), 45-54 (concerning the nature of the obligation); Ramstein, *A Manual of Canon Law,* p. 275.

[30] Donnellan, *op. cit.*, pp. 91-92; Cappello, *Summa Iuris Canonici,* II, 75-77.

[31] Can. 466, §§ 4-5. Cf. Donnellan, *op. cit.,* pp. 94-105.

[32] Can. 1327, § 1.

[33] Can. 1327, § 2.

[34] Cans. 467, § 2; 1328.

[35] Can. 1344, § 2. Cf. Cappello, *Summa Iuris Canonici,* II, 77-79.

[36] Can. 1344, § 1.

[37] Can. 1332. Cf. Cappello, *Summa Iuris Canonici,* II, 83.

[38] Can. 1329. Cf. Jansen, *Canonical Provisions for Catechetical Instructions,* The Catholic University of America Canon Law Studies, n. 107

aid of the other clergy or also of the pious laity in this work.[39] It is the pastor's duty also to see that a mission is held for the faithful at least every ten years,[40] and that special sermons are preached during the Lenten season.[41] Finally, in this matter the pastor is under obligation to admonish and exhort the faithful to be present at the parochial Mass and on other occasions to hear the preaching of the word of God.[42]

A pastor who is gravely neglectful of these duties must be admonished by the ordinary and may be punished with appropriate penalties according to the gravity of his neglect, not exclusive of the forfeiture of a proportionate part of the income of his benefice, and even of privation of the benefice itself.[43]

5. The pastor is obliged to celebrate the divine offices.[44] This broad statement points to many and varied duties for the pastor. In the matter of penalties the Code indicates that by the name of "divine offices" are to be understood those functions of the power of orders which by the institution of Christ or of the Church are destined to serve the purpose of the divine cult, and can be performed by clerics only.[45] In relation to the collegiate chapter the term "divine office" comprises the chanting of the canonical hours in choir and the celebration of the conventual Mass, besides other Masses as required by the rubrics of the Missal or by the agreement of the founders of the chapter.[46] In the matter of the obligation of a pastor it must be taken to extend to those liturgical functions which are enjoined in the Missal and the Roman Ritual, as well as those functions which may be prescribed either through custom, or in the common law, or by way of particular legislation.[47]

Some of these functions are reserved exclusively to the pastor in

(Washington, D. C.: The Catholic University of America, 1937), pp. 79-80.

[39] Can. 1333, § 1.

[40] Can. 1349.

[41] Can. 1346, § 1.

[42] Cans. 467, § 2; 1348.

[43] Cans. 2382; 2182-2185.

[44] Can. 467, § 1.

[45] Can. 2256, 1°.

[46] Can. 415, § 2.

[47] Cappello, *Summa Iuris Canonici*, II, 84; Wernz-Vidal, *Ius Canonicum*, II, 936-937.

such a way that others may not perform them without his permission except in certain circumstances in which the law makes special provisions.[48] A number of these reserved functions concern or are connected with the administration of the sacraments. These will be discussed later. Other functions reserved to the pastor include the right to conduct the funeral services of his parishioners, unless they themselves have selected another church for burial, or unless the law makes special provisions;[49] the right to bless homes on Holy Saturday, or on other days according to the custom of the place;[50] the right to bless the baptismal font on Holy Saturday;[51] the right to conduct public processions outside the church;[52] and the right to bestow solemn blessings outside the church.[53] The pastor also has the authority to bless the sacred furnishings of the church, although this is not a strictly reserved function.[54]

Besides the functions reserved to the pastor there are many other liturgical and non-liturgical services which the pastor is reasonably bound to supply for the souls under his care insofar as circumstances will allow. These include such things as daily Mass, the functions of Holy Week, occasional special services such as a novena or a triduum, Benediction of the Blessed Sacrament, the blessing of candles, ashes, palms, etc.[55] It should be noted that while the pastor is reasonably obliged to provide these services for his parishioners, so also the parishioners are under some obligation, though not by way of strict compulsion, to take advantage of the benefits to be gained from these services by frequenting the parish church.[56]

Certain other rights of the pastor may be included in this category. Such is the right of precedence after the pastor of the cathe-

---

[48] Can. 462. Cf. Kelly, *The Functions Reserved to Pastors,* The Catholic University of America Canon Law Studies, n. 250 (Washington, D. C.: The Catholic University of America Press, 1947), pp. 60-62.

[49] Cans. 462, 5°; 1216. Cf. Kelly, *op. cit.,* pp. 91-100.

[50] Can. 462, 6°. Cf. Kelly, *op. cit.,* pp. 105-106.

[51] Can. 462, 7°. Cf. Kelly, *op. cit.,* pp. 106-107.

[52] Cans. 462, 7°; 482; 1291. Cf. Kelly, *op. cit.,* pp. 111-113.

[53] Can. 462, 7°. Cf. Cappello, *Summa Iuris Canonici,* II, 58-59.

[54] Can. 1304, 3°.

[55] Cappello, *Summa Iuris Canonici,* II, 84.

[56] *Loc. cit.*

dral church and above parochial vicars, etc.[57] Also to be used for the good of souls is the authority of the pastor to dispense in single cases and for a just cause from the laws of fast and abstinence and the observance of feast days. This authority extends over his subjects whether they are actually in the territory of the parish or outside of it, and also to all non-residents who are actually in the parish.[58]

Finally, a word should be said about the obligaiton of the daily recitation of the canonical hours. The pastor must be an ordained priest,[59] and hence he is obliged to say the divine office in consequence of his ordination. But the same obligation to recite the canonical hours daily derives also from the added fact that he is the holder of a benefice.[60] This is an obligation which binds him in justice, and unless he is legitimately impeded, the pastor who does not satisfy this obligation may not claim the full revenue of his office. The proportionate amount of the revenue must be given to the diocesan seminary, to the church, or to the poor.[61] It should be noted that the amount of the income to be forfeited because of the omission of the recitation of the canonical hours is to be determined in a ratio with the entire daily duties of the pastor. Various opinions are expressed by the authors as to the portion of the daily obligations of the pastor which is represented in the recitation of the canonical hours. Some state that it represents a fourth or a fifth part of the obligation, while others say that it represents only a tenth part.[62]

6. The pastor is obliged to administer the sacraments to the

[57] Cans. 478, § 1; 106. Cf. Augustine, *A Commentary on the Code of Canon Law,* II, 578.

[58] Can. 1245.

[59] Can. 451, § 1.

[60] Can. 1475, §1.

[61] Can. 1475, § 2. Cf. Cappello, *Summa Iuris Canonici,* II, 576; Golden, *Parochial Benefices in the New Code,* The Catholic University of America Canon Law Studies, n. 10 (Washington, D. C.: The Catholic University of America, 1921), pp. 71-72; Cocchi, *Commentarium in Codicem Iuris Canonici,* VI, 241-242; Coronata, *Institutiones Iuris Canonici,* II, 418-420; Ramstein, *A Manual of Canon Law,* p. 522.

[62] Cf. Ayrinhac, *Administrative Legislation in the New Code of Canon Law,* p. 363; Beste, *Introductio in Codicem,* pp. 714-715; Coronata, *Institutiones Iuris Canonici,* II, 419.

faithful whenever they reasonably request them, even though it is not a case of the necessary reception of the sacrament.[63] This is a personal obligation of the pastor which should not be supplied by others indefinitely.[64] It is also in itself a grave obligation whose fulfillment is called for in justice. It exists for the pastor by reason of his office. The varying gravity of the obligation must, of course, be determined from the circumstances in each case.[65]

In the administration of the sacraments certain matters are reserved exclusively to the pastor in such a manner that for another to perform these functions the permission of the pastor is required for the licitness of the act, and sometimes even for its validity.[66] Those functions which are reserved to the pastor include the right to confer solemn baptism,[67] the right to carry the Holy Eucharist publicly to the sick within his parish,[68] the right to administer Holy Viaticum either publicly or privately and to administer the sacrament of extreme unction to those who are in danger of death,[69] the right to publish the announcements of ordinations,[70] the right to publish the banns of marriage,[71] to assist at the marriage of his subjects within the limits of his parish,[72] and to impart the nuptial blessing.[73]

The pastor also has ordinary jurisdiction to hear confessions in his parish,[74] and to hear the confessions of his parishioners also outside of his territory.[75] While this is ordinary jurisdiction, yet by way of exception to the general principle the pastor does not

---

[63] Can. 467, § 1.

[64] Wernz-Vidal, *Ius Canonicum,* II, 937; Cappello, *Summa Iuris Canonici,* II, 84.

[65] E.g., can. 892, § 1. Cf. Cappello, *Summa Iuris Canonici,* II, 85; Fanfani, *De Iure Parochorum,* pp. 202-207.

[66] E.g., can. 1094.

[67] Cans. 462, 1°; 738, §§ 1-2.

[68] Cans. 462, 2°; 848, §§ 1-2. Cf. Kelly, *The Functions Reserved to Pastors,* pp. 72-74.

[69] Cans. 462, 3°; 850; 938, § 2; 939. Cf. Kelly, *op. cit.,* pp. 75-76.

[70] Cans. 462, 4°; 998, § 1. Cf. Kelly, *op. cit.,* pp. 79-80.

[71] Cans. 462, 4°; 1022; 1023, § 1. Cf. Kelly, *op. cit.,* pp. 77-78.

[72] Cans. 462, 4°; 1095, § 1.

[73] Cans. 462, 4°; 1101, § 1. Cf. Kelly, *op. cit.,* pp. 86-88.

[74] Can. 873, § 1.

[75] Can. 881, § 1.

have *ex officio* the authority to delegate this power to another.[76] The pastor also has the authority to absolve during the paschal time from all sins reserved by the ordinary.[77]

Besides the general obligation of administering the sacraments to the faithful whenever they reasonably request them, the law places certain other specific obligations upon pastors in these matters. A few of the more important duties may be mentioned. The pastor has the obligation to take care that the faithful, especially midwives, doctors and surgeons know how to baptize properly in case of necessity.[78] It is the pastor's duty to see that the children are sufficiently instructed for the fruitful reception of the sacraments of penance, confirmation and the Holy Eucharist,[79] and to be vigilant that they opportunely receive these sacraments with the proper dispositions.[80]

The pastor is bound to investigate the freedom of those who seek to enter marriage, and to determine whether they are sufficiently instructed in Christian doctrine and regarding the rights and duties which flow from the reception of this sacrament.[81] If one or the other of the parties is in danger of death, or also in circumstances when all things are prepared for the marriage, the pastor has a limited authority to dispense from matrimonial impediments which derive their existence from ecclesiastical law.[82]

7. Beyond the matters already mentioned, the pastor is bound diligently to exercise a pastoral vigilance that in his parish, especially in the schools, both public and private, nothing be perpetrated against faith and morals.[83] In order to accomplish this purpose it is obviously necessary for him to become acquainted with his parishioners and to know the conditions and circumstances of their

---

[76] Can. 874, § 1; P. C. I., declaratio, 16 oct. 1919, n. 3—*AAS,* XI (1919), 477; Bouscaren, *Canon Law Digest,* I, 410-411.

[77] Can. 899, § 3.

[78] Can. 743. Cf. Woywod, *A Practical Commentary on the Code of Canon Law,* I, 331.

[79] Cans. 1330; 1331.

[80] Cans. 854, § 5; 787.

[81] Cans. 1020, §§ 1-2; 1033.

[82] Cans. 1044; 1045, § 3.

[83] Can. 469.

daily life.[84] To do this in an efficient manner it is necessary for him to keep a census record of the parishioners.[85]

Special vigilance is required of the pastor to see to it that infants are baptized as soon as possible. The faithful should be frequently reminded of this grave obligation.[86] The pastor should also be watchful that children are given a Christian name in baptism.[87] He should encourage the faithful to receive Holy Communion frequently and to attend Mass daily if possible.[88] The pastor should prudently instruct the people concerning the nature of the sacrament of matrimony and the canonical impediments to marriage,[89] and should caution young people not to enter marriage without the knowledge or the consent of their parents,[90] and not to contract marriage with non-Catholics.[91]

Cleanliness should be maintained in the church, and care should be taken to keep out anything which would occasion irreverence to or disrespect for the house of God.[92] Many other illustrations could be given in delineation of what is comprehended under the obligation of pastoral vigilance.

On the positive side the pastor must foster and establish works of charity, of faith and of piety.[93] In discussing this point the authors and commentators mention such works as parish societies, charitable organizations, ecclesiastical associations, sodalities, pious unions, confraternities, third Orders, etc.[94] The many pronouncements

---

[84] Can. 467, § 1.

[85] Can. 470, § 1. Cf. Letter of the Apostolic Delegate to the Bishops of the United States, June 12, 1941 (private)—Bouscaren, *Canon Law Digest*, II, 147-150.

[86] Can. 770.

[87] Can. 761.

[88] Can. 863.

[89] Cans. 1018; 1033.

[90] Can. 1034.

[91] Can. 1065, § 1.

[92] Can. 1178.

[93] Can. 469.

[94] Cf. Clark, *Parish Societies*, The Catholic University of America Canon Law Studies, n. 176 (Washington, D. C.: The Catholic University of America Press, 1943), pp. 88-89; Coronata, *Institutiones Iuris Canonici*, I, 588; Cappello, *Summa Iuris Canonici*, II, 86; Wernz-Vidal, *Ius Canonicum*, II, 938.

of the recent popes, especially those of Pope Pius XI and of the present Holy Father on the subject of Catholic Action, furnish abundant examples of the nature of the pastor's obligation in this matter.[95]

The pastor is also admonished by the law to take an interest in the spiritual welfare of the non-Catholics in his parish, and to regard them as commended to him in the Lord.[96]

8. The poor and the destitute are close to the pastor by special bonds of charity. The law vividly expresses this obligation of the pastor by saying that he ought to embrace the poor and the forlorn with paternal charity.[97] This obligation arises from divine law. It extends to the members of the parish in a special manner, and also to others who may actually reside in the parish.[98]

The pastor must also exercise special care and abundant charity toward the sick, and should be especially solicitous for the ones who are in danger of death by providing them with the strength of the sacraments and by recommending their souls to God.[99] The special rights of the pastor to administer the sacraments to the sick and the dying have already been discussed. Pastors, along with other priests who assist the sick, have the faculty to grant the apostolic blessing with a plenary indulgence at the moment of death according to the formula approved in liturgical books.[100] Special instructions and prayers are also given in the Ritual for the visits to the sick,[101] for the assistance to be given to the dying,[102] and for the commending of their souls to God.[103]

9. The obligations of the pastor with regard to the catechetical instructions for both adults and children have already been men-

---

[95] Cf. Pius XI, *allocutio,* 23 maii 1923—*AAS,* XV (1923), 245; Bouscaren, *Canon Law Digest,* I, 258. For a list of the principal documents on Catholic Action cf. Bouscaren, *op. cit.,* I, 137, and II, 73-75.

[96] Can. 1350.

[97] "Debet parochus . . . pauperes ac miseros paterna caritate complecti . . ." —Can. 467, § 1.

[98] Cappello, *Summa Iuris Canonici,* II, 86-87.

[99] Can. 468, § 1.

[100] Can. 468, § 2; *Rituale Romanum,* pp. 156-159.

[101] *Ibid.,* pp. 140-154.

[102] *Ibid.,* pp. 154-156.

[103] *Ibid.,* pp. 159-183.

tioned. Beyond this the pastor has a duty to give his special care to the Catholic instruction of children.[104] It is obvious that this obligation can best be fulfilled by means of conducting Catholic schools. The legislation of the Church cautions children not to attend non-Catholic, non-denominational, or so-called mixed schools. The local ordinary alone has the right to decide under what circumstances the attendance at such schools by Catholic children may be tolerated.[105]

Where Catholic schools do not yet exist, provisions should be made for their establishment, and the faithful should be encouraged to contribute according to their means toward their construction and support.[106] While the law places the principal responsibility in these matters upon the local ordinary, the burden of the pastor in this important work is easily recognized.[107] Special provisions for the establishment of parochial schools as an "almost essential part of a parish" were enacted by the III Plenary Council of Baltimore (1884).[108]

The pastor also has the right and the obligation to inspect the teaching in the public schools.[109] In the United States this right is not recognized, and religious instruction in the public schools is forbidden. But as a private citizen the pastor can exercise a strong influence especially to stem the spread of anti-religious teaching.[110]

10. A particular diligence is required of the pastor in maintaining and preserving the parish registers. These include the baptismal, confirmation, marriage and death records, and also the *liber status animarum* or census record.[111] At the end of each year the pastor

---

[104] Cans. 467, § 1; 1372, §§ 1-2. Cf. Jansen, *Canonical Provisions for Catechetical Instructions*, pp. 91-99.

[105] Can. 1374. Cf. Boffa, *Canonical Provisions for Catholic Schools*, The Catholic University of America Canon Law Studies, n. 117 (Washington, D. C.: The Catholic University of America Press, 1939), pp. 112-120.

[106] Can. 1379, §§ 1-3.

[107] Cf. Cappello, *Summa Iuris Canonici*, II, 88.

[108] *Acta et Decreta Concilii Plenarii Baltimorensis Tertii*, nn. 194-213.

[109] Cans. 469; 1381, § 1.

[110] Cf. Beste, *Introductio in Codicem*, p. 297; Augustine, *A Commentary on the New Code of Canon Law*, II, 555.

[111] Can. 470, § 1. Cf. O'Rourke, *Parish Registers*, The Catholic University

must send an authentic copy of these records, with the exception of the census record, to the diocesan curia.[112]

Local statutes may require that also a copy of the census record be sent to the chancery. It should be noted, however, that the ordinary may not take away from the pastor the right to keep the parish records on the pretext of preserving them in the diocesan curia, for this would take away the pastor's right to any remuneration which might legitimately be obtained from the copying of these records as public documents.[113]

The importance of carefully maintaining and preserving the parish records is evident from the fact that these records and all authentic copies of them constitute public documents which are admitted in judicial trials as full proof of the facts which are directly and primarily asserted.[114] The law also makes specific mention of the right to inflict penalties according to the gravity of the neglect upon those who are negligent in keeping the parish records.[115]

The baptismal record, besides the pertinent facts concerning the baptism,[116] should also include a notation if the person has received confirmation,[117] contracted marriage (unless it was a marriage of conscience),[118] received the sacred order of subdeaconship,[119] or made a solemn profession in religion.[120]

The confirmation record[121] is important for the reason that evidence of the reception of this sacrament is necessary in many instances.[122] The officially recorded assertion of the reception of this sacrament is also used in judicial trials as supporting evidence in proof of the Catholic background of the parties.

---

of America Canon Law Studies, n. 88 (Washington, D. C.: The Catholic University of America, 1934), pp. 45-84.

[112] Can. 470, § 3.

[113] Wernz-Vidal, *Ius Canonicum,* II, 940.

[114] Cans. 1813, § 1, 4° ; 1816.

[115] Can. 2383.

[116] Can. 777, §§ 1-2.

[117] Cans. 470, § 2; 798.

[118] Cans. 470, § 2; 1103; 1107; 1988.

[119] Cans. 470, § 2; 1011.

[120] Cans. 470, § 2; 576, § 2.

[121] Cans. 470, § 1; 798.

[122] Cans. 974, § 1; 544, § 1; 1363, § 2; 1021, § 2.

The necessity of accuracy in the marriage register[123] can easily be attested by anyone who has had to exercise the office of defender of the bond or of an advocate in a matrimonial tribunal. An accurate death record likewise furnishes important evidence in many judicial matters, especially concerning second marriages.[124] The obligation of keeping an accurate census record has already been mentioned.[125] Its importance for the efficient care of souls and for the successful administration of the parish cannot be ignored.

Since the pastor is obliged to compile the parish records diligently and accurately, it is clear that no changes, substitutions or corrections may be made in them unless the reason for the change is also indicated in the record. Cappello states that such changes must be previously approved by the ordinary, unless they are merely material changes.[126]

The pastor is also a qualified witness in those things which pertain to the duties of his office.[127] It is necessary, therefore, that there should be a proper parish seal as evidence of the authenticity and accuracy of the public documents as also of the copies of them which may be drawn up by the pastor.[128]

The parish registers together with the letters of the bishop and other documents of importance or utility to the parish[129] should be carefully preserved in the parish archives or in a safe place (*tabularium*).[130] The ordinary or his delegate should inspect the records and the place in which they are kept at the time of the parochial visitation or at other opportune times, and the pastor is

---

123 Cans. 470, § 1; 1103, §§ 1-3; 1107.

124 Cans. 470, § 1; 1238.

125 Can. 470, § 1.

126 *Summa Iuris Canonici,* II, 90.

127 Can. 1813, § 1, 4°.

128 Can. 470, § 4.

129 E.g., the decrees of the establishment of the parish, the articles of incorporation, insurance policies, deeds to the parish property, inventories of the movable and immovable property of the parish, records of parish foundations, etc.

130 The III Plenary Council of Baltimore (1884) requires the pastor to have an iron safe in the parish rectory or in some other safe and convenient place for the safekeeping of the parish records and documents—*Acta et Decreta Concilii Plenarii Baltimorensis* III, n. 278.

also cautioned to guard religiously the parish records so that they do not fall into profane hands.[131]

From this lengthy, even though not entirely complete, listing of the rights and duties of the pastor in regard to the care of souls, the obligation of a formal or *"laboriosa"* residence of the pastor in his parish becomes more understandable. Some of the penalties which may be inflicted upon pastors who are negligent in these duties have been indicated. A special procedure is prescribed for the taking of action against pastors who are seriously neglectful of their pastoral duties.[132]

Article 2. The Right to the Income of the Benefice

It has already been mentioned that the pastor who has been properly installed, or who validly has taken possession of his parochial benefice in some other way, is thereby entitled to many spiritual rights and is obligated by many spiritual duties, particularly in the care of souls. By virtue of the same law[133] he also receives many rights and many duties in temporal matters. Chief among his rights as a beneficiary is the right to those things which are necessary for his honorable and decent livelihood.[134] As the holder of a *parochial* benefice the pastor is also entitled to the offerings which are given to him in consequence of a legitimate custom or of legal taxation.[135]

To discuss intelligently the rights of the pastor to the income of his benefice it is necessary to understand the various types of clerical and beneficial property rights. These are commonly divided into patrimonial, quasi-patrimonial, beneficial and parsimonial rights.[136]

Patrimonial rights are those which come to a cleric through secular means, e.g., through inheritance or from gifts, etc. Quasi-

---

[131] Can. 470, § 4.

[132] Cans. 2182-2185.

[133] Can. 1472.

[134] Can. 1473.

[135] Can. 463, § 1.

[136] Wernz-Vidal, *Ius Canonicum,* II, 382; Augustine, *A Commentary on the New Code of Canon Law,* VI, 536-537; Golden, *Parochial Benefices in the New Code,* p. 63; Coronata, *Institutiones Iuris Canonici,* II, 416; Cappello, *Summa Iuris Canonici,* II, 574.

patrimonial rights are those which are acquired through the cleric's industry or diligence from work not directly related to his obligations in the holding of his benefice. This would include such things as the income from Mass stipends, from preaching outside of the parish, from writing, etc. It would also include stole fees and offerings given as the result of a legitimate custom or of legal taxation, unless these were officially made a part of the revenue of the benefice. In the former law these offerings were always considered as quasi-patrimonial income, but the present law allows them to be made a part of the revenue of a benefice if there is not a sufficient source of income for the benefice through an endowment or by means of other sources.[137]

The beneficial property rights which accrue to the beneficiary consist of the income from the benefice. These rights are called *necessary* if they relate to that income which is required for an honorable and decent livelihood for the beneficiary, and *superfluous* if they connote the surplus income which the beneficiary is obliged to distribute to the poor or to use for charitable purposes.[138] The revenue which the beneficiary by frugal living is able to save from the so-called *necessary* income is called parsimonial.[139]

A pastor may freely dispose of his patrimonial, quasi-patrimonial and parsimonial revenue in whatever manner he chooses, not only throughout his lifetime, but also by last will or testament.[140] Concerning the quasi-patrimonial revenue a question may be raised concerning the so-called stole fees and offerings of the faithful. Is the pastor always entitled to these offerings without restrictions? Canon 463, § 1, gives him the right to the offering which is established by an approved custom or by lawful taxation. A pastor who demands more than this amount is held to restitution,[141] and for

---

[137] Can. 1410. Cf. Golden, *Parochial Benefices in the New Code,* p. 63; Coronata, *Institutiones Iuris Canonici,* II, 416; Beste, *Introductio in Codicem,* p. 712.

[138] Coronata, *loc. cit.*

[139] Augustine, *A Commentary on the New Code of Canon Law,* VI, 537.

[140] Ayrinhac, *Administrative Legislation in the New Code of Canon Law,* p. 360; Coronata, *loc. cit.*; Golden, *Parochial Benefices in the New Code,* p. 63; Wernz-Vidal, *Ius Canonicum,* II, 382, footnote 1; Cappello, *Summa Iuris Canonici,* II, 574.

[141] Can. 463, § 2.

such a violation of the law he may be punished with severe penalties;[142] but if an amount in excess of the usual offering is freely given, he may legitimately accept it. He is also entitled to the customary offerings or fees even though the function is performed by another. This applies also to any amount in excess of the usual offering, unless it is clear from the will of the donor that the additional amount was intended for the priest who performed the ceremony.[143] A pastor may not, however, refuse to give his services gratuitously to those who are not able to make an offering.[144]

The amount of the stole fees or taxes which may be requested for the various functions is to be determined for the entire province by a provincial council or by an agreement of the bishops of the province, and the schedule of taxes is to be approved by the Holy See.[145] The same principle applies to the taxes which may be required for judicial expenses.[146] In the United States the Councils of Baltimore have not established a schedule of taxes,[147] and in many provinces no provincial council has been held. Oftentimes, therefore, the amount of the stole fees depends entirely upon custom.[148]

The right of the pastor to receive the stole fees or offerings is not, however, entirely exclusive. The present legislation on benefices allows the stole fees to be made a part of the income of the benefice if there are not sufficient sources of revenue from endowments, etc.[149] If such a provision is made in the establishment of a

---

[142] Can. 2408.

[143] Can. 463, § 3. For a fuller discussion of this subject cf. Ferry, *Stole Fees,* The Catholic University of America Canon Law Studies, n. 59 (Washington, D. C.: The Catholic University of America, 1930), pp. 52-57.

[144] Can. 463, § 4. Can. 2349 states that the ordinary may punish according to his prudent judgment those who refuse to make the prescribed offerings.

[145] Can. 1507, § 1.

[146] Can. 1909, § 1.

[147] Cf. the II Plenary Council of Baltimore (1866), n. 94, and the III Plenary Council of Baltimore (1884), n. 294, in which no schedule of taxes is established. It is, however, forbidden to accept any offering in connection with confession or even to accept Mass stipends offered at the time of confession. Cf. the II Plenary Council of Baltimore, n. 289.

[148] Bouscaren-Ellis, *Canon Law,* p. 209. Cf. Ferry, *Stole Fees,* pp. 38-42.

[149] Can. 1410. Cf. Ferry, *Stole Fees,* pp. 60-62.

benefice, the income derived from stole fees can no longer be considered as purely quasi-patrimonial revenue. It must then be considered as beneficial revenue, and as such it is subject to special provisions.

The pastor is entitled to receive the strictly beneficial income of the benefice even though he may have other sources of revenue. He may use this income to provide for himself a decent livelihood according to the circumstances of the locality in which he lives.[150] The law, however, states that the beneficiary is obliged to distribute to the poor or to pious causes that part of the beneficial income which is not needed for his decent support. This obligation is considered by some to be an obligation whose fulfillment falls due in strict justice,[151] but the more common opinion maintains that the obligation arises simply from a precept of the Church or from the virtue of religion, and that therefore the pastor, though he sin gravely in his neglect of this obligation, nevertheless is not bound to make restitution.[152]

In the case in which the stole fees are made a part of the beneficial revenue it does not seem that the pastor is under any special obligation beyond the obligation of charity to distribute to the poor or to pious causes the surplus income from this source. The fact that stole fees are made a part of the revenue of the benefice already places a restriction on the pastor's rights in comparison with other pastors, and hence further restrictions should be minimized rather than aggravated in accord with the ancient Rule of Law. Another argument for this opinion is deduced from the wording of canon 1410, which by the use of a disjunctive rather than a conjunctive particle seems to indicate that stole fees may be made a

---

150 Can. 1473. Cf. Coronata, *Institutiones Iuris Canonici,* II, 416; Augustine, *A Commentary on the New Code of Canon Law,* VI, 537; Ayrinhac, *Administrative Legislation in the New Code of Canon Law,* p. 361.

151 Augustine, *loc. cit.*; Pistocchi, *De Re Beneficiali,* pp. 416-418.

152 Coronata, *Institutiones Iuris Canonici,* II, 415; Cocchi, *Commentarium in Codicem Iuris Canonici,* VI, 239; Cappello, *Summa Iuris Canonici,* II, 575; Ayrinhac, *Administrative Legislation in the New Code of Canon Law,* p. 362; Beste, *Introductio in Codicem,* p. 713; Wernz-Vidal, *Ius Canonicum,* II, 382; Vermeersch-Creusen, *Epitome Iuris Canonici,* II, 554; Golden, *Parochial Benefices in the New Code,* pp. 65-66.

part of the income of the benefice only when other sources of revenue are lacking.[153]

In the United States the right of the pastor to receive the stole fees is sometimes restricted in various ways by diocesan legislation. The Councils of Baltimore recommended that diocesan regulations should be enacted regarding the distribution of stole fees.[154] Accordingly in some dioceses the stole fees are given to the treasury of the church, in others to the support of the parochial residence, and in some places the fees are divided in various portions for the pastor and the assistant pastors.[155] A question may be raised with regard to the validity of some of these statutes especially in view of canon 463 which states that the pastor has the right to the revenue to which legitimate custom or legal taxation entitles him. However, it is beyond the scope of this treatise to enter into a detailed discussion of that problem.

Of the same nature as the income from stole fees is the so-called parochial portion of the offering given on the occasion of a funeral.[156] The proper pastor of the deceased is entitled to receive this portion even though the funeral is held in another church, except in the case in which it would be difficult or inconvenient to bring the body of the deceased to the proper parish for burial or unless particular law ordains otherwise.[157]

Finally it should be noted that the pastor who is negligent in his parochial duties in regard to the temporal administration of the goods of his benefice or parish to the extent that the parish thereby suffers a serious loss must be compelled by the ordinary to make restitution for this loss, and if he is gravely neglectful of his duties, he may be removed from office.[158] Special mention is made in the law of the obligation to fulfil faithfully all of the duties connected with the benefice, and in particular the obligation of reciting the canonical hours.[159] A pastor who fails to say the divine office when

---

153 Vermeersch-Creusen, *loc. cit.*; Ferry, *Stole Fees*, p. 62.

154 II Plenary Council of Baltimore, n. 94; III Plenary Council of Baltimore, n. 294.

155 Cf. Bouscaren-Ellis, *Canon Law*, p. 210.

156 Cans. 1234, § 1; 1237, §§ 1-3.

157 Can. 1236, § 1. Cf. Ferry, *Stole Fees*, pp. 88-94.

158 Cans. 1476, § 2; 2147, § 2, 5°.

159 Can. 1475, § 1.

not legitimately impeded is obliged to give the proportionate part of the daily income to the church, to the diocesan seminary, or to the poor.[160]

Article 3. The Obligation of the Administration of the Temporal Goods of the Parish

Although it is said that the pastor "takes possession" of his parish by being installed, it is obvious that the property of the parish does not thereby become his property. The pastor is in reality only the guardian of the parish property, who obtains the right to use the income from the property for his decent support. The real *dominium* over the parochial property is held by the parochial benefice itself as a true moral person.[161] The pastor, as the holder of the parochial benefice, is obliged to administer the parish property according to the norms of the law in the manner of a guardian.[162]

The Church in its nature of a fully self-contained society has the right to demand of the faithful those things which are necessary for the conducting of divine worship, for the decent maintenance of the clergy and other ministers, and for the other things necessary to attain its proper ends.[163] Accordingly the pastor has the right to make reasonable demands upon the faithful for the material means necessary to enable him to properly carry out the purposes of the parish.[164]

It is not within the scope of this treatise to discuss in detail the many provisions of law concerning the administration of church property.[165] Canon 1522 prescribes that an administrator of ecclesiastical property in assuming the task of administration must in the presence of the ordinary or the rural dean take an oath which is accompanied with the promise to fulfill his duties faith-

---

160 Can. 1475, § 2.

161 Cans. 1495, § 2; 1499, §§ 1-2.

162 Can. 1476, § 1.

163 Can. 1496. Cf. Bouscaren-Ellis, *Canon Law*, p. 733.

164 For a fuller discussion of this subject cf. John Goodwine, *The Right of the Church to Acquire Property*, The Catholic University of America Canon Law Studies, n. 131 (Washington, D. C.: The Catholic University of America Press, 1941), pp. 6-13; 35-38.

165 Cf. cans. 1518-1528.

fully and well. He must also make an accurate inventory of all of the movable and immovable property of the church together with an estimate of its value. One copy of this inventory is to be retained in the church archives, and another copy is to be sent to the diocesan curia.[166] From the wording of this canon it seems that this prescription of law binds only the special administrators appointed by virtue of canon 1521. However, the general principles here enacted are also applied to pastors as the administrators of ecclesiastical property, except that they are not required to take the special oath.[167] Canon 1296, § 2, also prescribes that an accurate inventory should be made of all of the sacred furnishings of the church.

Canon 1523 lists a number of the duties which the administrator of ecclesiastical property must fulfill with the kind of diligence that attaches to the acts of a good and provident family-provider. The pastor, then, as the administrator of the parish property, must first of all be watchful that the parochial property does not suffer damage or loss in any way. If because of his negligence the parish suffers a serious loss, the pastor should be compelled by the ordinary to make compensation for the loss, and if the loss is gravely serious, the pastor may be removed from his office.[168] Necessary repairs to the parish property should be made promptly with a view to forestalling greater loss.[169] Diocesan regulations usually require that various types of insurance be carried on all parish property.

It should be noted also that very severe penalties are enacted against those who presume to usurp or appropriate for their own use ecclesiastical property of any kind.[170]

In the administration of the parish the pastor must observe the requirements of the civil law as well as those of canon law, and he must also execute the approved stipulations as imposed by the founder or by a donor, and follow the regulations enacted by the legitimate authority. He is obliged to collect the income of the

---

[166] Can. 1522, 2°-3°.

[167] Cf. III Plenary Council of Baltimore, n. 276.

[168] Cans. 1476, § 2; 2147, § 2, 5°.

[169] Can. 1477, § 3.

[170] Can. 2346.

parish accurately and in good time, and to keep it in a safe place. The money of the parish which is left over after expenses are paid should be invested with the consent of the ordinary for the good of the parish. An accurate account book of receipts and expenditures must be kept. All documents and legal papers pertaining to the property and to the rights of the parish must be properly kept in the parish archives or in a safe place, and, whenever it is conveniently possible, authentic copies should also be kept in the archives of the diocesan curia.[171]

The law makes a special mention of the obligation of the pastor to observe the dictates of social justice in dealing with the employees of the parish.[172] It is hardly necessary to emphasize that as the leader of the flock the pastor ought to be an example in this matter. Special provisions are also made for acts of extraordinary administration,[173] for the alienation of ecclesiastical property,[174] for the making of loans and the mortgaging of parish goods,[175] for the making of contracts of all kinds,[176] and for the entering into or contesting of law suits in the name of the parish.[177]

Finally, it should also be mentioned that the pastor is obliged to make an annual report of his administration of the parish to the local ordinary. This is a strict obligation. All contrary customs are disapproved, rejected and reprobated by the law.[178] Since the ordinary is obliged to exercise vigilance in order to make sure that the parish property is properly protected and rightly administered,[179] it follows that he may demand periodical inspections of the parish records. The rural dean is frequently delegated to perform this task.

---

[171] Can. 1523, 2°-6°. The III Plenary Council of Baltimore (1884) requires the pastor to have an iron safe in the parish rectory for the safekeeping of the parish records and documents—*Acta et Decreta Concilii Plenarii Baltimorensis III*, n. 278.

[172] Can. 1524.

[173] Can. 1527, § 1.

[174] Cans. 1530-1534.

[175] Can. 1538.

[176] Can. 1529.

[177] Can. 1526.

[178] Can. 1525, § 1.

[179] Cans. 1478; 1519.

Article 4. The Tacit Renunciation of an Incompatible Benefice

Since the time of the Council of Trent, which re-established earlier legislation on this subject, it has been contrary to ecclesiastical discipline for a beneficiary to hold two or several incompatible benefices at the same time.[180] This legislation is reaffirmed in various canons of the Code. Canon 156, § 1, states that two incompatible offices may not be conferred upon the same person. Canon 460, § 1, states that a pastor may hold the title to only one parish at the same time unless it should happen that two or more parishes are united *aeque principaliter,* i.e., each parish retaining its legal personality. The same regulations are enacted for incompatible benefices.[181]

Canon 156, § 2, further states that ecclesiastical offices when held by a single incumbent become incompatible in character whenever the duties inherent in them cannot be duly and properly executed by him. Canon 1439, § 2, goes still further to state that benefices are incompatible not only when not all of their inherent obligations can be duly fulfilled by the same beneficiary, but also when the income of one or the other suffices to supply a decent livelihood for the incumbent.

It is obvious, therefore, that parochial benefices are incompatible in relation to each other, since the care of souls which is imposed upon the pastor obligates him to reside in or near the parish, a duty which can hardly be fulfilled in two parishes at the same time. It is possible, of course, that because of necessity or utility two parishes may be joined together in such a way that each retains its own identity, and yet only one pastor is appointed for administering both parishes.[182] Likewise a pastor may have possession of one parish in title, i.e., in his own right, and at the same time have charge of another parish as a temporary administrator.[183]

---

[180] Cf. sess. XXIV, *de ref.,* c. 17; cc. 1, 2, C. XXI, q. 1; c. 3, X, *de clericis non residentibus in ecclesia vel praebenda,* III, 4; c. 32, *de praebendis et dignitatibus,* III, 4, in VI°; cc. 13, 14, X, *de praebendis et dignitatibus,* III, 5; Wernz-Vidal, *Ius Canonicum,* II, 274-276.

[181] Can. 1439, § 1. Cf. Berutti, *Institutiones Iuris Canonici,* Vol. II, pars I, p. 197.

[182] Cans. 1419, 2°; 1423, § 1. Cf. Bouscaren-Ellis, *Canon Law,* p. 200.

[183] Bouscaren-Ellis, *loc. cit.*; Ramstein, *A Manual of Canon Law,* p. 552.

This practice is often followed in the United States in the erection of new parishes in sparsely settled areas or in areas where there are not many Catholics. Until the new parish is sufficiently well established to be able to support a pastor, it is placed under the charge of a neighboring pastor. In some areas the pastor of one parish may have charge of several small neighboring parishes.

In view of these various provisions of the law it is easily understandable that the law should also demand the resignation of a previously held benefice upon the completion of installation or the taking of possession of a second incompatible benefice. By virtue of canon 188, 3°, the acceptance or the obtaining of peaceful possession of an office automatically implies the tacit renunciation of any previous incompatible office. The first office becomes vacant *ipso facto* without the need of any declaration of the vacancy. Peaceful possession is that which is not contested, or about which there is no controversy in law or in fact, judicially or extrajudicially.[184]

This law is strengthened by the force of canon 2396, which prescribes the punishment of deprivation of office or benefice for anyone who presumes to retain possession of a previous incompatible office or benefice after obtaining the peaceful possession of the second office or benefice. He who is guilty of this offense is deprived by law (*ipso iure*) of both benefices or offices. Since the law requires presumption on the part of the offender before this penalty applies, it must be clear that the offices or benefices are incompatible, and that the peaceful possession of the second benefice has actually been obtained.[185]

It should be noted that the bishop is not able to dispense from this law. If because of necessity or because of the utility for the Church it would be advisable to have the same person as a pastor of more than one parish in real title at the same time, a dispensation would have to be obtained from the Holy See.[186]

---

[184] Coronata, *Institutiones Iuris Canonici,* I, 316, footnote 3.

[185] Ayrinhac-Lydon, *Penal Legislation in the New Code of Canon Law,* p. 311.

[186] Wernz-Vidal, *Ius Canonicum,* II, 278; Berutti, *Institutiones Iuris Canonici,* Vol. II, pars I, p. 196.

Article 5. The Presumption of Actual Possession and Restrictions Concerning Petitory Actions

One of the important effects of installation in office is the presumption of law that the person who has been installed in office, or who has taken peaceful possession of an office or benefice in some other way, has received possession of that office or benefice with a true and valid title.[187] Accordingly his possession of the office is protected in such a way that anyone who wishes to contest the right to the office is under certain restrictions in the petitory action which he must introduce in order to contest this right. In the bill of complaint (*libellus*) he must indicate the name of the possessor of the office, the duration of his possession, and the definite and special cause on account of which it is claimed that the possessor actually has no right to the possession. In the meantime the office may not be conferred upon the person contesting the right of possession until the petitory action is decided according to the norms of law.[188]

This legislation has its origin in the Rules of the Apostolic Chancery from the time of Pope Nicholas V (1450).[189] *Regula 35* of these Rules, entitled *"De annali possessore,"* gave the protection now afforded by canon 1447 to a beneficiary. But this protection was then given only after the possessor had held his benefice peacefully for one year.[190]

The legislation of this canon is entirely in accord with the laws concerning the conferral of office. Canon 150, § 1, provides that the conferral of an office which is not vacant *de iure* is *ipso facto* invalid, and the subsequent vacancy of the office does not convalidate the appointment. Likewise an office which is vacant *de iure,* but which is perhaps still held unlawfully by another, cannot be conferred unless it has first been declared, according to the norms of the canons, that this possession is unlawful. Mention of this declaration must also be made in the letter of appointment.[191]

---

187 Can. 1447.

188 Can. 1447.

189 Cf. Cicognani, *Canon Law,* pp. 322-324; Pistocchi, *De Re Beneficiali,* p. 242.

190 Ferraris, I, s. v., *Beneficium,* art. IX, n. 35.

191 Can. 151.

In the consideration of this legislation several points in canon 1447 should be noted. The beneficiary must be in peaceful possession of the benefice. A benefice is held in peaceful possession when there is no dispute either as to the title of possession or as to the actual possession.[192] This does not mean that the possession may not have been contested previously, provided only that the controversy was judicially decided in favor of the incumbent of the benefice.

The legislation under consideration establishes a presumption of law that the incumbent of the benefice is in rightful possession of it. Hence he is not obliged to prove his right to possession. The burden of proof lies with the plaintiff in this case.[193] Since the fact of possession establishes only a presumption of its rightful character in law, the possession may be impugned by means of a legitimate action. Hence the person who contests this possession may introduce a petitory action according to the norms of law. A petitory action is one in which the plaintiff attempts to vindicate unto himself a claim to a thing or to prosecute a right given to him by the law.[194] In a possessory action the plaintiff attempts to protect his possession of a thing or his quasi-possession of a right.[195]

The person who introduces a petitory action to obtain a benefice held by another must contend that the incumbent's possession of the benefice is invalid for a certain and definite reason.[196] In other words, he cannot attack the possession merely on general grounds. This provision is obviously made to protect the incumbent of a benefice from annoying suits for which there does not exist any real basis. The special reason on account of which it is contended that the benefice is vacant must be mentioned in the bill of complaint which introduces the action. Such a cause could be the invalidity of the title to the benefice in view of an invalid election or appointment, in view of simony in the making of the appointment, in view of the invalid taking of possession of the office, etc.[197]

---

[192] Augustine, *A Commentary on the New Code of Canon Law,* VI, 522.

[193] Ayrinhac, *Administrative Legislation in the New Code of Canon Law,* p. 345.

[194] Can. 1668, § 1.

[195] Can. 1668, § 2.

[196] ". . . quod certo modo vacare contendat . . ."—Can. 1447.

[197] Cf. Pistocchi, *De Re Beneficiali,* p. 241.

Likewise the name of the possessor and the duration of his peaceful possession of the benefice must be indicated in the bill of complaint. The indicated name of the possessor will serve as a factor for determining whether the court has competence for considering the action. The indicated duration of the possession will reveal whether or not sufficient time has elapsed to allow legal prescription to have effect. These various provisions are in accord with the general requirements for an introductory *libellus.*[198]

Finally, canon 1447 provides that the benefice in dispute may not be conferred upon the plaintiff until a decision is given in the petitory action according to the norms of law. As has already been mentioned, this is in accord with the legislation on the conferral of office, which makes invalid the conferring of an office which is not *de iure* vacant.[199]

Article 6. The Right to Possession through Prescription after Three Years of Peaceful Possession

Although a pastor may have obtained possession of his parish through an invalid title, he may retain possession of the parish in consequence of the extant factor of legal prescription if he can prove that he was in peaceful possession of the parochial benefice in good faith for at least three years, and that there was no simony involved in connection with his obtaining this possession.[200] The effect of this law is to heal by means of legal prescription the illegal possession of a benefice, if certain conditions are fulfilled.

This law also has its origin in the Rules of the Apostolic Chancery as well as in earlier decretal legislation.[201] The commentators of the early legislation did not always agree on the interpretation of this Rule, principally because of the first of the *Regulae Iuris* of Boniface VIII, which stated that a benefice could not be obtained licitly without canonical institution.[202] Because of this rule it was felt that prescription could not have any effect in the obtain-

[198] Cf. can. 1708, 1°-3°.

[199] Cf. cans. 150, §§ 1-2; 151.

[200] Can. 1446.

[201] Cf. c. un., *de sequestratione possessionum et fructum,* II, 6, in Clem.; Reg. 36, Reg. Canc., *de triennali possessione*—Ferraris, I, s. v., *Beneficium,* art. IX, n. 36; Wernz, *Ius Decretalium,* IV, n. 448.

[202] Cf. *supra,* pp. 33-34.

ing of a benefice unless there was some semblance of a title. Consequently some of the authors concluded that at least a colored title (*titulus coloratus*) was necessary before legal prescription could achieve an operative effect.[203]

Another controversy among the canonists centered about the question whether in virtue of Rule 36 the factor of legal prescription accorded an actual title to the possession of a benefice, or whether it merely protected the person in possession from suits by others who wished to contest the right to the benefice.[204] Those who held the latter view maintained that although a beneficiary who held peaceful possession of a benefice for more than three years, though with an invalid title, could not be dispossessed by means of a judicial action instituted by another who desired to obtain the benefice, nonetheless the legitimate ecclesiastical superior could *ex officio* begin proceedings for the removal of the beneficiary on condition that it became clearly demonstrated that his title to possession was invalid.[205]

These various questions are now settled by the detailed provisions of the law contained in canon 1446. Five conditions are prescribed by this canon before legal prescription can achieve its full effect. The beneficiary must be able to prove: 1) that he has been in peaceful possession of the benefice; 2) that he has been in peaceful possession for the continuous period of three full years; 3) that he was acting in good faith; 4) that he possessed a title to the benefice, even though it may have been invalid; and 5) that there was no simony involved in the conferral of the benefice.

1. Peaceful possession of a benefice is that which is without violence in its inception and which has not been interrupted either physically or morally. In other words there must be quiet enjoyment of possession without interruption and without disturbance in order to have peaceful possession.[206] The interruption can occur in various ways. It can arise from the intervention of a third party or

---

[203] Leurenius, *Forum Beneficiale,* pars II, q. 853; Garcia, *Tractatus de Beneficiis,* pars V, c. 4, nn. 298-308; Reiffenstuel, *Ius Canonicum Universum,* lib. III, tit. 5, n. 526.

[204] Leurenius, *Forum Beneficiale,* pars II, q. 827, nn. 1-2; qq. 857-858; Wernz, *Ius Decretalium,* IV, n. 449; Rossi, *De Paroecia,* pp. 180-181.

[205] Rossi, *loc. cit.*

from natural causes. It can be interrupted either physically or morally.

It may be interrupted physically by the introduction of a legal action by another who wishes to contest the title to the benefice,[207] or by the actual physical removal from the benefice through the action of an intruder or in consequence of the hostility of enemies, etc. These latter actions would seem to cause undue hardship upon the beneficiary by denying him the right of prescription in such circumstances, but it must be remembered that to invoke the right of prescription the beneficiary must be in *actual* possession of the benefice.[208]

Peaceful possession of a benefice may be interrupted morally by the loss of good faith in the beneficiary.[209] Many other factors might also cause a moral interruption of the peaceful possession. Thus an *excommunicatus vitandus* is automatically deprived of his benefice.[210] It seems also that the legal incapacity of the beneficiary to acquire a valid title to a benefice because of an irregularity,[211] because of the censure of excommunication,[212] or the censure of suspension from his office or benefice[213] would also interrupt the peaceful possession of a benefice obtained through an invalid title, and consequently the right of prescription would cease.

It is obvious that the beneficiary must be in possession of the benefice in his own name before legal prescription can take effect. This requirement was expressed in the earlier legislation in the *Regulae Juris.*[214]

2. The peaceful possession of the benefice must be continuous

---

[206] Cf. Martin, *Adverse Possession, Prescription and Limitation of Actions. The Canonical* "Praescriptio," The Catholic University of America Canon Law Studies, n. 202 (Washington, D. C.: The Catholic University of America Press, 1944), pp. 77-78.

[207] Can. 1447.

[208] Cf. Martin, *op. cit.*, pp. 72-74.

[209] Pistocchi, *De Re Beneficiali,* pp. 234-235.

[210] Can. 2266.

[211] Cans. 983-989.

[212] Can. 2265, §§ 1-2.

[213] Cans. 2279-2280; 2283.

[214] "Sine possessione praescriptio non procedit,"—Reg. 3, R. J., in VI°. Cf. Pistocchi, *loc. cit.*; Wernz-Vidal, *Ius Canonicum,* Tom. IV, Vol. II, pp. 307-308.

over a period of three full years.[215] Since no interruption is permissible in the computation of the time that is required if legal prescription is to take effect, it is obvious that the so-called *tempus utile* is precluded from consideration here.[216] In the determination of whether or not the three-year period has elapsed the rules for the computation of time must be followed. The *terminus a quo* will be the day of the installation in office or of the actual taking of possession, and the completion of the three year period will be determined by the respective rules given in canon 34, § 3.

3. No prescription is valid in ecclesiastical law unless it is based on good faith not only at the time of the entering into possession but also during the whole time required for the ultimate culmination of the legal prescription.[217] This rule is also found in the *Regulae Juris* of Boniface VIII.[218] Good faith may be described as the judgment by which a person prudently thinks that he justly possesses a thing as his own without injury to the rights of another.[219] It is logical, therefore, that the factor of legal prescription cannot take effect for the obtaining of possession of a benefice unless the beneficiary is in good faith.

To be in peaceful possession of a benefice in good faith it is necessary that the beneficiary possess a title to the benefice which he considers to be valid, even though in reality it may be invalid. If during the period of adverse possession he finds out that his title is not a valid title, he cannot retain possession in good faith. If accusations are raised against the validity of his title of possession or against the manner in which he has taken possession of the benefice, he must prudently feel that these accusations are without proof. If he cannot prudently justify his own view, he can hardly be considered to retain possession in good faith. If such accusations are made the basis of a legal claim or petitory action, the beneficiary is no longer considered to be in peaceful possession of the benefice. If doubts arise regarding the validity of the possession,

---

215 "... per integrum triennium ..."—can. 1446.

216 Cf. can. 35; Pistocchi, *loc. cit.*; Wernz-Vidal, *loc. cit.*

217 Can. 1512.

218 "Possessor malae fidei ullo tempore non praescribit"—Reg. 2, R. J., in VI°.

219 Wernz-Vidal, *Ius Canonicum*, Tom. IV, Vol. II, p. 311; Cappello, *Summa Iuris Canonici*, III, 19-25.

the beneficiary must be able to clear up such doubts in order to be able to claim title through legal prescription at a later date.[220]

4. Canon 1446 does not explicitly state that a beneficiary must have an actual title to possession in order to obtain possession of a benefice by way of legal prescription, but at least by implication it does, since it requires that the beneficiary must be in good faith. It also speaks of possession "even though with an invalid title," implying that some kind of a title is necessary.[221]

Reiffenstuel described the title as the *"iusta causa possidendi quod nostrum non est."*[222] Van Hove says that a title is the instrument of proof of a juridical act or of the quality in virtue of which one can take part in the performance of such an act.[223] In canon law the term *"titulus,"* or title, can have various meanings. In reference to sacred orders it refers to the canonical right to a proper sustenance which must be given to one promoted to sacred orders.[224] In connection with a benefice or office the title is the canonical reason or justification by which one is given the possession of a benefice or office.

It should be noted that a true title is that which is validly received from a competent superior. An invalid title may be putative or colored (*titulus coloratus*), sometimes also called an apparent title. A putative title is present when the beneficiary erroneously thinks—or perhaps in bad faith pretends—that he has received a title to the benefice when in reality there has been no act of the legitimate superior. A colored title is one which has the appearance of a true title inasmuch as it is conferred by a competent superior, but labors under an occult defect which makes it invalid. The defect may be on the part of the one conferring the title, e.g., if the superior, though perhaps unaware of the fact, should have been deprived of the right to confer the title; it may be on the part of the one receiving the title, e.g., if he is legally incapable of re-

---

220 Cf. Martin, *Adverse Possession, Prescription and Limitation of Actions. The Canonical* "Praescriptio," pp. 53-54.

221 ". . .etsi forte cum titulo invalido . . ."—can. 1446. Cf. Woywod, "Law of the Code on Benefices," *HPR,* XXIX (1929), 388.

222 *Ius Canonicum Universum,* lib. II, tit. 26, n. 127.

223 *Commentarium Lovaniense in Codicem Iuris Canonici,* Tom. I, vol. I, p. 24.

224 Cans. 979-980.

ceiving the title; or the defect may arise from the manner of conferring the title, e.g., if a substantial formula is neglected in the conferral of the title, or if simony is involved.[225]

From the wording of canon 1446 it may, therefore, be concluded that a beneficiary must possess at least a colored or apparent title to the possession of his benefice in order to claim possession by way of legal prescription. Canon 1509, 6°, also prohibits the operation of legal prescription with reference to an ecclesiastical benefice that was obtained without a title.

5. Finally, for prescription to take effect there must be no simony involved in the conferral of the benefice or in the maintaining of peaceful possession. Since a simoniacal pact in connection with the bestowal of an ecclesiastical benefice constitutes simony forbidden by the divine law,[226] the Church not only forbids this practice, but also has enacted stringent regulations to prevent the parties to such a simoniacal pact from profiting thereby.

Over and above the fact that the penalties which the law has enacted against the parties of a simoniacal pact still have their force, the contract moreover is null and void; and if simony is committed in connection with benefices, offices or dignities, the subsequent act of canonical appointment to them is also null and void, even though the simony was committed by a third person apart from all knowledge on the side of the person who obtains the benefice, provided it was not done fraudulently with a calculated view to rendering the appointment invalid, or over the protest of the one who obtained the benefice.[227] Hence, even before the sentence of a judge, the price given and received in the simoniacal act must be restored, if possible, and the benefice or office must be vacated.[228] Likewise the person who has received the office or benefice through simony is not entitled to the income of the

---

[225] Cf. Miaskiewicz, *Supplied Jurisdiction According to Canon 209*, The Catholic University of America Canon Law Studies, n. 122 (Washington, D. C.: The Catholic University of America Press, 1940), p. 15.

[226] "Studiosa voluntas emendi vel vendendi pro pretio temporali . . . rem temporalem rei spirituali adnexam ita ut res temporalis sine spirituali nullo modo esse possit, ex. gr., beneficium ecclesiasticum, etc., . . . est simonia iuris divini."—Can. 727, § 1.

[227] Can. 729.

[228] Can. 729, 1°.

office or the benefice. If he has already received a part of the income in good faith, it is left to the prudent judgment of the judge or the ordinary to decide whether he may keep this income.[229]

These general prinicples concerning simoniacal acts are repeated in various canons of the Code. Renunciation of an office or of a benefice made as the result of simony is *ipso facto* invalid.[230] Deductions from the income of the benefice, or compensatory payments made by the beneficiary at the time of receiving the benefice, are forbidden as simoniacal.[231] The presentation of a candidate by a patron which is vitiated by simony is *ipso iure* null and void, and the appointment which may have followed this presentation is also invalid.[232] Besides nullifying the appointment to a benefice or an office, the crime of simony also makes the persons who commit this sin in connection with offices or benefices subject to severe penalties. They automatically incur an excommunication reserved simply to the Apostolic See, they are automatically deprived forever of any right they may have obtained to elect, present, or nominate a candidate for the office or benefice, and, if they are clerics, they are also subject to suspension.[233] In view of these stringent regulations it is compellingly logical that no rights to a benefice can be allowed by way of legal prescription if simony has occurred.[234]

It is beyond the scope of this treatise to discuss in detail the various ways in which simony may be committed in connection with the bestowal of an office or a benefice, or to enter into a discussion of the controversy among authors concerning the question whether confidential simony is still treated in the Code.[235]

A particular problem arises, however, when the simony is com-

---

229 Can. 729, 2°.

230 Can. 185.

231 Cans. 1440-1441.

232 Can. 1465, § 2.

233 Can. 2392, 1°-3°.

234 Can. 1446.

235 For a fuller discussion of these topics cf. Woywod, *A Practical Commentary on the Code of Canon Law,* I, 315-320; Coronata, *Institutiones Iuris Canonici,* II, 3-21; Ryder, *Simony,* The Catholic University of America Canon Law Studies, n. 65 (Washington, D. C.: The Catholic University of America, 1931), pp. 66-99; Beste, *Introductio in Codicem,* pp. 473-480.

mitted by a third party without the knowledge of the holder of the benefice. Since the beneficiary is in good faith, may he claim a title to the benefice in consequence of legal prescription after three years of peaceful possession, regardless of the simony committed by a third party? Coronata holds that he may claim this title as long as he remains in good faith during the entire three-year period and does not obtain knowledge of the simony until after that time. He bases his argument on the fact that the law of canon 1446 grants a favor to the possessor in good faith, and since laws which grant a favor may be widely interpreted, he holds that the phrase "*dummodo absit simonia*" applies only if the possessor of the benefice has been a party to the simony, or at least knew that simony was committed by another.[236] Some authors before the Code also applied a similar interpretation to the 36th Rule of the Apostolic Chancery.[237]

Ryder, however, maintains that the Code legislation in this matter is more stringent than the former rule of the Apostolic Chancery, since canon 729 specifically nullifies an appointment to a benefice even though the simony was committed by a third party apart from the knowledge of the beneficiary. Consequently he argues that no distinction can be made in this case, for when the law does not distinguish neither should the commentator.[238] Rossi also inclines to this view.[239]

It seems, however, that the law concerning simony does allow for some distinctions in this matter, since it does not penalize the innocent party involved in the act of simony if he protests against it, or if the simony is committed fraudulently with the purpose of depriving him of the benefice.[240] Likewise the law allows the judge or the ordinary to condone the receipt of the income of the benefice in whole or in part if it was received in good faith.[241] Also,

---

236 *Institutiones Iuris Canonici*, II, 12.

237 Reiffenstuel, *Ius Canonicum Universum*, lib. V, tit. 3, n. 278; Schmalzgrueber, *Ius Ecclesiasticum Universum*, lib. V, tit. 3, n. 267; Wernz, *Ius Decretalium*, VI, p. 347, n. 77.

238 *Simony*, p. 98.

239 *De Paroecia*, p. 145, footnote 30, n. 2.

240 ". . . dummodo hoc non fiat in fraudem eiusdem provisi aut eo contradicente."—Can. 729.

241 Can. 729, 2°.

inasmuch as canon 1446 is largely a restatement of the former law, it seems that the opinions of the approved authors of the former law may be safely followed.

In concluding the discussion regarding the acquisition of a valid title to a benefice by way of legal prescription, one may note that the present law definitely settles the former controversy as to whether three years of peaceful possession gave a real title to the benefice, or whether it merely protected the possessor from being dispossessed by another who desired to obtain the benefice. The present law explicitly states that the possessor obtains the benefice by way of legitimate prescription.[242]

---

[242] ". . . beneficium ex legitima praescriptione obtinet."—Can. 1446. Cf. Martin, *Adverse Possession, Prescription and Limitation of Actions. The Canonical* "Praescriptio," p. 54.

CONCLUSIONS

1. It is sometimes stated that the canonical institute of the installation of pastors in office is merely an outgrowth of the sacramentary system in the Church. While this may be a theoretical explanation for this development, historical facts indicate that this institute had its origin in the early Middle Ages and developed along with the system of benefices and the system of the so-called proprietary church. Under feudalism and during the so-called Investiture Struggle installation in office came to be considered as a most important part in the conferral of an office. The crystallization of legislation concerning investiture and installation was reached in the twelfth and thirteenth centuries, especially through the decretal letters of Popes Alexander III and Innocent III.

2. Some authors from the fourteenth through the sixteenth centuries held that an act of actual installation was necessary for the valid possession of an office or a benefice, but from the seventeenth century onward the authors more generally agreed that installation was necessary simply for the lawfulness of the possession, except in certain obvious cases in which it was necessary for the validity of the possession as well.

3. In the present legislation the canonical installation of pastors is to be considered as an important and an integral part of the complete conferral of office, but it cannot be called an essential part or a substantial form in the conferral of office to the extent that it is required for the valid possession of the pastoral office. In other words, the laws of canons 1443 and 461 are not expressly invalidating laws; neither are they in themselves equivalently invalidating laws. At most one may admit that there exists in these laws a *dubium iuris* which would consequently leave them without an invalidating effect.

4. Particular legislation or a legitimate local custom which requires for validity a definite rite or manner to be observed for the installation of pastors has the same effect as the establishing of an invalidating character in the general law. In these circumstances

the manner or rite thus prescribed must be observed for the valid possession of the pastoral office.

5. The penalty of disqualification contained in canon 2394 does not seem to apply to one who takes possession of a parochial benefice without being canonically installed after he has obtained a *ius in re* to the benefice, unless he uses force or fraud, or in other ways acts unjustly to obtain possession of the benefice.

6. A dispensation from the law of the installation of pastors must be expressly stated and in writing. A presumed dispensation in this matter cannot be admitted. The requirement that the dispensation must be in writing is necessary only for the licitness of the dispensation, and not for its validity.

7. Quasi-pastors and acting vicars are also bound by the law of installation in office, but parochial administrators, substitute vicars, adjutant vicars and assistant pastors are not subject to this law, unless their office is established as a true canonical benefice.

8. Although it is legally possible, it is not likely that there are legitimate contrary customs in the United States which derogate from the law requiring the installation of pastors in office, since any such customs which previously existed would have been abolished with the advent of the present Code of Canon Law, unless the ordinary had expressly allowed them to continue because he felt that they could not prudently be removed.

9. The profession of faith required either before or in the act of installation of pastors is not required for the valid possession of the parochial benefice, but only for the lawfulness of possession.

10. A pastor must have at least a colored or apparent title (*titulus coloratus*) in order to claim possession of his parochial benefice by means of legal prescription after three years of peaceful possession of the benefice.

APPENDIX I

A Typical Rite of the Formal Installation of Pastors

The following rite of installation is a typical example of the more formal manner of the installation of pastors in office as it is carried out in a number of dioceses in the United States. It is reproduced *verbatim* from the *Liber Synodalis* of the Diocese of Fargo[1] with the kind permission of the Vicar General of the Diocese of Fargo, the Very Reverend Howard Smith.

Rite of Installation of Pastors

Holy Mother Church desires that the installation of a pastor be conducted with dignified solemnity.

Canonical Possession

For the canonical possession of the parish it is herewith ordered that the new pastor make the required profession of faith and take the oath against modernism. This solemnity shall take place in the rectory before the dean or someone delegated by him, unless uncontrollable circumstances make another arrangement advisable. The priests of the deanery as well as of neighboring parishes should attend the installation ceremony.

It is suggested that the new pastor, in the presence of the installator, the clergy, and a parish committee, kneeling before a crucifix with lighted candles one on each side of it, place his hand on the Holy Gospels and make the required profession of faith as well as take the oath against modernism. The clergy should be vested as becomes a religious ceremony. If the rectory has a house chapel, the ceremony should be held in the chapel.

Ceremony of Installation

It is fitting that an appropriate ceremony of installation be held before all the congregation in the church. If the installation takes

[1] *Synodus Dioecesana Fargensis Prima Iuxta Canones Sacros et Decreta Conciliorum Baltimorensium in Ecclesia Cathedrali Stae Mariae Virginis ab Excellentissimo ac Reverendissimo Aloisio Joseph Muench, S.T.D., Episcopo Fargensi Diebus XXIX et XXX Septembris A.D. MCMXLI, pp. 203-207.*

place in the morning the newly installed pastor will say the Mass; if in the afternoon or evening, he will give Benediction of the Blessed Sacrament.

Procession from the Rectory to the Church. After the signing of the documents the procession will form in front of the rectory to escort the new pastor to the church by way of the front entrance.

Amidst the ringing of bells all proceed to the church as follows: the procession is led by the *Vexillum* of Christ the King, or the banner of the Church Patron. Then follow in order, the children, first boys then girls, societies of men and women with their respective banners, nuns, cross-bearer with acolytes carrying lighted candles, altar boys in cassocks and surplices, the clergy, the installator with the new pastor at his left, both wearing cassock, surplice, and biretta, or, in case of prelates, rochet and mantelletta.

Upon entering the church an appropriate hymn should be sung. If capable, the choir should sing the antiphon *Ego sum pastor bonus,* taken from the communion prayer of the second Sunday after Easter, with psalm 22 *Dominus regit me,* repeating the antiphon after every second verse.

Installation. At the altar the installator and the new pastor kneel and adore. The first and last verses of the *Veni Creator* are sung, whereupon the installator sings the versicle and oration.

Both rise; the new pastor then sits at the epistle side. The installator, or the notary appointed by him, reads from some convenient place in the sanctuary or from the pulpit the letter of appointment. The installator then introduces the new pastor to his people and, after reading the Gospel of the Good Shepherd, preaches an appropriate homily on the gospel text without, however, delivering a panegyric.

Thereupon the installator proceeds to the altar, ascends its steps, and sits down on a chair that has been placed in the middle of the predella. The new pastor advances and kneels before him.

The installator hands the new pastor the keys of the church and says in a loud voice for all the congregation to hear:

"These Keys symbolize your power to open the gates of heaven. Open them to the worthy and close them to the unworthy. Gather into one fold your flock in the charity of Christ and as a good shepherd protect them against all evil." The new pastor responds: "Amen."

Handing him the Gospel Book the installator says:

"Receive these Holy Gospels. God has sent you to preach its truths. Preach them in season and out of season; reprove, entreat, rebuke with all patience and teaching. Do not put light for darkness, nor darkness for light. Do not call evil good, nor good evil. Be faithful to the ministry of the word of the Lord in dispensing His truths to your flock." The new pastor responds: "Amen."

After this the installator hands him the baptismal shell saying:

"Receive this symbol of the Laver of Regeneration. From it flow the life-giving waters of a new birth in God. Be a faithful custodian of the font of regeneration, the immaculate bosom of the Church, from which are brought forth children of God, a heavenly progeny, members of the Mystical Body of Christ, and parishioners of the parish committed this day to your care." The new pastor responds: "Amen."

Handing him the purple stole the installator says:

"Take charge of the Tribunal of God's Mercy. Be a kind father, a prudent judge, a consoling physician, to all who confess their sins in a spirit of humility and with a contrite heart, that they may obtain plentiful forgiveness and divine grace through the merits of Christ Jesus." The new pastor responds: "Amen."

The new pastor now takes in his hands both the chalice and ciborium while the installator says:

"These are the sacred vessels for the celebration of the Mysteries of our Redemption. Take charge of them, keep them spotless, that your flock may know that you love the beauty of God's house." The new pastor responds: "Amen."

The installator then says to the new pastor as he hands him the oil stocks:

"Receive the holy oils, the Oil of the Catechumens that God may open to them His gates of mercy; the Holy Chrism for the salvation of His chosen generation and kingly priesthood; and the Oil of the Sick, that, if they be in sins, their sins shall be forgiven unto them." The new pastor responds: "Amen."

The installator now rises, takes the new pastor by the hand and leads him to the altar and says:

"The Altar of Holy Church is Christ. May you, for many years, with pure hands and a clean heart offer the Sacrifice of our Lord Jesus Christ, and through Him, with Him, and in Him render to God, the Father Almighty, in the unity of the Holy Ghost, all honor and glory." The new pastor responds: "Amen."

The installator and the new pastor kiss the altar and give each other the liturgical greeting of peace. As an expression of fraternal fellowship and brotherly unity the new pastor then gives his peace greeting to his fellow priests who, coming to the foot of the altar at the middle, one by one, receive it from him. Immediately after, the new pastor blesses his people:

"Benedictio Dei omnipotentis Patris, et Filii et Spiritus Sancti, descendat super vos et maneat semper. Amen."

The official document attesting to the canonical taking over of the parish is now read by the installator, or the notary appointed by him. The new pastor now delivers to his flock a short sermon, couched in simple, prudent words, and appropriate to the occasion.

Thereupon the new pastor vests and Holy Mass begins. If the installation takes place in the evening, the ceremony closes with Benediction of the Blessed Sacrament. This service concludes with "Holy God, We Praise Thy Name."

Transmissal of Documents

Without delay the installator shall send to the chancery office: the attestation of the act of canonical possession duly signed and sealed; the profession of faith and oath against modernism properly signed; notification of the canonical installation of the pastor and of the observance of the rite of installation.

APPENDIX II

An Informal Manner for the Installation of Pastors

On the appointed day the new pastor, the dean of the respective deanery (or other delegate of the ordinary), the administrator during the vacancy of the parish (or the previous pastor) and the trustees of the parish (or two members of the parish committee) shall meet at the parochial residence.

After it has been determined by the dean that the parish is vacant *de iure* and *de facto,* the new pastor shall present his letter of appointment to the parish to the dean who will determine the authenticity of the document. The administrator will then present the parish records and the parish seal (required by canon 470), a copy of the inventory of the parochial property and the books of receipts and expenditures together with a duplicate financial report from the beginning of the current year. If the report is found to be satisfactory, it shall be signed by the administrator and the parish trustees, and the new pastor shall indicate in writing his acceptance of the report.

The new pastor shall then make the profession of faith and take the oath against modernism. The new pastor and the dean shall then sign these documents. When this is completed, the dean will hand to the new pastor the keys of the tabernacle and of the church, and with appropriate words he shall indicate that he thereby grants the canonical possession of the parish.

When the new pastor has indicated his acceptance of the canonical possession, the dean, the new pastor, the administrator and the trustees shall sign in duplicate the certificate of the installation of the pastor, and the seal of the parish shall be attached thereto. One copy of the certificate and of the financial report, and the signed profession of faith and the oath against modernism shall be sent to the Chancery Office, and the other copies shall be kept in the parish records.

APPENDIX III

SUGGESTED FORMS FOR THE DOCUMENTS USED IN INSTALLATION

1. *Attestation of the Formal Installation of the Pastor*[1]

In the name of the Most Holy Trinity. Amen.

Under the Roman Pontificate of His Holiness, Pope Pius XII, His Excellency, the Most Reverend ____________________, being Bishop of the Diocese of ____________________, I, the Reverend ____________________, by delegation of the Most Reverend Ordinary, having seen and verified the letters of appointment of the Reverend ______________ ______________ as pastor of this church of ______________ in the city of ____________________, do hereby give to the aforesaid Reverend ____________________ the canonical possession of this parochial benefice.

I therefore declare that the Reverend ____________________ is now canonically installed in the possession of this parochial benefice and is endowed with all of the rights, duties and emoluments pertaining thereto.

I further attest that the act of installation was publicly proclaimed and that the canonical requirements were properly fulfilled.

Given at ____________________ this __________ day of ______________ in the year of Our Lord __________.

____
Dean or other Delegate

(CHURCH SEAL)

____
New Pastor

____
Witness

____
Witness

[1] This form has been adapted from various forms now in use in various dioceses.

2. *Certificate of the Installation of the Pastor*[2]

This is to certify that I, the Reverend ...., as a delegate of the Most Reverend ...., Bishop of the Diocese of ...., having seen and verified the letters of appointment of the Reverend .... as pastor of the Church of .... in the city of ...., have installed him as the pastor with the prescribed ceremonies and have given to him the true and actual canonical possession of the parochial Church of ...., with all rights, duties and emoluments pertaining thereto.

Given at ...., on the .... day of ...., A. D., 19..........

....
Dean or other Delegate

....
Administrator or previous Pastor

(Church Seal)

....
New Pastor

....
Witness

....
Witness

---

[2] This form has been adapted from various forms now in use in several dioceses.

BIBLIOGRAPHY

SOURCES

Acta Apostolicae Sedis, Commentarium Officiale, Romae, 1909—

Acta et Decreta Concilii Plenarii Baltimorensis Tertii, A.D. MDCCCXXXIV, Baltimorae: John Murphy, 1886.

Acta et Decreta Sacrorum Conciliorum Recentiorum, Collectio Lacensis, 7 vols., Friburgi Brisgoviae, 1870-1890.

Acta Sanctae Sedis, 41 vols., Romae, 1865-1908.

Bizzarri, A., *Collectanea in Usum Secretariae Sacrae Congregationis Episcoporum et Regularium,* Romae, 1885.

Bouscaren, T. L., *The Canon Law Digest,* 2 vols., Milwaukee, Wis.: Bruce Publishing Co., 1934-1943.

Bruns, H. T., *Canones Apostolorum et Conciliorum Saeculorum IV-VII,* 2 vols., Berolini, 1839.

Codex Iuris Canonici Pii X Pontificis Maximi iussu digestus Benedicti Papae XV auctoritate promulgatus, praefatione, fontium annotatione et indice analytico—alphabetico ab Emo Petro Card. Gasparri auctus, Romae: Typis Polyglottis Vaticanis, 1917.

Codicis Iuris Canonici Fontes, cura Emi Petri Card. Gasparri editi, 9 vols., Romae (postea Civitate Vaticana): Typis Polyglottis Vaticanis, 1923-1939 (Vols. VII-IX ed. cura et studio Emi Iustiniani Card. Serédi).

Collectanea S. Congregationis de Propaganda Fide, 2 vols., Romae: Typographia Polyglotta S. C. de Propaganda Fide, 1907.

Concilii Plenarii Baltimorensis II, in Ecclesia Metropolitana Baltimorensi, a die VII ad diem XXI Octobris, A.D. MDCCCLXVI, Habiti, et a Sede Apostolica Recogniti, Acta et Decreta, ed. altera, Baltimore: Joannes Murphy, 1894.

Concilii Tridentini, Diariorum, Actorum, Epistularum, Tractatuum, Nova Collectio, ed. Societas *Goerresiana,* 13 vols., Friburgi Brisgoviae: apud B. Herder, 1901-1938.

Constitutiones Dioeceseos Sinus Viridis Quae in Synodo Dioecesana Quarta Latae et Promulgatae Fuerunt, Pulaski, Wis.: Typis Franciscanae Typographiae, 1921.

Corpus Iuris Canonici, ed. Lipsiensis secunda, post Aemilii Ludovici Richteri curas . . . instruxit Aemelius Friedberg, 2 vols., Lipsiae: Tauchnitz, 1879-1881; ed. anatastice repetita, 1928.

Decreta Authentica Congregationis Sacrorum Rituum, 6 vols., Romae: Ex Typographia Polyglotta, 1898-1927.

Decretales D. Gregorii Papae IX, suae integritati, una cum glossis restituta, Romae, 1582.

Decretum Gratiani, emendatum et notationibus illustratum, una cum glossis, 2 vols., Romae, 1682.

Denzinger, H., *Enchiridion Symbolorum Definitionum et Declarationum de Rebus Fidei et Morum,* ed. 18.20., a C. Bannwart denuo compositum, iteratis curis edidit J. Umberg, Friburgi Brisgoviae: Herder and Co., 1932.

Hardouin, Jean, *Acta Conciliorum et Epistolae Decretales ac Constitutiones Summorum Pontificum,* 12 vols., Parisiis, 1714-1715.

Jaffé, Philipus, *Regesta Pontificum Romanorum ab condita Ecclesia ad annum post Christum natum MCXCVIII,* 2. ed., (G. Wattenbach, Kaltenbrunner, Ewald, Loewenfeld), 2 vols., Lipsiae, 1885-1888.

Mansi, Joannes, *Sacrorum Conciliorum Nova et Amplissima Collectio,* 53 vols. in 60, Parisiis, 1901-1927.

Monumenta Germaniae Historica, 188 vols. incomplete, Hanoverae, 1826—
Leges in 4°, Sectio II (*Capitularia Regum Francorum*) Tom. 1, ed. A. Boretius, 1883;
Sectio III (*Concilia*) Tom. I (*Concilia Aevi Merovingici*), ed. F. Maassen, 1893; Tom II (*Concilia Aevi Karolini*), ed., A. Werminghoff, 1904.

Pallottini, S., *Collectio Omnium Conclusionum et Resolutionum Quae in Causis Propositis apud Sacrum Congregationem Cardinalium S. Concilii Tridentini Interpretum Prodierunt ab eius Institutione Anno MDLXIV ad Annum MDCCCLX, Distinctis Titulis Alphabetico Ordine per Materias Digesta,* 18 vols., Romae, 1868-1895.

Pontificale Romanum, Ratisbonae, 1891.

Potthast, Augustus, *Regesta Pontificum Romanorum inde ab anno post Christum natum MCXCVIII ad annum MCCCIV,* 2 vols., Berolini, 1874-1875.

Quinque Compilationes Antiquae necnon Collectio Canonum Lipsiensis, ad librorum mani scriptorum fidem recognivit et adnotatione critica instruxit Aemelius Friedberg, Lipsiae, 1882.

Rituale Romanum Paul V Pontificis Maximi Jussu Editum Aliorumque Pontificum Cura Recognitum atque Auctoritate Sanctissimi D. N. Pii XI ad Norman Codicis Iuris Canonici Accomodatum, ed. iuxta typicam, Romae-Tornaci-Parisiis: Desclée et Socii, 1927.

Schroeder, H. J., *Canons and Decrees of the Council of Trent,* St. Louis: Herder, 1941.

Statuta Archidioecescos Indianapolitanae Lata ac Promulgata ab Exm̃o ac Revm̃o Paulo Schulte, D. D., Archiepiscopo Indianapolitano in Synodo Archidioecesana (I) Septima Die 21 Mensis Maii 1947 Habita, Indianapolis, Ind.: Standard Printing Co., 1947.

Statuta Archidioecesis Sancti Francisci, Lata ac Promulgata ab Exm̃o ac Revm̃o Joanne J. Mitty, Archiepiscopo Sancti Francisci in Synodo Dioecesana Secunda, San Francisco, Calif.: The Monitor Publishing Co., 1936.

Synodus Dioecesana Fargensis Prima iuxta Canones Sacros et Decreta Conciliorum Baltimorensium in Ecclesia Cathedrali Sanctae Mariae Virginis ab Excellentissimo ac Reverendissimo Aloisio Joseph Muench,

S.T.D., Episcopo Fargensi Diebus XXIX et XXX Septembris A.D. MCMLI Habita, Milwaukee: The Bruce Publishing Co., 1941.

Synodus Dioecesana Omahensis Quarta, Omaha, Nebraska: Typis Burkley Envelope and Printing Co., 1934.

Thesaurus Resolutionum Sacrae Congregationis Concilii, 167 vols., Romae, 1718-1908.

AUTHORS

Augustine, Charles, *A Commentary on the New Code of Canon Law,* 8 vols., Vol. I, 3. ed., 1920; Vol. II, 3. ed., 1919; Vol. III, 2. ed., 1919; Vol. IV, 1. ed., 1920; Vol. V, 2. ed., 1920; Vol. VI, 3. ed., 1931; Vol. VII, 1. ed., 1921; Vol. VIII, 3. ed., 1931, St. Louis: Herder & Co., 1919-1931.

Ayrinhac, H. A., *Administrative Legislation in the New Code of Canon Law,* New York: Longmans, Green and Co., 1930.

———, -Lydon, P. J., *Penal Legislation in the New Code of Canon Law,* rev. ed., New York: Benziger Bros., Inc., 1944.

Badii, C., *Institutiones Iuris Canonici,* 2 vols., Florentiae: Libreria Editrice Fiorentina, 1921-1922.

Barbosa, Augustinus, *De Officio et Potestate Parochi, Animadversiones et Addimenta Ubaldi Giraldi,* Romae, 1831.

———, *Iuris Ecclesiastici Universi Libri Tres,* 3 vols., Lugdini, 1660.

Bastnagel, Clement V., *The Appointment of Parochial Adjutants and Assistants,* The Catholic University of America Canon Law Studies, n. 58, Washington, D. C.: The Catholic University of America, 1930.

Bernardus Papiensis, *Summa Decretalium,* ed. E. Laspeyres, Ratisbonae, 1860.

Berutti, Crisostomo, *Institutiones Iuris Canonici,* 6 vols. in 7, Vol. II, pars I, Taurini-Romae: Marietti, 1943.

Beste, Udalricus, *Introductio in Codicem,* 2. ed., Collegeville, Minn.: St. John's Abbey Press, 1944.

Blat, A., *Commentarium Textus Codicis Iuris Canonici,* 5 vols. in 7, Lib. I, *Normae Generales,* 1921; Lib. III, *De Rebus,* Partes II-VI, 1923, Romae: Collegio "Angelico," 1921-1927.

Boffa, Conrad, *Canonical Provisions for Catholic Schools,* The Catholic University of America Canon Law Studies, n. 117, Washington, D. C.: The Catholic University of America Press, 1939.

Bouix, D., *Tractatus de Parocho,* 3. ed., Parisiis, 1880.

Bouscaren, T. L., -Ellis, Adam C., *Canon Law,* Milwaukee, Wis.: Bruce Publishing Co., 1946.

Canavan, Walter, *The Profession of Faith,* The Catholic University of America Canon Law Studies, n. 151, Washington, D. C.: The Catholic University of America Press, 1942.

Cance, Adrien, *Le Code de Droit Canonique,* 7. ed., 3 vols., Paris: Librairie LeCoffre, 1946.

Cappello, Felix M., *Summa Iuris Canonici,* 3 vols., Romae: Apud Aedes

Universitatis Gregorianae, 1932-1936. Vol. I, 2. ed., 1932; Vol. II, 2. ed., 1934; Vol. III, 1936.

———, *Tractatus Canonico-Moralis de Sacramentis,* 3 vols. in 5, Vol. III, 3. ed. 1933, Taurinorum Augustae-Romae: Apud Marietti et Aedes Universitatis Gregorianae, 1932-1938.

Catholic Encyclopedia, The, 15 vols. with Index and 2 Supplements, New York, 1907-1922.

Chelodi, J., *Ius Canonicum de Delictis et Poenis et de Iudiciis Criminalibus,* 5. ed. a P. Ciprotti recognita et aucta, Trento: Libreria Moderna Editrice, 1943.

———, *Ius Canonicum de Personis,* 3. ed., curavit P. Ciprotti, Trento: Libreria Moderna Editrice, 1942.

Cicognani, Amleto, *Canon Law,* 2. rev. ed., authorized English version by J. M. O'Hara and Francis Brennan, Westminster, Maryland: The Newman Bookshop, 1946.

Ciesluk, J. E., *National Parishes in the United States,* The Catholic University of America Canon Law Studies, n. 190, Washington, D. C.: The Catholic University of America Press, 1944.

Claeys-Bouuaert, F., *De Canonica Cleri Saecularis Obedientia,* Lovanii, 1904.

Clarke, T. J., *Parish Registers,* The Catholic University of America Canon Law Studies, n. 176, Washington, D. C.: The Catholic University of America Press, 1943.

Coady, John, *The Appointment of Pastors,* The Catholic University of America Canon Law Studies, n. 52, Washington, D. C.: The Catholic University of America, 1929.

Cocchi, G., *Commentarium in Codicem Iuris Canonici,* 8 vols. in 5, Vol. I, Lib. I, *Normae Generales,* 5. ed. recognita, 1938; Vol. VI, Lib. III, *De Rebus,* Partes IV-VI, 5. ed. recognita, 1947; Vol. VIII, Lib. V, *De Delictis et Poenis,* 4. ed. recognita, 1938, Torino: Marietti, 1932-1947.

Coronata, Matthaeus Conte a, *Institutiones Iuris Canonici,* 2. ed., 5 vols., Taurini: Marietti, 1939-1947.

———, *Institutiones Iuris Canonici de Sacramentis,* 3 vols., Taurini-Romae: Domus Editorialis Marietti, 1943-1946.

D'Annibale, J., *Summula Theologiae Moralis,* 3. ed., 3 vols., Romae, 1892.

De Becker, J., *Praelectiones Canonicae de Matrimonio,* ed. nova, Louvain: Etabliss. Fr. Ceuterick, 1931.

De Meester, A., *Juris Canonici et Juris Canonico-Civilis Compendium,* nova ed., 3 vols. in 4, Brugis: Desclée, De Brouwer, 1921-1928.

Donnellan, T., *The Obligation of the* MISSA PRO POPULO, The Catholic University of America Canon Law Studies, n. 155, Washington, D. C.: The Catholic University of America Press, 1942.

DuCange, Carolus du Fresne, *Glossarium Mediae et Infimae Latinitatis,* 9. ed., 10 vols., Paris: Librairie des Sciences et des Arts, 1938.

Eichmann, E., *Das Strafrecht des* CODEX IURIS CANONICI, Paderborn: Druck und Verlag von Ferdinand Schöningh, 1920.

———, *Lehrbuch des Kirchenrechts,* 2. ed., Paderborn: Druck und Verlag von Ferdinand Schöningh, 1926.

Engel, Ludovicus, *Collegium Universi Iuris Canonici,* 9. ed., cum annotationibus Caspari Barthel, Beneventi, 1760.

Fanfani, L., *De Iure Parochorum,* Taurini-Romae: Marietti, 1924.

Ferraris, Lucius, *Prompta Bibliotheca Canonica, Iuridica, Moralis, Theologica, necnon Ascetica, Polemica, Rubristica, Hsitorica,* 9 vols., Romae, 1885-1899.

Ferreres, J., *Institutiones Canonicae,* 2. ed., 2 vols., Barcinone: Eugenius Subirana, 1920.

Ferry, W., *Stole Fees,* The Catholic University of America Canon Law Studies, n. 59, Washington, D. C.: The Catholic University of America, 1930.

Fuchs, Vinzenz, *Der Ordinationstitel von seiner Entstehung bis auf Innozenz III,* Bonn: Kurt Schroeder Verlag, 1930.

Galvin, W. A., *The Administrative Transfer of Pastors,* The Catholic University of America Canon Law Studies, n. 232, Washington, D. C.: The Catholic University of America Press, 1946.

Garcia, Nicholaus, *De Beneficiis Ecclesiasticis,* Venetiis, 1618.

Golden, H., *Parochial Benefices in the New Code,* The Catholic University of America Canon Law Studies, n. 10, Washington, D. C.: The Catholic University of America, 1921.

Gonzalez-Tellez, Manuel, *Commentaria in Quinque Libros Decretalium,* 5 vols., Venetiis, 1699.

Goodwine, John, *The Right of the Church to Acquire Property,* The Catholic University of America Canon Law Studies, n. 131, Washington, D. C.: The Catholic University of America Press, 1941.

Haydt, John J., *Reserved Benefices,* The Catholic University of America Canon Law Studies, n. 161, Washington, D. C.: The Catholic University of America Press, 1942.

Hefele, Charles-Clark, Wm., *A History of the Councils of the Church,* 2. ed., 5 vols., Edinburg, 1883-1896.

Hinschius, Paul, *System des katholischen Kirchenrechts,* 6 vols., Berlin, 1869-1897.

Hostiensis (Henricus de Segusio), *Commentaria in Quinque Libros Decretalium,* 5 vols. in 3, Venetiis, 1581.

———, *Summa Aurea,* Venetiis, 1570.

Ioannes Andreae, *In Decretalium Libros Novella Commentaria,* 5 vols., Venetiis, 1584.

Jansen, R., *Canonical Provisions for Catechetical Instructions,* The Catholic University of America Canon Law Studies, n. 107, Washington, D. C.: The Catholic University of America, 1937.

Kelly, B., *The Functions Reserved to Pastors,* The Catholic University of America Canon Law Studies, n. 250, Washington, D. C.: The Catholic University of America Press, 1947.

Koudelka, C., *Pastors, Their Rights and Duties According to the New*

Code of Canon Law, The Catholic University of America Canon Law Studies, n. 11, Washington, D. C.: The Catholic University of America, 1921.

Leurenius, Petrus, *Forum Beneficiale,* 2 vols., Venetiis, 1752.

Lexikon für Theologie und Kirche, 10 vols., Freiburg im Breisgau: Herder & Co. G. M. B. H. Verlagsbuchhandlung, 1930-1938.

Maroto, P., *Institutiones Iuris Canonici,* 2 vols., Vol. I, 3. ed., 1921, Madrid: Editorial del Corazón de Maria, 1919-1921.

Martin, T., *Adverse Possession, Prescription and Limitation of Actions. The Canonical* "PRAESCRIPTIO," The Catholic University of America Canon Law Studies, n. 202, Washington, D. C.: The Catholic University of America Press, 1944.

McDevitt, G. V., *The Renunciation of an Ecclesiastical Office,* The Catholic University of America Canon Law Studies, n. 218, Washington, D. C.: The Catholic University of America Press, 1946.

Miaskiewicz, F., *Supplied Jurisdiction According to Canon 209,* The Catholic University of America Canon Law Studies, n. 122, Washington, D. C.: The Catholic University of America Press, 1940.

Michiels, G., *Normae Generales Iuris Canonici,* 2 vols., Lublin, Polonia: Universitas Catholica, 1929.

Migne, J. P., *Patrologiae Cursus Completus, Series Graeca,* 161 vols., Parisiis, 1857-1866.

———, *Patrologiae Cursus Completus, Series Latina,* 221 vols., Parisiis, 1844-1864.

Mourret, F.-Thompson, N., *A History of the Catholic Church,* 6 vols., St. Louis: Herder Book Co., 1930-1946.

Nabuco, J., *Pontificalis Romani Exposito Juridico-Practica,* 3 vols., Petropoli, Brasilia: Sumptibus Editora Vozes Ltda., 1945.

Nicholaus de Tudeschis (Abbas Panormitanus), *Commentaria in Quinque Libros Decretalium,* 5 vols. in 8, Venetiis, 1581-1588.

Ojetti, B., *Commentarium in Codicem Iuris Canonici,* 4 vols., Vol. I, *Normae Generales* (1927), Romae: Apud Aedes Universitatis Gregorianae, 1927-1931.

O'Rourke, J. J., *Parish Registers,* The Catholic University of America Canon Law Studies, n. 88, Washington, D. C.: The Catholic University of America, 1934.

Peltier, A.-Migne, *Dictionnaire des Conciles,* 2 vols., Parisiis, 1847.

Pirhing, Ernricus, *Ius Canonicum in Quinque Libros Decretalium Distributum,* 5 vols. in 4, Dilingae, 1674-1678.

Pistocchi, M., *De Re Beneficiali,* Taurini: Marietti, 1928.

———, *I Canoni Penali del Codice Ecclesiastico,* Torino-Roma: Marietti, 1925.

Prümmer, D., *Manuale Iuris Canonici,* 5. ed., Friburgi Brisgoviae: Herder & Co., 1927.

Raia, S., *De Parochis,* Roma: Desclée, 1921.

Ramstein, M., *A Manual of Canon Law*, Hoboken, N. J.: Terminal Printing and Publishing Co., 1947.

Raus, J. B., *Institutiones Canonicae*, 2. ed., Parisiis: Typis Emmanuelis Vitte, 1931.

Reiffenstuel, Anacletus, *Ius Canonicum Universum*, 5 vols. in 7, Parisiis, 1864-1870.

Reilly, P., *Residence of Pastors*, The Catholic University of America Canon Law Studies, n. 97, Washington, D. C.: The Catholic University of America, 1935.

Rossi, J., *De Paroecia*, Romae: Pustet, 1923.

Rufinus, *Summa Decretorum*, ed. H. Singer, Paderborn, 1902.

Ryder, R., *Simony*, The Catholic University of America Canon Law Studies, n. 65, Washington, D. C.: The Catholic University of America, 1931.

Sägmüller, Johannes B., *Lehrbuch des katholischen Kirchenrechts*, 4 ed., Freiburg im Breisgau: Herdersche Verlagshandlung, 1925-1934.

Salucci, R., *Il Diritto Penale*, 2 vols., Subiaco: Tipografia dei Monasteri, 1926-1930.

Santi, Franciscus, *Praelectiones Iuris Canonici*, 2. ed., 5 vols. in 2, Ratisbonae, 1892.

Scharnagl, Anton, *Der Begriff der Investitur in den Quellen und der Literatur des Investiturstreites*, Kirchenrechtliche Abhandlungen, hrsg. von U. Stutz, 56 Heft, Stuttgart: Verlag Enke, 1908.

Schmalzgrueber, Franciscus, *Ius Ecclesiasticum Universum*, 5 vols. in 12, Romae, 1843-1845.

Sebastianelli, Gulielmus, *Praelectiones Iuris Canonici*, 2. ed., 3 vols., Romae, 1905.

Sipos, Stephanus, *Enchiridion Iuris Canonici*, 4 ed., Pećs: Ex Typographia "Haladas R. T.," 1940.

Stutz, Ulrich, "The Proprietary Church as an Element of Medieval Germanic Ecclesiastical Law," *Studies in Medieval History, Medieval Germany (911-1250)*, translated by Geoffrey Barraclough, 2 vols., Oxford: Blackwell, 1938.

Toso, A., *Ad Codicem Iuris Canonici Commentaria Minora*, 5 vols., Romae: Marietti, 1920-1927.

Van Hove, A., *Commentarium Lovaniense in Codicem Iuris Canonici*, 5 toms., Tom. I, *Prolegomena*, 2. ed., 1945; Tom. II, *De Legibus Ecclesiasticis*, 1930, Mechliniae: Dessain, 1930-1945.

Vermeersch, A.-Creusen, J., *Epitome Iuris Canonici*, 6. ed., 3 vols., Mechliniae-Romae: H. Dessain, 1937-1946.

Victor a Jesu Maria (Tirado), *De Iurisdictionis Acceptione in Iure Ecclesiastico*, Romae: Soc. Tip. A. Manuzio, 1940.

Vinogradoff, Sir Paul, "Feudalism," *The Cambridge Medieval History*, planned by J. Bury and edited by Gwatkin and Whitney, 8 vols., New York: Macmillan & Co., 1911-1936.

Wernz, F. X., *Ius Decretalium*, 3. ed., 6 vols., Prati, 1913-1915.

———, -Vidal, P., *Ius Canonicum*, 7 vols. in 9. Tom. II, *De Personis*, 3. ed.

a P. Aguirre recognita, 1943; Tom IV, *De Rebus,* Vol. II, 1935; Tom. VII, *Ius Poenale Ecclesiasticum,* 1937, Romae: Apud Aedes Universitatis Gregorianae, 1927-1946.

Woywod, S., *A Practical Commentary on the Code of Canon Law,* 7. ed. revised by Callistus Smith, 2 vols., New York: Joseph F. Wagner, Inc., 1945.

ARTICLES

Benedetti, I., "Presa di Possesso"—*Perfice Munus!,* IV (1929), 365.

Biccari, S., "Giuramento e Possesso"—*Perfice Munus!,* III (1928), 541.

———, "Presa di Possesso"—*Perfice Munus!,* III (1928), 227-228, 542-543.

Cappello, F., "De Vicario Substituto"—*Periodica,* XIX (1930), 1*-10*.

Claeys-Bouuaert, F., "De Vicariis Substitutis"—*Jus Pontificium,* VII (1927), 72-81.

D'Angelo, S., "De Possessione Beneficii"—*Apollinaris,* I (1928), 411-415.

———, "De Professione Fidei"—*Apollinaris,* I (1928), 415-417.

Goyeneche, S., "An Canon 461 Applicandus Sit Parochis Religiosis"—*Commentarium pro Religiosis,* VI (1925), 484-486.

———, "An Valida Sint necne Acta a Superiore Maiore Posita, Qui necdum Fidei Professionem Emisit?"—*Commentarium pro Religiosis,* XIII (1932), 265.

Hanrahan, P. J., "The Induction of Parish Priests"—*The Clergy Review,* IX (1939), 338-340.

Löffler, Klemens, "Conflict of Investitures," *The Catholic Encyclopedia,* VIII (1910), 84-89.

Maroto, P., "De Missa pro Populo"—*Apollinaris,* VI (1933), 421-431.

Park, Charles, "The Necessity of Installation of Pastors," *The Homiletic and Pastoral Review,* XXXV (1935), 579-592.

Roelker, E., "The Interpretation of Invalidating Laws"—*The Jurist,* III (1943), 364-403.

———, "The Power to Enact Invalidating Laws"—*The Jurist,* III (1943), 231-257.

Romani, S., "Be Beneficiis Paroecialibus Conferendis"—*Ius Pontificum,* XIII (1933), 88-96, 172-185.

Schaaf, Valentine, "Corporal Installation of Pastors," *The Ecclesiastical Review,* XCI (1934), 620-624.

Wasner, F., "De Institutione Corporali in Jure Canonico. Delibatio Juridico-Historica"—*Jus Pontificium,* XVII (1937), 131-143.

Woywod, S., "Law of the Code on Benefices"—*The Homiletic and Pastoral Review,* XXIX (1929), 386-394.

Anonymous, "Parishes Without Boundaries"—*The Ecclesiastical Review,* LXXXIII (1930), 391-397.

Anonymous, "De die qua Parochus existimandus sit adeptus esse Possessionem Beneficii, vel Officium inivisse ut Matrimoniis in Paroecia valide assistat"—*Periodica,* V (1913), 184, n. 427A.

Anonymous, "Uber den Sinn 'adepta possessio' im Ehedekret 'Ne temere' vom 2. Aug. 1907"—*Archiv für katholisches Kirchenrecht,* LXXXIX (1909), 327-329.

PERIODICALS

American Ecclesiastical Review, The, Philadelphia, 1889-1943; Washington, 1944—. From Vol. XXXIII (1905) to Vol. CIX (1943), *The Ecclesiastical Review.*

Apollinaris, Romae, 1928—

Archiv für katholisches Kirchenrecht, Innsbruck, 1857-1861; Mainz, 1862—

Clergy Review, The, London, 1931—

Commentarium pro Religiosis, Romae, 1920-1934; from 1935, *Commentarium pro Religiosis et Missionariis.*

Homiletic and Pastoral Review, The, New York, 1900—

Jurist, The, Washington, D. C., 1941—

Jus Pontificium, Romae, 1921-1940.

Perfice Munus!, Torino, 1926—

Periodica de Re Morali, Canonica, Liturgica, Brugis, 1905-1936; Romae, 1937—. 8 vols., from 1905 to 1919, *Periodica de Religiosis et Missionariis*; 7 vols., from 1920 to 1927, *Periodica de Re Canonica et Morali utili praesertim Religiosis et Missionariis.*

ABBREVIATIONS

AAS—*Acta Apostolicae Sedis.*
AER—*The American Ecclesiastical Review.*
ASS—*Acta Sanctae Sedis.*
Bruns—*Canones Apostolorum et Conciliorum Saeculorum IV-VII.*
Collectanea—*Collectanea Sacrae Congregationis de Propaganda Fide.*
Coll. Lac.—*Collectio Lacensis.*
ER—*The Ecclesiastical Review.*
Ferraris—*Prompta Bibliotheca Canonica, etc.*
Fontes—*Codicis Iuris Canonici Fontes . . . cura . . . Gasparri editi.*
Hardouin—*Acta Conciliorum et Epistolae Decretales, etc.*
Hefele—*A History of the Councils of the Church.*
HPR—*The Homiletic and Pastoral Review.*
Jaffé—*Regesta Pontificum Romanorum, etc.*
Mansi—*Sacrorum Conciliorum Nova et Amplissima Collectio.*
MGH—*Monumenta Germaniae Historica.*
MPG—Migne, *Patrologia Graeca.*
MPL—Migne, *Patrologia Latina.*
Pallottini—*Collectio Omnium Conclusionum et Resolutionum, etc.*
P. C. I.—Pontifical Commission for the Authentic Interpretation of the Code.
Periodica—*Periodica de Re Morali, Canonica, Liturgica, etc.*
Potthast—*Regesta Pontificum Romanorum, etc.*
S. C. C.—Sacred Congregation of the Council.
S. C. Consist.—Sacred Congregation of the Consistory.
S. C. de Prop. Fide—Sacred Congregation for the Propagation of the Faith.
S. C. Ep. et Reg.—Sacred Congregation of Bishops and Regulars.
S. C. S. Off.—Sacred Congregation of the Holy Office.
S. R. C.—Sacred Congregation of Rites.
Thesaurus—*Thesaurus Resolutionum Sacrae Congregationis Concilii.*

ALPHABETICAL INDEX

Acting vicars, 43, 77.
  and installations, 78.
Adjutant vicars, 82-83.
Administration of the goods of the parish, 159 sq.
Administrators,
  of parishes, 40, 81.
  of temporal goods, 159, 160.
  of vacant sees, 32, 126.
Archdeacons,
  abuse of power, 23, 26.
  duties of, 28-29.
  lessening of authority, 32, 46, 53, 127.
  rights of, 25, 28-29, 31, 37, 53.
Assistant pastors, 84.
Authors, 186.

Bad faith, 45.
Benefices, 5, 86.
  and moral persons, 79.
  definition of, 86.
  incompatible, 162.
  non-consistorial, 119, 126.
  origin and history of, 8, 13, 21.
  parishes in U. S. as, 74.
  rights and duties connected with, 139 sq., 154.
Bibliography, 184.

Canonical installation, 67.
  and assistance at marriage, 99.
  definition of, 67-70.
  essential part of *provisio,* 96.
  integral part of *provisio,* 70.
  in various offices, 71.
  see also Installation.
Canonica provisio, 68 sq.
  see also Institution.
Carolingian reform, 16.
Chorepiscopi, 3, 10.
Collatio,
  meaning of, 6, 34, 36, 56, 58.
  see also *institutio tituli collativa,* or conferral of office.
Common error, 111.
Conclusions, 175.
  concerning doctrine of commentators, 63.
  concerning necessity of installation, 102.
  concerning penalties, 116.
  general, 175.
Concordat of Worms, 22.
Conferral of office, 67-68, 164.
Confirmation in office, 32, 34, 36, 38, 68.
  see also *institutio auctorizabilis.*
Cura animarum, 72, 87, 121, 139 sq.
Customs, 107.
  concerning manner of installation, 54.
  concerning validity of possession, 62, 97, 103.
  contrary to law, 108, 110.
  immemorial, 109, 110, 134.
  ordinary, 108-109.

Deans, 50, 127, 161, 177.
Delegated installing officer, 88, 127, 132.
Dispensation, 88, 104-106, 130.
  express, 105.
  implicit, 105.
  just cause for, 104.
  presumed, 106.
  tacit, 105.
  written, 106.
Disqualifying law, 92, 116.
Dubium iuris, 103.

Effects of installation, 138 sq.
Equivalently invalidating law, 93-95, 111.
Excommunication, 19, 46.
Expressly invalidating law, 93-95.

Faith, profession of, 131 sq., 141.
Force, use of, 32, 57, 61, 113.
Forms, 182.
  formal installation, 177.
  informal installation, 181.
  profession of faith, 41.
  substantial, 94, 95.

Good faith, 35, 45, 166, 169.
Gratian, Decree of, 8, 11.
Gregorian reform, 18.

Gregory IX, 26.

Impediments to installation, 130.
Incompatible benefices, 162.
Installation, 67.
  and assistance at marriage, 99.
  by proxy, 29, 135.
  canonical, 67, 139.
  corporal, 67, 69.
  definition of, 67.
  elements of, 125.
  formal, 122, 177.
  informal, 45, 122, 181.
  in the Council of Trent, 39.
  manner of, 54, 119 sq.
  necessity of, 54, 86, 96.
    for licitness, 55, 59, 89 sq.
    for validity, 55, 59, 89 sq.
  origin of term, 5.
  purpose of, 70, 87, 88, 120.
  rite of, 120, 177.
  symbols of, 124, 178.
  time of, 128 sq., 178.
  time within which it must take place, 128 sq.
  verbal, 57, 58, 61, 97, 123.
Installing officer, 50, 126.
  delegate as, 50, 127, 132.
  layman as, 121, 127.
  vicar capitular as, 126.
  vicar general as, 126, 131.
Institutio, 6, 36, 67, 68.
  auctorizabilis, 6, 34, 38.
  corporalis, 6, 25, 38, 67.
  meaning of, 6, 36, 85.
  realis et actualis, 6, 34, 46, 57, 58.
  tituli collativa, 6, 25, 34, 38.
Institution in office, 29, 30, 33, 34, 36, 55, 68.
Intrusion in office, 113.
  see also usurpation.
Invalidating laws, 92, 103.
Investiture, 6, 37, 67.
  decrees against lay, 19, 20, 21, 26, 27, 46.
  evils of lay, 17, 19, 22.
  forms of, 14, 15, 44.
  in re absenti, 30, 37.
  in re praesenti, 30, 37.
  meaning of, 6, 30, 34, 37.
  symbols of, 15, 54, 58, 124.
Ius ad rem, 56, 59, 69, 101, 113.
Ius in re, 56, 58, 59, 61, 69, 97, 101, 113, 114.
Ius patronatus, 21, 24, 27, 38, 40.

Juridic effects of installation, 138 sq.

Laity and installation, 121-123, 177.

Missio in possessionem, 6, 25, 67, 86.
  see installation, corporal.
Modernism, oath against, 50-52, 125, 134.
Moral person, 72, 77, 79.

Notary, 48, 178, 180.
Notification of installation, 124, 180, 181.

Oath against Modernism, 50-52, 125, 134.
Obligations of pastors, 139, 141, 154, 159.
Ordinary, the local, 126.
  authority of, 126, 129, 131.
  delegate of, 126, 131.

Parallelism, 98, 99.
Parish, 72, 74.
  as a benefice in U. S., 74.
  definition of, 74.
  union with moral body, 77.
Parish priest, 72.
  in the U. S., 73, 75.
Parish registers, 151-153.
Parochial vicars, 71.
Parochus, 5, 72.
Parsimonial rights, 154.
Pastor, 72.
  and installation, 72, 75.
  definition of, 5, 72.
  income of, 154.
  origin of term, 5, 72.
  residence of, 74, 142, 154.
  rights and obligations of, 138 sq.
Pastoral office, 71.
  and installation, 71.
  as a benefice, 87.
  in the U. S., 73.
  origin of, 4, 9-11, 39.
Pastoral vigilance, 148.
Patrimonial rights, 154.
Peaceful possession of office, 35, 165, 167.
Penal sanctions, 46, 110, 144, 158, 160, 163.
  for absence from parish, 142.
  for omitting installation, 100, 111.
  for omitting profession of faith, 133-134.

for simony, 171.
for usurpation of office, 100, 111.
Petitory action, 164, 165.
Possession of office, 164.
canonical, 139, 177.
corporal, 31, 60, 62.
of more than one, 29, 45, 162.
peaceful, 35, 164, 165, 166, 167.
time of, 121, 139, 143.
Prescription, 35, 45, 166.
Presentation to office, 67.
meaning of, 36, 67.
Presumed dispensation, 106.
Presumption of law, 164, 165.
Procurator, use of, 132, 135, 136, 141.
layman as, 137.
Profession of faith, 41, 42, 49, 51, 125, 131, 141.
accepted by layman, 132.
by proxy, 132, 137.
for validity of installation, 133.
Proprietary church, 12-14.
Proxy, use of, 130, 132, 135, 136, 141.
cause necessary for, 136.
layman as, 137.

Quasi-pastors, 75-76.
Quasi-patrimonial rights, 155.

Record of installation, 124, 180, 181.
Renunciation of office, 129, 142, 162.
Rite of installation, 120, 177.
Rural deans, 50, 127, 161, 177.

Simony, 171.
in obtaining office, 18, 22, 40, 47, 49, 128, 171.
penalties for, 171.
Sources, 184.
Substantial form, 98.
Substitute vicar, 82.

Tacit dispensation, 105.
Tacit renunciation of office, 129, 142, 162.
Time of installation, 128, 178.
for prescription, 169.
within which it must be held, 128-130.
Title of possession, 45, 48, 57, 72, 114, 121, 164, 170.
colored, 167, 170.
invalid, 166, 167, 170.
Transfer of pastors, 120.

Usurpation of office, 11, 15, 32, 57, 59, 61, 100, 110, 112, 114.
penalties against, 100, 110.

Vacant *de facto*, 70, 113.
Vacant *de iure*, 70, 113, 121, 164, 166.
Vicar capitular, 126.
Vicar general, 126, 131.
Vicarii curati, 43, 77.
Vicarius cooperator, 84.
Vicarius oeconomus, 40, 81.
Vicars regular, 44, 77, 80.

Witnesses, 125, 153, 182, 183.
Written dispensation, 106.

BIBLIOGRAPHICAL NOTE

Frederick William Freking was born on August 11, 1913, at Heron Lake, Minnesota. He received his elementary schooling at Sacred Heart Grade School and his secondary education at the Public High School of that city. In the fall of 1930 he entered St. Mary's College in Winona, Minnesota, and was graduated from that institution with the degree of Baccalaureate of Arts in June, 1934.

In the fall of that year he entered the North American College in Rome, and completed his philosophical and theological courses at the Gregorian University in June, 1939. He was ordained to the priesthood at St. Ignatius Church in Rome on July 31, 1938, for service in the Diocese of Winona.

He was engaged in parish work in that Diocese for six years. During that time he was also Superintendent of Lourdes High School at Rochester, Minnesota, from 1941 to 1943, and the first Editor of the Winonan Edition of Our Sunday Visitor from 1943 to 1945. He enrolled in the School of Canon Law at the Catholic University of America in September, 1945, and received the degree of Baccalaureate in Canon Law in June, 1946, and the degree of Licentiate in Canon Law in June, 1947.

CANON LAW STUDIES*

1. Freriks, Rev. Celestine A., C.PP.S., J.C.D., Religious Congregations in Their External Relations, 121 pp., 1916.
2. Galliher, Rev. Daniel M., O.P., J.C.D., Canonical Elections, 117 pp., 1917.
3. Borkowski, Rev. Aurelius L., O.F.M., J.C.D., De Confraternitatibus Ecclesiasticis, 136 pp., 1918.
4. Castillo, Rev. Cayo, J.C.D., Disertacion Historico-Canonica sobre la Potestad del Cabildo en Sede Vacante o Impedida del Vicario Capitular, 99 pp., 1919 (1918).
5. Kubelbeck, Rev. William J., S.T.B., J.C.D., The Sacred Penitentiaria and Its Relation to Faculties of Ordinaries and Priests, 129 pp., 1918.
6. Petrovits, Rev. Joseph J. C., S.T.D., J.C.D., The New Church Law on Matrimony, X-461 pp., 1919.
7. Hickey, Rev. John J., S.T.B., J.C.D., Irregularities and Simple Impediments in the New Code of Canon Law, 100 pp., 1920.
8. Klekotka, Rev. Peter J., S.T.B., J.C.D., Diocesan Consultors, 179 pp., 1920.
9. Wanenmacher, Rev. Francis, J.C.D., The Evidence in Ecclesiastical Procedure Affecting the Marriage Bond, 1920 (Printed 1935).
10. Golden, Rev. Henry Francis, J.C.D., Parochial Benefices in the New Code, IV-119 pp., 1921 (Printed 1925).
11. Koudelka, Rev. Charles J., J.C.D., Pastors, Their Rights and Duties According to the New Code of Canon Law, 211 pp., 1921.
12. Melo, Rev. Antonius, O.F.M., J.C.D., De Exemptione Regularium, X-188 pp., 1921.
13. Schaaf, Rev. Valentine Theodore, O.F.M., S.T.B., J.C.D., The Cloister, X-180 pp., 1921.
14. Burke, Rev. Thomas Joseph, S.T.D., J.C.D., Competence in Ecclesiastical Tribunals, IV-117 pp., 1922.
15. Leech, Rev. George Leo, J.C.D., A Comparative Study of the Constitution "Apostolicae Sedis" and the "Codex Juris Canonici," 179 pp., 1922.
16. Motry, Rev. Hubert Louis, S.T.D., J.C.D., Diocesan Faculties According to the Code of Canon Law, II-167 pp., 1922.
17. Murphy, Rev. George Lawrence, J.C.D., Delinquencies and Penalties in the Administration and the Reception of the Sacraments, IV-121 pp., 1923.
18. O'Reilly, Rev. John Anthony, S.T.B., J.C.D., Ecclesiastical Sepulture in the New Code of Canon Law, II-129 pp., 1923.

* All published numbers of this series are available from the Catholic University Press, 621 Michigan Avenue, N.E., Washington 17, D.C., except the following Nos. 1-114 inclusive, 116, 118, 120, 122, 123, 136, 162 and 198.

19. Michalicka, Rev. Wenceslas Cyrill, O.S.B., J.C.D., Judicial Procedure in Dismissal of Clerical Exempt Religious, 107 pp., 1923.
20. Dargin, Rev. Edward Vincent, S.T.B., J.C.D., Reserved Cases According to the Code of Canon Law, IV-103 pp., 1924.
21. Godfrey, Rev. John A., S.T.B., J.C.D., The Right of Patronage According to the Code of Canon Law, 153 pp., 1924.
22. Hagedorn, Rev. Francis Edward, J.C.D., General Legislation on Indulgences, II-154 pp., 1924.
23. King, Rev. James Ignatius, J.C.D., The Administration of the Sacraments to Dying Non-Catholics, V-141 pp., 1924.
24. Winslow, Rev. Francis Joseph, M.M., J.C.D., Vicars and Prefects Apostolic, IV-149 pp., 1924.
25. Correa, Rev. Jose Servelion, S.T.L., J.C.D., Lo Potestad Legislativa de la Iglesia Catolica, IV-127 pp., 1925.
26. Dugan, Rev. Henry Francis, A.M., J.C.D., The Judiciary Department of the Diocesan Curia, 87 pp., 1925.
27. Keller, Rev. Charles Frederick, S.T.B., J.C.D., Mass Stipends, 167 pp., 1925.
28. Paschang, Rev. John Linus, J.C.D., The Sacramentals According to the Code of Canon Law, 129 pp., 1925.
29. Piontek, Rev. Cyrillus, O.F.M., S.T.B., J.C.D., De Indulto Exclaustrationis necnon Saecularizationis, XIII-289 pp., 1925.
30. Kearney, Rev. Richard Joseph, S.T.B., J.C.D., Sponsors at Baptism According to the Code of Canon Law, IV-127 pp., 1925.
31. Bartlett, Rev. Chester Joseph, A.M., LL.B., J.C.D., The Tenure of Parochial Property in the United States of America, V-108 pp., 1926.
32. Kilker, Rev. Adrian Jerome, J.C.D., Extreme Unction, V-425 pp., 1926.
33. McCormick, Rev. Robert Emmett, J.C.D., Confessors of Religious, VIII-266 pp., 1926.
34. Miller, Rev. Newton Thomas, J.C.D., Founded Masses According to the Code of Canon Law, VII-93 pp., 1926.
35. Roelker, Rev. Edward G., S.T.D., J.C.D., Principles of Privilege According to the Code of Canon Law, XI-166 pp., 1926.
36. Bakalarczyk, Rev. Richardus, M.I.C., J.U.D., De Novitiatu, VIII-208 pp., 1927.
37. Pizzuti, Rev. Lawrence, O.F.M., J.U.L., De Parochis Religiosis, 1927. (Not Printed.)
38. Bliley, Rev. Nicholas Martin, O.S.B., J.C.D., Altars According to the Code of Canon Law, XIX-132 pp., 1927.
39. Brown, Mr. Brendan Francis, A.B., LL.M., J.U.D., The Canonical Juristic Personality with Special Reference to its Status in the United States of America, V-212 pp., 1927.
40. Cavanaugh, Rev. William Thomas, C.P., J.U.D., The Reservation of the Blessed Sacrament, VIII-101 pp., 1927.
41. Doheny, Rev. William J., C.S.C., A.B., J.U.D., Church Property: Modes of Acquisition, X-118 pp., 1927.

42. FELDHAUS, REV. ALOYSIUS H., C.PP.S., J.C.D., Oratories, IX-141 pp., 1927.
43. KELLY, REV. JAMES PATRICK, A.B., J.C.D., The Jurisdiction of the Simple Confessor, X-208 pp., 1927.
44. NEUBERGER, REV. NICHOLAS J., J.C.D., Canon 6 or the Relation of the Codex Juris Canonici to the Preceding Legislation, V-95 pp., 1927.
45. O'KEEFE, REV. GERALD MICHAEL, J.C.D., Matrimonial Dispensations, Powers of Bishops, Priests, and Confessors, VIII-232 pp., 1927.
46. QUIGLEY, REV. JOSEPH A. M., A.B., J.C.D., Condemned Societies, 139 pp., 1927.
47. ZAPLOTNIK, REV. JOHANNES LEO, J.C.D., De Vicariis Foraneis, X-142 pp., 1927.
48. DUSKIE, REV. JOHN ALOYSIUS, A.B., J.C.D., The Canonical Status of the Orientals in the United States, VIII-196 pp., 1928.
49. HYLAND, REV. FRANCIS EDWARD, J.C.D., Excommunication, Its Nature, Historical Development and Effects, VIII-181 pp., 1928.
50. REINMANN, REV. GERALD JOSEPH, O.M.C., J.C.D., The Third Order Secular of Saint Francis, 201 pp., 1928.
51. SCHENK, REV. FRANCIS J., J.C.D., The Matrimonial Impediments of Mixed Religion and Disparity of Cult, XVI-318 pp., 1929.
52. COADY, REV. JOHN JOSEPH, S.T.D., J.U.D., A.M., The Appointment of Pastors, VIII-150 pp., 1929.
53. KAY, REV. THOMAS HENRY, J.C.D., Competence in Matrimonial Procedure, VIII-164 pp., 1929.
54. TURNER, REV. SIDNEY JOSEPH, C.P., J.U.D., The Vow of Poverty, XLIX-217 pp., 1929.
55. KEARNEY, REV. RAYMOND A., A.B., S.T.D., J.C.D., The Principles of Delegation, VII-149 pp., 1929.
56. CONRAN, REV. EDWARD JAMES, A.B., J.C.D., The Interdict, V-163 pp., 1930.
57. O'NEILL, REV. WILLIAM H., J.C.D., Papal Rescripts of Favor, VII-218 pp., 1930.
58. BASTNAGEL, REV. CLEMENT VINCENT, J.U.D., The Appointment of Parochial Adjutants and Assistants, XV-257 pp., 1930.
59. FERRY, REV. WILLIAM A., A.B., J.C.D., Stole Fees, V-136 pp., 1930.
60. COSTELLO, REV. JOHN MICHAEL, A.B., J.C.D., Domicile and Quasi-Domicile, VII-201 pp., 1930.
61. KREMER, REV. MICHAEL NICHOLAS, A.B., S.T.B., J.C.D., Church Support in the United States, VI-136 pp., 1930.
62. ANGULO, REV. LUIS, C.M., J.C.D., Legislation de la Iglesia sobre la intencion en la application de la Santa Misa, VII-104 pp., 1931.
63. FREY, REV. WOLFGANG NORBERT, O.S.B., A.B., J.C.D., The Act of Religious Profession, VIII-174 pp., 1931.
64. ROBERTS, REV. JAMES BRENDAN, A.B., J.C.D., The Banns of Marriage, XIV-140 pp., 1931.

65. Ryder, Rev. Raymond Aloysius, A.B., J.C.D., Simony, IX-151 pp., 1931.
66. Campagna, Rev. Angelo, Ph.D., J.U.D., Il Vicario Generale del Vescovo, VII-205 pp., 1931.
67. Cox, Rev. Joseph Godfrey, A.B., J.C.D., The Administration of Seminaries, VI-124 pp., 1931.
68. Gregory, Rev. Donald J., J.U.D., The Pauline Privilege, XV-165 pp., 1931.
69. Donohue, Rev. John F., J.C.D., The Impediment of Crime, VII-110 pp., 1931.
70. Dooley, Rev. Eugene A., O.M.I., J.C.D., Church Law on Sacred Relics, IX-143 pp., 1931.
71. Orth, Rev. Clement Raymond, O.M.C., J.C.D., The Approbation of Religious Institutes, 171 pp., 1931.
72. Pernicone, Rev. Joseph M., A.B., J.C.D., The Ecclesiastical Prohibition of Books, XII-267 pp., 1932.
73. Clinton, Rev. Connell, A.B., J.C.D., The Paschal Precept, IX-108 pp., 1932.
74. Donnelly, Rev. Francis B., A.M., S.T.L., J.C.D., The Diocesan Synod, VIII-125 pp., 1932.
75. Torrente, Rev. Camilo, C.M.F., J.C.D., Las Procesiones Sagradas, V-145 pp., 1932.
76. Murphy, Rev. Edwin J., C.PP.S., J.C.D., Suspension Ex Informata Conscientia, XI-122 pp., 1932.
77. MacKenzie, Rev. Eric F., A.M., S.T.L., J.C.D., The Delict of Heresy in its Commission, Penalization, Absolution, VII-124 pp., 1932.
78. Lyons, Rev. Avitus E., S.T.B., J.C.D., The Collegiate Tribunal of First Instance, XI-147 pp., 1932.
79. Connolly, Rev. Thomas A., J.C.D., Appeals, XI-195 pp., 1932.
80. Sangmeister, Rev. Joseph V., A.B., J.C.D., Force and Fear as Precluding Matrimonial Consent, V-211 pp., 1932.
81. Jaeger, Rev. Leo A., A.B., J.C.D., The Administration of Vacant and Quasi-Vacant Episcopal Sees in the United States, IX-229 pp., 1932.
82. Rimlinger, Rev. Herbert T., J.C.D., Error Invalidating Matrimonial Consent, VII-79 pp., 1932.
83. Barrett, Rev. John D. M., S.S., J.C.D., A Comparative Study of the Third Plenary Council of Baltimore and the Code, IX-221 pp., 1932.
84. Carberry, Rev. John J., Ph.D., S.T.D., J.C.D., The Juridical Form of Marriage, X-177 pp., 1934.
85. Dolan, Rev. John L., A.B., J.C.D., The Defensor Vinculi, XII-157 pp., 1934.
86. Hannan, Rev. Jerome D., A.M., S.T.D., LL.B., J.C.D., The Canon Law of Wills, IX-517 pp., 1934.
87. Lemieux, Rev. Delise A., A.M., J.C.D., The Sentence in Ecclesiastical Procedure, IX-131 pp., 1934.

88. O'Rourke, Rev. James J., A.B., J.C.D., Parish Registers, VII-109 pp., 1934.
89. Timlin, Rev. Bartholomew, O.F.M., A.M., J.C.D., Conditional Matrimonial Consent, X-381 pp., 1934.
90. Wahl, Rev. Francis X., A.B., J.C.D., The Matrimonial Impediments of Consanguinity and Affinity, VI-125 pp., 1934.
91. White, Rev. Robert J., A.B., LL.B., S.T.B., J.C.D., Canonical Ante-Nuptial Promises and the Civil Law, VI-152 pp., 1934.
92. Herrera, Rev. Antonio Parra, O.C.D., J.C.D., Legislacion Ecclesiastica sobra el Ayuno y la Abstinencia, XI-191 pp., 1935.
93. Kennedy, Rev. Edwin J., J.C.D., The Special Matrimonial Process in cases of Evident Nullity, X-165 pp., 1935.
94. Manning, Rev. John J., A.B., J.C.D., Presumption of Law in Matrimonial Procedure, XI-111 pp., 1935.
95. Moeder, Rev. John M., J.C.D., The Proper Bishop for Ordination and Dimissorial Letters, VII-135 pp., 1935.
96. O'Mara, Rev. William A., A.B., J.C.D., Canonical Causes for Matrimonial Dispensations, IX-155 pp., 1935.
97. Reilly, Rev. Peter, J.C.D., Residence of Pastors, IX-81 pp., 1935.
98. Smith, Rev. Mariner T., O.P., S.T.Lr., J.C.D., The Penal Law for Religious, VII-169 pp., 1935.
99. Whalen, Rev. Donald W., A.M., J.C.D., The Value of Testimonial Evidence in Matrimonial Procedure, XIII-297 pp., 1935.
100. Cleary, Rev. Joseph F., J.C.D., Canonical Limitations on the Alienation of Church Property, VIII-141 pp., 1936.
101. Glynn, Rev. John C., J.C.D., The Promoter of Justice, XX-337 pp., 1936.
102. Brennan, Rev. James H., S.S., M.A., S.T.B., J.C.D., The Simple Convalidation of Marriage, VI-135 pp., 1937.
103. Brunini, Rev. Joseph Bernard, J.C.D., The Clerical Obligations of Canons 139 and 142, X-121 pp., 1937.
104. Connor, Rev. Maurice, A.B., J.C.D., The Administrative Removal of Pastors, VIII-159 pp., 1937.
105. Guilfoyle, Rev. Merlin Joseph, J.C.D., Custom, XI-144 pp., 1937.
106. Hughes, Rev. James Austin, A.B., A.M., J.C.D., Witnesses in Criminal Trials of Clerics, IX-140 pp., 1937.
107. Jansen, Rev. Raymond J., A.B., S.T.L., J.C.D., Canonical Provisions for Catechetical Instruction, VII-153 pp., 1937.
108. Kealy, Rev. John James, A.B., J.C.D., The Introductory Libellus in Church Court Procedure, XI-121 pp., 1937.
109. McManus, Rev. James Edward, C.SS.R., J.C.D., The Administration of Temporal Goods in Religious Institutes, XVI-196 pp., 1937.
110. Moriarty, Rev. Eugene James, J.C.D., Oaths in Ecclesiastical Courts, X-115 pp., 1937.
111. Rainer, Rev. Eligius George, C.SS.R., J.C.D., Suspension of Clerics, XVII-249 pp., 1937.

112. REILLY, REV. THOMAS F., C.SS.R., J.C.D., Visitation of Religious, VI-195 pp., 1938.

113. MORIARITY, REV. FRANCIS E., C.SS.R., J.C.D., The Extraordinary Absolution from Censures, XV-334 pp., 1938.

114. CONNOLLY, REV. NICHOLAS P., J.C.D., The Canonical Erection of Parishes, X-132 pp., 1938.

115. DONOVAN, REV. JAMES JOSEPH, J.C.D., The Pastor's Obligation in Prenuptial Investigation, XII-322 pp., 1938.

116. HARRIGAN, REV. ROBERT J., M.A., S.T.B., J.C.D., The Radical Sanation of Invalid Marriages, VIII-208 pp., 1938.

117. BOFFA, REV. CONRAD HUMBERT, J.C.D., Canonical Provisions for Catholic Schools, VII-211 pp., 1939.

118. PARSONS, REV. ANSCAR JOHN, O.M.Cap., J.C.D., Canonical Elections, XII-236 pp., 1939.

119. REILLY, REV. EDWARD MICHAEL, A.B., J.C.D., The General Norms of Dispensation, XII-156 pp., 1939.

120. RYAN, REV. GERALD ALOYSIUS, A.B., J.C.D., Principles of Episcopal Jurisdiction, XII-172 pp., 1939.

121. BURTON, REV. FRANCIS JAMES, C.S.C., A.B., J.C.D., A Commentary on Canon 1125, X-222 pp., 1940.

122. MIASKIEWICZ, REV. FRANCIS SIGISMUND, J.C.D., Supplied Jurisdiction According to Canon 209, XII-340 pp., 1940.

123. RICE, REV. PATRICK WILLIAM, A.B., J.C.D., Proof of Death in Prenuptial Investigation, VIII-156 pp., 1940.

124. ANGLIN, REV. THOMAS FRANCIS, M.S., J.C.D., The Eucharistic Fast, VIII-183 pp., 1941.

125. COLEMAN, REV. JOHN JEROME, J.C.D., The Minister of Confirmation, VI-153 pp., 1941.

126. DOWNS, REV. JOHN EMMANUEL, A.B., J.C.D., The Concept of Clerical Immunity, XI-163 pp., 1941.

127. ESSWEIN, REV. ANTHONY ALBERT, J.C.D., Extrajudicial Penal Powers of Ecclesiastical Superiors, X-144 pp., 1941.

128. FARRELL, REV. BENJAMIN FRANCIS, M.A., S.T.L., J.C.D., The Rights and Duties of the Local Ordinary Regarding Congregations of Women Religious of Pontifical Approval, V-195 pp., 1941.

129. FEENEY, REV. THOMAS JOHN, A.B., S.T.L., J.C.D., Restitutio in Integrum, VI-169 pp., 1941.

130. FINDLAY, REV. STEPHEN WILLIAM, O.S.B., A.B., J.C.D., Canonical Norms Governing the Deposition and Degradation of Clerics, XVII-279 pp., 1941.

131. GOODWINE, REV. JOHN, A.B., S.T.L., J.C.D., The Right of the Church to Acquire Property, VIII-119 pp., 1941.

132. HESTON, REV. EDWARD LOUIS, C.S.C., Ph.D., S.T.D., J.C.D., The Alienation of Church Property in the United States, XII-222 pp., 1941.

133. HOGAN, REV. JAMES JOHN, A.B., S.T.L., J.C.D., Judicial Advocates and Procurators, XIII-200 pp., 1941.

134. KEALY, REV. THOMAS M., A.B., Litt.B., J.C.D., Dowry of Women Religious, IX-152 pp., 1941.
135. KEENE, REV. MICHAEL JAMES, O.S.B., J.C.D., Religious Ordinaries and Canon 198, V-164 pp., 1942.
136. KERIN, REV. CHARLES A., S.S., M.A., S.T.B., J.C.D., The Privation of Christian Burial, XVI-279 pp., 1941.
137. LOUIS, REV. WILLIAM FRANCIS, M.A., J.C.D., Diocesan Archives, X-101 pp., 1941.
138. MCDEVITT, REV. GILBERT JOSEPH, A.B., J.C.D., Legitimacy and Legitimation, X-247 pp., 1941.
139. MCDONOUGH, REV. THOMAS JOSEPH, A.B., J.C.D., Apostolic Administrators, X-217 pp., 1941.
140. MEIER, REV. CARL ANTHONY, A.B., J.C.D., Penal Administrative Procedure Against Negligent Pastors, XI-240 pp., 1941.
141. SCHMIDT, REV. JOHN ROGG, A.B., J.C.D., The Principles of Authentic Interpretation in Canon 17 of the Code of Canon Law, XII-331 pp., 1941.
142. SLAFKOSKY, REV. ANDREW LEONARD, A.B., J.C.D., The Canonical Episcopal Visitation of the Diocese, X-197 pp., 1941.
143. SWOBODA, REV. INNOCENT ROBERT, O.F.M., J.C.D., Ignorance in Relation to the Imputability of Delicts, IX-271 pp., 1941.
144. DUBÉ, REV. ARTHUR JOSEPH, A.B., J.C.D., The General Principles for the Reckoning of Time in Canon Law, VIII-299 pp., 1941.
145. MCBRIDE, REV. JAMES T., A.B., J.C.D., Incardination and Excardination of Seculars, XX-585 pp., 1941.
146. KRÓL, REV. JOHN T., J.C.D., The Defendant in Contentious Trials, XII-207 pp., 1942.
147. COMYNS, REV. JOSEPH J., C.SS.R., A.B., J.C.D., Papal and Episcopal Administration of Church Property, XIV-155 pp., 1942.
148. BARRY, REV. GARRETT FRANCIS, O.M.I., J.C.D., Violation of the Cloister, XII-260 pp., 1942.
149. BOLDUC, REV. GATIEN, C.S.V., A.B., S.T.L., J.C.D., Les Études dans les Religions Cléricales, VIII-155 pp., 1942.
150. BOYLE, REV. DAVID JOHN, M.A., J.C.D., The Juridic Effects of Moral Certitude on Pre-Nuptial Guarantees, XII-188 pp., 1942.
151. CANAVAN, REV. WALTER JOSEPH, M.A., Litt.D., J.C.D., The Profession of Faith, XII-143, pp., 1942.
152. DESROCHERS, REV. BRUNO, A.B., Ph.L., S.T.B., J.C.D., Le Premier Concile Plénier de Québec et le Code de Droit Canonique, XIV-186 pp., 1942.
153. DILLON, REV. ROBERT EDWARD, A.B., J.C.D., Common Law Marriage, X-148 pp., 1942.
154. DODWELL, REV. EDWARD JOHN, Ph.D., S.T.B., J.C.D., The Time and Place for the Celebration of Marriage, X-156 pp., 1942.
155. DONNELLAN, REV. THOMAS ANDREW, A.B., J.C.D., The Obligation of the Missa pro Populo, VII-311 pp., 1942.

156. ELTZ, REV. LOUIS ANTHONY, A.B., J.C.D., Cooperation in Crime, XII-208 pp., 1942.
157. GASS, REV. SYLVESTER FRANCIS, M.A., J.C.D., Ecclesiastical Pensions, XI-206 pp., 1942.
158. GUINIVEN, REV. JOHN JOSEPH, C.SS.R., J.C.D., The Precept of Hearing Mass, XIV-188 pp., 1942.
159. GULCYNSKI, REV. JOHN THEOPHILUS, J.C.D., The Desecration and Violation of Churches, X-126 pp., 1942.
160. HAMMILL, REV. JOHN LEO, M.A., J.C.D., The Obligations of the Traveler According to Canon 14, VIII-204 pp., 1942.
161. HAYDT, REV. JOHN JOSEPH, A.B., J.C.D., Reserved Benefices, XI-148 pp., 1942.
162. HUSER, REV. ROGER JOHN, O.F.M., A.B., J.C.D., The Crime of Abortion in Canon Law, XII-187 pp., 1942.
163. KEARNEY, REV. FRANCIS PATRICK, A.B., S.T.L., J.C.D., The Principles of Canon 1127, X-162 pp., 1942.
164. LINAHEN, REV. LEO JAMES, S.T.L., J.C.D., De Absolutione Complicis In Peccato Turpi, 114 pp., 1942.
165. MCCLOSKEY, REV. JOSEPH ALOYSIUS, A.B., J.C.D., The Subject of Ecclesiastical Law According to Canon 12, XVII-246 pp., 1942.
166. O'NEILL, REV. FRANCIS JOSEPH, C.SS.R., J.C.D., The Dismissal of Religious in Temporary Vows, XIII-220 pp., 1942.
167. PRINCE, REV. JOHN EDWARD, A.B., S.T.B., J.C.D., The Diocesan Chancellor, X-136 pp., 1942.
168. RIESNER, REV. ALBERT JOSEPH, C.SS.R., J.C.D., Apostates and Fugitives from Reliigous Institutes, IX-168 pp., 1942.
169. STENGER, REV. JOSEPH BERNARD, J.C.D., The Mortgaging of Church Property, 186 pp., 1942.
170. WALDRON, REV. JOSEPH FRANCIS, A.B., J.C.D., The Minister of Baptism, XII-197 pp., 1942.
171. WILLETT, REV. ROBERT ALBERT, J.C.D., The Probative Value of Documents in Ecclesiastical Trials, X-124 pp., 1942.
172. WOEBER, REV. EDWARD MARTIN, M.A., J.C.D., The Interpellations, XII-161 pp., 1942.
173. BENKO, REV. MATTHEW ALOYSIUS, O.S.B., M.A., J.C.D., The Abbot *Nullius*, XVI-148 pp., 1943.
174. CHRIST, REV. JOSEPH JAMES, M.A., S.T.L., J.C.D., Dispensation from Vindicative Penalties, XIV-285 pp., 1943.
175. CLANCY, REV. PATRICK M. J., O.P., A.B., S.T.Lr., J.C.D., The Local Religious Superior, X-229 pp., 1943.
176. CLARKE, REV. THOMAS JAMES, J.C.D., Parish Societies, XII-147 pp., 1943.
177. CONNOLLY, REV. JOHN PATRICK, S.T.L., J.C.D., Synodal Examiners and Parish Priest Consultors, X-223 pp., 1943.
178. DRUMM, REV. WILLIAM MARTIN, A.B., J.C.D., Hospital Chaplains, XII-175 pp., 1943.

179. Flanagan, Rev. Bernard Joseph, A.B., S.T.L., J.C.D., The Canonical Erection of Reliigous Houses, X-147 pp., 1943.
180. Kelleher, Rev. Stephen Joseph, A.B., S.T.B., J.C.D., Discussions with Non-Catholics: Canonical Legislation, X-93 pp., 1943.
181. Lewis, Rev. Gordian, C.P., J.C.D., Chapters in Religious Institutes, XII-169 pp., 1943.
182. Marx, Rev. Adolph, J.C.D., The Declaration of Nullity of Marriages Contracted Outside the Church, X-151 pp., 1943.
183. Matulenas, Rev. Raymond Anthony, O.S.B., A.B., J.C.D., Communication, a Source of Privileges, XII-225 pp., 1943.
184. O'Leary, Rev. Charles Gerard, C.SS.R., J.C.D., Religious Dismissed After Perpetual Profession, X-213 pp., 1943.
185. Power, Rev. Cornelius Michael, J.C.D., The Blessing of Cemeteries, XII-231 pp., 1943.
186. Shuhler, Rev. Ralph Vincent, O.S.A., J.C.D., Privileges of Regulars to Absolve and Dispense, XII-195 pp., 1943.
187. Ziolkowsky, Rev. Thaddeus Stanislaus, A.B., J.C.D., The Consecration and Blessing of Churches, XII-151 pp., 1943.
188. Heneghan, Rev. John Joseph, S.T.D., J.C.D., The Marriages of Unworthy Catholics: Canons 1065 and 1066, XVI-213 pp., 1944.
189. Carroll, Rev. Coleman Francis, M.A., S.T.L., J.C.L., Charitable Institutions.
190. Ciesluk, Rev. Joseph Edward, Ph.B., S.T.L., J.C.D., National Parishes in the United States, VI-178 pp., 1944.
191. Coburn, Rev. Vincent Paul, A.B., J.C.D., Marriages of Conscience, XII-172 pp., 1944.
192. Connors, Rev. Charles Paul, C.S.Sp., A.B., J.C.D., Extra-Judicial Procurators in the Code of Canon Law, X-94 pp., 1944.
193. Coyle, Rev. Paul Raymond, A.B., J.C.D., Judicial Exceptions, X-142 pp., 1944.
194. Fair, Rev. Bartholomew Francis, A.B., S.T.L., J.C.D., The Impediment of Abduction, XII-122 pp., 1944.
195. Gallagher, Rev. Thomas Raphael, O.P., A.B., S.T.Lr., J.C.D., The Examination of the Qualities of the Ordinand, X-166 pp., 1944.
196. Gannon, Rev. John Mark, S.T.L., J.C.D., The Interstices Required for the Promotion to Orders, XII-100 pp., 1944.
197. Goldsmith, Rev. J. William, B.C.S., S.T.L., J.C.D., The Competence of Church and State over Marriage—Disputed Points, X-128 pp., 1944.
198. Goodwine, Rev. Joseph Gerard, A.B., S.T.B., J.C.D., The Reception of Converts, XIV-326 pp., 1944.
199. Kowalski, Rev. Romuald Eugene, O.F.M., A.B., J.C.D., Sustenance of Religious Houses of Regulars, X-174 pp., 1944.
200. McCoy, Rev. Alan Edward, O.F.M., J.C.D., Force and Fear in Relation to Delictual Imputability and Penal Responsibility, XII-160 pp., 1944.
201. McDevitt, Rev. Vincent John, Ph.B., S.T.L., J.C.L., Perjury.

202. MARTIN, REV. THOMAS OWEN, Ph.D., S.T.D., J.C.D., Adverse Possession, Prescription and Limitation of Actions: The Canonical "Praescriptio," XX-208 pp., 1944.

203. MIKLOSOVIC, REV. PAUL JOHN, A.B., J.C.L., Attempted Marriages and Their Consequent Juridic Effects.

204. MUNDY, REV. THOMAS MAURICE, A.B., S.T.L., J.C.D., The Union of Parishes, X-164 pp., 1944.

205. O'DEA, REV. JOHN COYLE, A.B., J.C.D., The Matrimonial Impediment of Nonage, VIII-126 pp., 1944.

206. OLALIA, REV. ALEXANDER AYSON, S.T.L., J.C.D., A Comparative Study of the Christian Constitution of States and the Constitution of the Philippine Commonwealth, XII-136 pp., 1944.

207. POISSON, REV. PIERRE-MARIE, C.S.C., A.B., Ph.L., Th.L., J.C.L., Droits Patrimoniaux des Maisons et des Églises Religieuses.

208. STADALNIKAS, REV. CASIMIR JOSEPH, M.I.C., J.C.D., Reservation of Censures, X-141 pp., 1944.

209. SULLIVAN, REV. EUGENE HENRY, S.T.L., J.C.D., Proof of the Reception of the Sacraments, X-165 pp., 1944.

210. VAUGHAN, REV. WILLIAM EDWARD, J.C.D., Constitutions for Diocesan Courts, X-210 pp., 1944.

211. PARO, REV. GINO, S.T.D., J.C.L., The Right of Apostolic Legation.

212. BALZER, REV. RALPH FRANCIS, C.P., J.C.D., The Computation of Time in a Canonical Novitiate, X-227 pp., 1945.

213. DOUGHERTY, REV. JOHN WHELAN, A.B., S.T.L., J.C.D., De Inquisitione Speciali, XII-195 pp., 1945.

214. DZIOB, REV. MICHAEL WALTER, J.C.D., The Sacred Congregation for the Oriental Church, XII-181 pp., 1945.

215. EIDENSCHINK, REV. JOHN ALBERT, O.S.B., B.A., J.C.D., The Election of Bishops in the Letters of Pope Gregory the Great, VII-200 pp., 1945.

216. GILL, REV. NICHOLAS, C.P., J.C.D., The Spiritual Prefect in Clerical Religious Houses of Study, X-140 pp., 1945.

217. HYNES, REV. HARRY GERARD, S.T.L., J.C.D., The Privileges of Cardinals, XII-183 pp., 1945.

218. MCDEVITT, REV. GERALD VINCENT, S.T.L., J.C.D., The Renunciation of an Ecclesiastical Office, XIV-179 pp., 1945.

219. MANNING, REV. JOSEPH LEROY, J.C.D., The Free Conferral of Offices, VIII-116 pp., 1945.

220. MEYER, REV. LOUIS G., O.S.B., A.B., S.T.B., J.C.D., Alms-Gathering by Religious, XII-163 pp., 1945.

221. O'DONNELL, REV. CLETUS FRANCIS, M.A., J.C.D., The Marriage of Minors, XII-268 pp., 1945.

222. PRUNSKIS, REV. JOSEPH, J.C.D., Comparative Law, Ecclesiastical and Civil, in Lithuanian Concordat, X-161 pp., 1945.

223. SWEENEY, REV. FRANCIS PATRICK, C.SS.R., J.C.D., The Reduction of Clerics to the Lay State, X-199 pp., 1945.

224. VOGELPOHL, REV. HENRY JOHN, J.C.D., The Simple Impediments to Holy Orders, XVI-190 pp., 1945.

225. BROCKHAUS, REV. THOMAS AQUINAS, O.S.B., A.B., J.C.D., Religious who Are Known as *Conversi*, X-127 pp., 1945.

226. GRIESE, REV. N. ORVILLE, S.T.D., J.C.D., The Marriage Contract and the Procreation of Offspring, XVI-224 pp., 1946.

227. BOUDREAUX, REV. WARREN LOUIS, J.C.D., The *"ab acatholicis nati"* of Canon 1099, § 2, XII-110 pp., 1946.

228. BOWE, REV. THOMAS JOSEPH, A.B., J.C.D., Religious Superioresses, VIII-206 pp., 1946.

229. DIEDERICHS, REV. MICHAEL FERDINAND, S.C.J., J.C.D., The Jurisdiction of the Latin Ordinaries over their Oriental Subjects, XIV-153 pp., 1946.

230. DINGMAN, REV. MAURICE JOHN, A.B., S.T.L., J.C.L., The Plaintiff in Contentious Trials.

231. FRISON, REV. BASIL, C.M.F., M.Mus., J.C.D., The Retroactivity of Law, X-221 pp., 1946.

232. GALVIN, REV. WILLIAM ANTHONY, M.A., J.C.D., The Administrative Transfer of Pastors, XII-288 pp., 1946.

233. GORACY, REV. JOSEPH C., J.C.L., The Diriment Matrimonial Impediment of Major Orders.

234. HALE, REV. JOSEPH FRANCIS, M.A., S.T.L., J.C.L., The Pastor of Burial.

235. HENRY, REV. JOSEPH ARTHUR, A.B., J.C.D., The Mass and Holy Communion: Inter-Ritual Law, XII-138 pp., 1946.

236. LINENBERGER, REV. HERBERT, C.PP.S., J.C.D., The False Denunciation of an Innocent Confessor, VIII-205 pp., 1946 (1949).

237. LOWRY, REV. JAMES MARTIN, A.B., J.C.D., Dispensation from Private Vows, XII-266 pp., 1946.

238. LYNCH, REV. GEORGE EDWARD, A.B., S.T.L., J.C.D., Coadjutors and Auxiliaries of Bishops, X-107 pp., 1947.

239. LYNCH, REV. TIMOTHY, M.S.SS.T., J.C.D., Contracts between Bishops and Religious Congregations, XIV-232 pp., 1946.

240. MCCLUNN, REV. JUSTIN DAVID, A.B., S.T.L., J.C.D., Administrative Recourse, VII-142 pp., 1946.

241. LOHMULLER, REV. MARTIN NICHOLAS, A.B., J.C.D., The Promulgation of Law, XII-140 pp., 1947.

242. MCGRATH, REV. JAMES, A.B., J.C.D., The Privilege of the Canon, XII-156 pp., 1946.

243. MARBACH, REV. JOSEPH FRANCIS, A.B., J.C.D., Marriage Legislation for the Catholics of the Oriental Rites in the United States and Canada, XIV-314 pp., 1946.

244. SHIMKUS, REV. BERNARD ALOYSIUS, A.B., J.C.L., The Determination and Transfer of Rite.

245. SMITH, REV. VINCENT MICHAEL, A.B., S.T.L., J.C.L., Ignorance Affecting Matrimonial Consent.

246. Wachtrle, Rev. Paul Anthony, A.B., J.C.L., The Baptism of the Children of Non-Catholics.
247. Crotty, Rev. Matthew Michael, J.C.D., The Recipient of First Holy Communion, X-142 pp., 1947.
248. Eagleton, Rev. George, J.C.D., The Quinquennial Faculties, Formula IV, XIV-199 pp., 1947 (1948).
249. Gibbons, Rev. Marion Leo, C.M., J.C.D., Domicile of the Wife Unlawfully Separated from Her Husband, XIV-171 pp., 1947.
250. Kelly, Rev. Bernard Matthew, S.T.L., J.C.D., The Functions Reserved to Pastors, X-150 pp., 1947.
251. Kilcullen, Rev. Thomas John, LL.M., J.C.D., The Collegiate Moral Person as Party Litigant, X-150 pp., 1947.
252. Lafontaine, Rev. Germain Joseph, W.F., J.C.D., Relations Canoniques entre le Missionaire et Ses Superieurs, X-118 pp., 1947.
253. Lane, Rev. Loras Thomas, J.C.L., Matrimonial Procedure in Ordinary Court of Second Instance.
254. Lover, Rev. James Francis, C.Ss.R., J.C.D., The Master of Novices, X-168 pp., 1947.
255. McNicholas, Rev. Timothy Joseph, J.C.L., The *Septimae Manus* Witness.
256. Marositz, Rev. Joseph John, M.S.C., J.C.D., Obligations and Privileges of Religious Promoted to the Episcopal or Cardinalitial Dignities, XII-180 pp., 1947.
257. Murphy, Rev. Francis Joseph, J.C.D., Legislative Powers of the Provincial Council, XII-158 pp., 1947.
258. O'Brien, Rev. Romaeus William, O.Carm., J.C.D., The Provincial Superior in Religious Orders of Men, X-294 pp., 1947.
259. Pfaller, Rev. Benedict Anthony, O.S.B., J.C.D., The *ipso facto* Effected Dismissal of Reliigous, XII-225 pp., 1947.
260. Popek, Rev. Alphonse Sylvester, J.C.D., The Rights and Obligations of Metropolitans, XVIII-460 pp., 1947.
261. Ristuccia, Rev. Bernard Joseph, C.M., J.C.L., Quasi-Religious.
262. Sonntag, Rev. Nathaniel Louis, O.F.M.Cap., J.C.D., Censorship of Special Classes of Books, XII-147 pp., 1947.
263. Stadler, Rev. Joseph Nicholas, J.C.D., Frequent Holy Communion, X-158 pp., 1947.
264. Szal, Rev. Ignatius Joseph, J.C.D., The Communication of Catholics with Schismatics, XII-217 pp., 1947.
265. Wagner, Rev. Urban Stanley, O.F.M.Conv., J.C.D., Parochial Substitute Vicars and Supplying Priests, IX-126 pp., 1947.
266. Quinn, Rev. Joseph, M.A., J.C.D., Documents Required for the Reception of Orders, XII-207 pp., 1948.
267. Bennington, Rev. James Clement, A.B., J.C.L., The Recipient of Confirmation.
268. Blaher, Rev. Damian Joseph, O.F.M., A.B., J.C.L., The Ordinary Processes in Causes of Beatification and Canonization.

269. CLUNE, REV. ROBERT BELL, B.A., J.C.L., The Judicial Interrogation of the Parties.

270. COURTEMANCHE, REV. BASIL F., B.A., J.C.L., The Total Simulation of Matrimonial Consent.

271. DLOUHY, REV. MAUR JOHN, O.S.B., A.B., J.C.L., The Ordination of Exempt Religious

272. DONOVAN, REV. JOHN THOMAS, Ph.B., S.T.L., J.C.L., The Clerical Obligations of Canons 138 and 140.

273. FREKING, REV. FREDERICK W., A.B., S.T.B., J.C.L., The Canonical Installation of Pastors.

274. FULTON, REV. THOMAS B., J.C.L., Prenuptial Investigation.

275. GODLEY, REV. JAMES P., J.C.L., The Time and the Place for the Celebration of Mass.

276. KANE, REV. THOMAS A., A.B., B.S., J.C.L., Jurisdiction of Patriarchs until 1439.

277. KENNEDY, REV. ANDREW A., J.C.L., The Annual Pastoral Report to the Local Ordinary.

278. KONRAD, REV. JOSEPH GEORGE, J.C.L., Transfer of Religious.

279. KRESS, REV. ALPHONSE, J.C.L., Contumacy in Ecclesiastical Trials.

280. MCCARTNEY, REV. MARCELLUS ANTHONY, O.F.M., M.A., J.C.L., Faculties of Regular Confessors.

281. MCCASLIN, REV. EDWARD PATRICK, M.A., S.T.L., J.C.L., The Division of Parishes.

282. MCELROY, REV. FRANCIS J., A.B., J.C.L., The Privileges of Bishops.

283. QUINN, REV. STEPHEN, M.S.SS.T., J.C.L., Relation between the Local Ordinary and Religious of Diocesan Approval.

284. SCHNEIDER, REV. EDELHARD LOUIS, S.D.S., M.A., J.C.D., The Status of Secularized Ex-Religious Clerics, X-155 pp., 1948.

285. THOMPSON, REV. CHESTER J., A.B., J.C.L., The Simple Removal from Office.

www.ingramcontent.com/pod-product-compliance
Lightning Source LLC
LaVergne TN
LVHW050243080826
844660LV00012B/587

* 9 7 8 0 8 1 3 2 2 4 5 1 0 *